PELICAN BOOKS

A385

SENSE AND NONSENSE IN PSYCHOLOGY

H. J. EYSENCK

SENSE AND NONSENSE
IN PSYCHOLOGY

By

H. J. EYSENCK

*

PENGUIN BOOKS

Penguin Books Ltd, Harmondsworth, Middlesex
U.S.A.: Penguin Books Inc., 3300 Clipper Mill Road, Baltimore 11, Md
AUSTRALIA: Penguin Books Pty Ltd, 762 Whitehorse Road,
Mitcham, Victoria

—

First published 1957
Reprinted with revisions 1958
Reprinted 1960, 1961

—

Made and printed in Great Britain
by Richard Clay & Company, Ltd,
Bungay, Suffolk

CONTENTS

EDITORIAL FOREWORD

THE building of a science is in many ways like the building of a cathedral or the building of a city. It is rarely, if ever, a matter of starting on a virgin site and of executing in detail a preconceived plan. More often than not it is a matter of continuous alteration, of repeated destruction and reconstruction. At any time the edifice will display the styles of many ages.

This is certainly so with Psychology. The science so described is an edifice which today has some of the features of the Parthenon, and some of the features of the new Coventry Cathedral. If its original architect could be named it would be Aristotle, but the system incorporates elements deriving from the pre-Socratics and elements from primitive thought; and like other ancient foundations it embodies much picturesque but functionless ornamentation.

It follows that a good psychologist must be a man of several parts. He must be original and creative, but he must also be critical and destructive. The needed qualities of mind are rarely combined, and in general the progress of psychology depends upon the kind of cooperation that consists in conflict. 'Bold creative thinkers' (as we describe them when they have our approval) or 'armchair speculators' (as we describe them when they have not) submit their creative thoughts to be manhandled and mauled by carping destructive critics and by the manipulators of slide rules. Never does a grand overall theory survive in the form in which it was originally conceived. Rarely, if ever, is it utterly destroyed. Something comes out of this conflict which neither the creative thinker nor the destructive critic could have produced alone.

Sometimes the qualities of the destructive critic are combined with those of the constructive thinker – as in the case of the author of this book. Dr Eysenck can manipulate slide rules, but he can also manipulate concepts. He has displayed these skills not only in his many contributions to the research journals, but also in works adapted to the needs and interests of the layman. Among the latter is the earlier volume in this series on *Uses and Abuses of Psychology*.

The layman can be pardoned for his belief that there is an essential incompatibility between an interest in interesting things and the capacity to discuss these things in a scientific way; and he can be pardoned for his belief that there is an essential association of scientific ability with dry-as-dustiness. The author of this book is an awkward negative case for those who would defend either generalization. He certainly discusses interesting questions and he discusses them in both a scientific and an interesting way. Of course there are other scientists, equally expert and equally fair-minded, who arrive at conclusions different from some of those presented in this book. The author would certainly not be the last to agree to this. But that is neither here nor there. What is important is that interesting and potentially explosive issues should be matters of rational discussion. *Sense and Nonsense in Psychology*, like *The Uses and Abuses of Psychology*, is a book which contributes not only to entertainment and instruction but also to the diffusion of a certain quality characteristic of the intellectual life of those who live in civilized societies.

C. A. MACE

October 1956

Acknowledgements for permission to quote are
due to the authors and publishers of the following two books:

Clark L. Hull. *Hypnosis and Suggestibility*.
New York: Appleton-Century-Crofts,
Inc., 1933.

F. E. Inbau & J. E. Reid. *Lie Detection
and Criminal Interrogation*. Third Edition.
Baltimore: The Williams & Wilkins Co.,
1953.

The author is indebted to *Modern Experiments in
Telepathy* by Soal and Bateman for many of the
criticisms of card-guessing on pages 1–228.

Science is nothing but trained and organized common-sense, differing from the latter only as a veteran may differ from a raw recruit: and its methods differ from those of common-sense only as far as the guardsman's cut and thrust differ from the manner in which a savage wields his club.

The chess board is the world; the pieces are the phenomena of the universe; the rules of the game are what we call the laws of nature. The player on the other side is hidden from us. We know his play is always fair, just, and patient. But also we know, to our cost, that he never overlooks a mistake or makes the smallest allowance for ignorance.

*

T. H. HUXLEY

INTRODUCTION

In a sense, this book is a sequel to *Uses and Abuses of Psychology*, but it has been written to stand on its own feet. In the first book I was concerned with problems of social usefulness and the contribution which psychology can make to society, and with the many unfounded claims which have been made in its name and which have caused so many intelligent critics to discount psychological contributions almost completely. In the present book I have taken a rather wider field. There is no doubt that a great deal of nonsense is talked, even by educated people, on a large number of subjects, but it is unlikely that there is any subject where the ratio of sense to nonsense is smaller than in matters psychological. I have picked out a few fields in an attempt to sort out the chaff from the wheat, and to put before the reader the facts as well as the speculations, the sense as well as the nonsense, which have grown up around these topics.

There is little obvious usefulness in most of the subjects discussed, although it is not out of the question that, in due course, hypnosis or dream interpretation, or even telepathy, may reach a status where claims in that direction could be substantiated. However, the discussion is certainly not slanted in that direction; our interest has been purely in the subject-matter as such; in the facts, and in the theories woven around these facts in an attempt to explain them.

It is interesting to consider for a moment why there are so many misconceptions about psychological topics. I vividly remember an occasion, not so very many years ago, when the Vice-Chancellor of one of our main universities, on seeing that on the occasion of a celebration dinner his wife had been placed next to the Professor of Psychology at the table, hurriedly changed the cards around, explaining that it would not be quite proper for a lady to sit next to a psychologist! Times may have changed a little since then, and a few people may have learned that the aura of sex, licentiousness, and promiscuity which, in the popular mind, attaches to psychoanalysis cannot justifiably be transferred to the innocent psychologist running his rats in the animal laboratory, or eliciting the laws of learning by conditioning university students to give an involuntary eye-blink to the sound of a buzzer. Yet, the great majority of people still have little idea of what it is that the psychologist tries to do. An oft-repeated reaction of the layman – and even more of the laywoman – on being introduced to a psychologist is the stereotyped sentence, 'Oh dear, I bet you'll know all that's in my mind!' While the psychologist as a private person would occasionally like to know what is in the other person's mind, he would certainly not regard this as his professional job. What he is trying to do is simply to discover the laws according to which human and animal behaviour takes place; the laws of learning, of memory, of emotion; the rules governing the development of motor and perceptual skills; the ways in which intellectual abilities develop and grow; and the laws of social and interpersonal relationships. This is quite a full programme, and by and large surely a sensible one; there is no black magic in all this, but simply the application of the usual scientific methods to a relatively complex and difficult subject.

In practice, most people show a rather odd and interesting ambivalence to a programme such as this. On the one hand, there is considerable verbal acclaim and approval. Most people realize that our knowledge of the physical world has vastly outstripped our knowledge of mankind, and that unless we can find some way of correcting this balance there may be very little left of mankind to study. This view, indeed, has become so much a commonplace that one feels almost ashamed of putting it down in black and white again. Yet, curiously enough, this almost universal verbal approval is not in any way reflected in action. The total amount of money spent on all the social sciences in this country is less than one thousandth of what is spent on the physical sciences; indeed, when we take into account the money spent by industry, the ratio becomes much more unfavourable still. In the whole country there are, at most, one dozen small, under-staffed, and under-developed departments of psychology lacking mostly even the elementary laboratory facilities required for teaching. On the practical side, then, it is reasonably safe to say that the lofty aspirations voiced by our so-called leaders of thought remain precisely that – aspirations – and that their translation into reality is put off until the Greek calends.

It often appears as if people, while paying lip-service to the desirability of basing conclusions on facts, prefer the meretricious sesquipedalianism of the kind offered by the late C. E. M. Joad and his many successors. Psychological topics of which there is some factual knowledge in existence are often dealt with by the BBC, but they are nearly always dealt with by philosophers, zoologists, mathematicians, journalists, theologians, or unspecified dons of ancient vintage, who clearly do not know even that there is any factual knowledge available, and who speculate and pontificate to their hearts' content in a manner they would never dare to assume in their own specialty.

This is only one example of what appears to be an almost universal belief to the effect that anyone is competent to discuss psychological problems, whether he has taken the trouble to study the subject or not, and that while everybody's opinion is of equal value, that of the professional psychologist must be excluded at all costs because he might spoil the fun by producing some facts which would completely upset the speculation and the wonderful dream-castles so laboriously constructed by the layman.

This tendency is most noticeable, of course, when the facts provided by the psychologist have a bearing on political matters. It is then that we find the finest flower of nonsense. Care is, naturally, always taken that the discussion should be pursued by people not contaminated in any way by factual knowledge, and motivated almost exclusively by a desire to score party points. One example may illustrate the sort of thing that is happening almost every day. In *Uses and Abuses of Psychology*, I described in some detail the construction of intelligence tests, the methods of validating them, and their usefulness in selection. In recent years there has been a considerable degree of criticism of selection, particularly at the 11-plus level, and it is worth-while to have a look at the most common of these objections. It is argued, for instance, that many children are so anxious on the occasion of the test that they do not do themselves justice. It is argued again that coaching produces a considerable effect on test scores, and that therefore the results are worthless. It is argued that the age at which selection takes place is too early in the life of a child, and that either no selection should take place at all, or that some form of 'streaming' should be introduced, with the constant possibility of changing the child from one stream to another. Whatever the objection, the argument usually ends by saying that intelligence tests are either useless or actively malfeasant in their influence.

Much of this argument arises from a very praiseworthy desire to give all children an equal chance, and to act on the principle that all men are created equal. Unfortunately, the facts make it quite certain that all men are not created equal, and that heredity clearly discriminates between the bright and the dull. In fact, the more we equalize the opportunities of education, the greater will be the influence of heredity in determining the final intellectual status of each child. This point is often argued by Communists, whose strange dogma seems to favour the conception of human beings as emerging with perfect uniformity from some conceptual conveyor belt, but no such view can be maintained for one moment in the face of the evidence.

Given innate differences in ability, we must next stress a fact which again has ample experimental foundation, namely that teaching is much more effective when the members of the class are of relatively uniform ability. It has often been shown that to teach the same material to a group containing bright, average, and dull members takes considerably longer and is considerably less effective than teaching the same material to a group consisting only of bright, or average, or dull members. It might, at first sight, seem surprising that it should be easier to teach a dull class than one of average ability, but the answer, of course, is that with a dull class the teacher can adapt himself and his methods to the level of his students, while with a class of average ability, containing both bright and dull students, the same method of teaching simply will not be applicable to all members of the class, so that time-wasting duplication is necessary. Unless, therefore, we want to have highly inefficient teaching, we must segregate – quite apart from the fact that certain subjects at a reasonably advanced level are quite unsuitable for children with low I.Q.s.

Given that for these, as well as for many other reasons, some form of segregation is desirable, is eleven too early an age at which to estimate children's abilities? Follow-up studies have usually shown that there is very little overlap between the abilities of children in grammar and in modern schools, even when they reach the age of fifteen or sixteen, so that prediction in the vast majority of cases appears to have been remarkably accurate. What, then, about the criticisms of coaching and examination nerves? Both are justified, but they are criticisms, not of psychological tests and psychological theory, but of political and social pressures which prevent the best use being made of available knowledge. There is ample evidence that coaching produces a rise in I.Q. of about ten points or so, which is quite a considerable increase. It has also been shown, however, that simply giving children a few hours practice in doing intelligence tests has much the same effect as coaching, and brings them to a point beyond which no coaching and no practice is found to increase their scores. The answer to the coaching problem, therefore, is quite a simple one. All children should be given five hours of practice on tests of intelligence before the crucial test is taken. This would counteract the effects of any coaching they would be given additionally, and give them all the same start. At the same time, this would reduce nervousness due to having to face an entirely new experience.

It would be preferable in many ways to have these five hours of testing spaced throughout the child's school period from six to eleven so that some knowledge could be gained at the same time of his intellectual growth pattern, because this might be of considerable value in making any predictions. Also it would reduce the importance of any particular single test, and would thus again have some effect in reducing examination nervousness. Children who did not come up to their expected level could be re-tested individually to determine whether this failure was due to nervousness or other extraneous causes. There are other ways in which the experienced psychologist could help education committees to overcome the difficulties involved in the administration of testing programmes and obviate the criticisms mentioned. Why, then, is nothing of this kind done?

The reason is a very simple one. If it costs 9*d* per child to give one test of intelligence and score it, then it would cost almost 4*s* to give five tests. The decision that a child's future happiness is worth only 9*d* rather than 3*s* 9*d* is not made by the psychologist, but by the general public through their elected members of local government bodies. All one can say is that for 9*d* the public is getting quite incredibly good value for its money. To have a fairly superficial examination of a car carried out costs several pounds. A reasonably complete health examination costs at least as much. To get a child's intelligence investigated for 9*d* can hardly be considered an extravagant expenditure. The degree of accuracy of this measurement, of course, is directly dependent on the amount of money spent on it. The higher the degree of accuracy required, the more money will have to be spent on the examination. During my recent visit to California I was shown a large series of laboratories constructed at a cost of several million dollars for the sole purpose of getting a few thousandths of one degree nearer to absolute zero temperature! Our society is willing to pay large sums of money like this for a slight increase in the accuracy of physical measurement, but it is content with an expenditure of 9*d* a child in the measurement of a psychological variable of great importance to both the child and society.

It is not my purpose in making this comparison to say whether this social decision is right or wrong. It is my purpose rather to point out some of the facts of the situation, and to show that if the accuracy of the measurement performed of a child's ability at the age of 11-plus is not all it might be, and is subject to various types of criticism, then it is not the psychologist who should be blamed, but society itself. By refusing to spend money on research, or refusing to implement the findings of private research because of a slight increase in cost, society has made a decision which may or may not be a correct one, yet discussion in the Press heaps all the resulting blame on the head of the psychologist for not performing miracles at the price of 9d, and fails to put before the public the facts of the situation so that it may have a chance to reconsider its verdict.

One of the reasons why popular discussions on psychological matters are so uninformed is perhaps the fact that psychology, being a science, uses methods and discussions of a highly technical nature. In particular, it uses statistical methods, and most people have developed a strong avoidance reaction to statistics. This reaction is both interesting and odd because it seems to be rather one-sided. A discussion of odds in horse-racing, or permutations and combinations in football pools, is no less statistical for being popular and widespread, yet when the psychologist attempts to employ statistical methods in relation to serious subjects he encounters the usual obscurantist notion that you can prove anything with statistics. In a sense, this is true. You can 'prove' anything with statistics, but only to a person who is completely ignorant of elementary statistical notions. In fact, faulty arguments, which the statistician would recognize as such immediately, often pass muster in the popular Press because they are disguised in such a way that their statistical nature is not recognized.

Let me give two examples of this: It is well known that about half the hospital beds in Britain are occupied by mental patients. On quite a number of occasions I have seen journalists argue from this as if half the medical patients in the country were suffering from mental disorders. Superficially, this may not seem a statistical point at all, yet the fallacy quite definitely is a statistical one. The equation of 'half the beds' with 'half the patients' would be correct only if we make the assumption that the length of time a patient stays in his bed is the same for mental and physical disorders. It is quite obvious that if, on the average, the patient suffering from a physical disorder stays in for two days and is then discharged, whereas the mental patient on the average stays for twenty years, then the number of patients suffering from physical disorders is 3,650 times as great as the number of patients suffering from mental disorders. Now, it is a fact that a large number of mental patients stay in hospital for very long periods, whereas patients suffering from physical disorders tend, in the great majority of cases, to stay only a few days. Unless the exact proportions are known it is impossible to argue from the proportion of beds to the proportion of patients.

Another example may be taken from the controversy on the causes of recidivism, i.e. the question of why certain offenders return to prison again and again. I was visiting Alcatraz, the famous American prison located on an island in San Francisco Bay, where the most serious offenders in the United States are punished. This prison is one of the harshest and best guarded in the world, and it is claimed that no one has ever succeeded in escaping from it. On this visit I happened to be accompanied by a few penologists and sociologists whose strong anti-statistical bias emerged during the boat trip across the Bay. We were shown round the prison by one of the deputy governors who had heard part of this argument regarding the use of statistics. He winked at me when the discussion turned to recidivism, and told the group that Alcatraz had practically stamped out recidivism because, of all the prisons in the country, it was right at the bottom of the list with respect to the number of persons returning to crime. This very much impressed his listeners, who kept discussing the possible reasons for this phenomenon for quite a long time. It did not occur to them that as most of the prisoners in Alcatraz are there for life, or for a very long period, they would have very little chance of ever committing a crime again, simply because very few had ever been released! This may seem an elementary point, hardly worthy of being called statistical, but it is precisely the kind of point so often missed by the unsophisticated journalist or reader who attempts to dismiss the modern logic of probability with a few damning phrases.

Sometimes society's reaction to psychological research appears to be not only unenthusiastic, but actively malevolent. As an example, let me take the recent inquiry into the effects of television. There was considerable social interest in this matter, and hundreds of people voiced their opinions and attitudes in the complete absence of any known facts. Some deplored the effects of television on children, saying that it kept them indoors, kept them from reading, made them incapable of initiative and enterprise, and had a great variety of other disastrous consequences. Others countered this by saying that it broadened their horizon, made them more knowledgeable, and kept them from doing other things which would be even less acceptable from the point of view of society. Now here, clearly, is a point where factual information is absolutely essential, and, indeed, the papers clamoured for such information to be supplied.

Finally, one of our best-known social psychologists was appointed by a Research Foundation to carry out and direct a research into this problem. Numerous questionnaires, diaries, and other instruments of research were circulated to thousands of children forming a well-selected sample of the school population. Out of this very large number, one or two, in talking about the questionnaires to their parents, giving an extremely garbled version of some of the questions, caused their parents to complain, and these complaints were prominently featured in the national Press. Certain points about the treatment by the Press of this matter are of considerable interest. The investigators had especially asked the newspapers not to print any of the actual questions used because doing that would invalidate the further use of the questionnaires containing these questions. Few of the papers complied. Not only that, but what most of them printed were not the actual questions but the garbled version of the questions obtained at third or fourth hand from the parents of children who had answered the original questionnaires. These questions, inaccurately quoted and taken out of their context, bore very little relation to those which formed part of the actual inquiry. When a Press conference was held and the correct questions were given to the papers, most persisted in printing the garbled version and did not print the corrections, nor did they apologize.

This is the bare outline of only some of the reactions encountered in the course of this work, and the obvious hostility and factual carelessness characterizing the Press treatment of this issue is only too typical of what is happening every day in journalistic discussions of psychological issues. It is hardly to be wondered at that the amount of nonsense talked about psychological matters is as great as it is.

It should not be thought, however, that the purveyors of nonsense in this field are entirely to be found in the ranks of non-psychologists. Alas, many members of the psychological fraternity – and particularly the psychological sorority! – have been equally guilty in this respect. It is hardly necessary to document this assertion in any detail, as few people are in any doubt about the facts of the matter. Let me illustrate my contention with just one example, namely, that of the bringing up of children. The psychological literature on this subject has always been one of the most amusing and unedifying examples of faddism in the history of civilization. During one decade all the books say the children should be fed only at stated intervals, so that it is a crime for the mother to feed her baby at five to one, while she has all the blessings of science when she feeds him at one o'clock. Soon the pendulum swings and everyone is instructed to feed her children on demand, regardless of the time of day or night. Parents recalcitrant to obey the currently fashionable demands are threatened that their children will develop all sorts of psychological disorders of a neurotic or psychotic kind if these alleged psychological laws are not punctiliously obeyed.

An interesting point about this controversy, as well as about so many other rules laid down on the bringing-up of children, is that at no time is any factual evidence of an experimental kind brought forward to support the views favoured by the text-book writers. Occasionally anecdotal examples are given of terrible things which happen to certain children when brought up according to the non-favoured rules and dictates, but the possibility that these children might have suffered quite the same fate, regardless of their upbringing, is never even canvassed.

Similarly absurd are the general notions current about the later upbringing of children. Advocates of *laisser faire* and excessive leniency are on the left; those of 'spare the rod, spoil the child' on the right. Both schools have no hesitation in telling the parent what to do, while neither appears to be conscious of the fact that their precepts are based on unverified theories and idle speculation and that, in the absence of any factual knowledge regarding the consequences of certain types of upbringing, the giving of advice is not far removed from sheer impudence.

Quite generally, the notion that any set of precepts can be useful as a general guide to human behaviour is one of the finest exhibits in our museum of nonsense. The type of upbringing suitable for a child which forms conditioned reflexes easily might not be at all suited to a child who forms conditioned reflexes only with difficulty; we shall discuss this point at some length in a later chapter. Rules which apply to the bright child do not necessarily apply to the dull child. Upbringing suitable for the emotionally unstable child may be quite unsuitable for the emotionally stable child, and *vice versa*. Much painstaking research will be required before we can even begin hesitantly to give advice in this field, which is anything but the projection of our own prejudices and emotions. We may regret that times have not advanced far enough to enable us to answer the many questions and problems in this field, but a recognition of the facts of our ignorance is a more likely precursor to knowledge than the pretence of omniscience.

What is true of child upbringing is, *a fortiori*, true of such complex social problems as war and peace, industrial unrest, and delinquency. Many people still have a pathetic faith that if only everyone could be psychoanalysed, wars, strikes, and crime could be wiped out as if by some magic wand. Alack, the most likely effect, as far as the evidence indicates, would be to leave matters precisely where they are now, neither better nor worse. Science does not peddle vade-mecums of this kind, and no credence should be given to those who pretend to be able to solve all our problems by some simple form of magic.

Why, it may be asked, is society so ambivalent in its attitude towards the scientific factual and experimental study of psychological phenomena, and why does it so readily accept the unfounded claims for all sorts of psychological panaceas? It is difficult to know for certain, but one likely possibility is perhaps this: politicians and journalists are used to what Humpty Dumpty called a knock-down argument, i.e. a purely verbal discussion, depending entirely on the manipulation of symbols mostly quite unrelated to reality. Having once tasted the exhilaration of being accepted as 'expert' on social and psychological matters because of their ability to manipulate linguistic symbols, such people are naturally not too eager to see factual research expose the half-truths and vague generalizations which are their stock-in-trade. This would account for the fact that while verbally praising the efforts of the experimentalist, they yet put every obstacle in the way of his successfully completing his investigations, and pay no attention to his conclusions once the experiment is finished. They are much more at home with the non-factual, semantic arguments of the psychological crusaders who have a system to sell and who therefore meet them on their own ground. No need to be bothered here by hard facts; acceptance and rejection can proceed in terms of emotion and prejudice rather than in terms of proof and disproof.

So much, then, for a brief introduction to the general topic of this volume. The arrangement of the different subjects and their classification have caused me a good deal of thought, particularly the attempt to find general terms to denote the two main parts of the book. My difficulties here are very similar to those faced by the Royal Commission investigating prostitution, one of whose first tasks was to find a collective noun for its objects of study. The first suggestion made, 'A jam of tarts', was rejected because of the objections of one of the Bishops, who thought it a trifle vulgar. The second suggestion, 'A novel of Trollope's', was received with more favour, but was considered a trifle on the literary side. The third suggestion, 'An anthology of pros', was finally rejected for the same reason, and agreement finally reached on the fourth and last term proposed, namely, 'A fanfare of strumpets'. I was unable to match this inventiveness in relation to my own problem, but hope that the two descriptive phrases finally chosen – *Borderlands of Knowledge* and *Personality and Social Life* – will give some impression to the reader of the subjects dealt with in the two parts of this book.

PART ONE

BORDERLANDS OF KNOWLEDGE

1

HYPNOSIS AND SUGGESTIBILITY

THE theory and practice of hypnosis is certainly a topic which must have a place of honour in any book dealing with sense and nonsense in psychology. Very few topics in the whole history of mankind can have given rise to so many absurdities, misunderstandings, and misconceptions. From the very beginning the study of hypnosis has been tied up with fantastic conceptions like animal magnetism, the influence of the stars, and similar tarradiddle. Even nowadays popular conceptions of hypnosis are extremely confused, and journalistic reports in newspapers have done but little to clarify the issues involved.

Most of the experimental work done in this field in recent years has been concerned with clearing up the errors committed by the early hypnotists, and consequently it is necessary to provide the reader with a brief historical circumspect. This inevitably begins with the rather mysterious personality of Franz Anton Mesmer, born in 1733 in the little Austrian village of Isnang, near Lake Constance. Mesmer was intended for the priesthood and went to a monk's school until the age of fifteen. He decided against the Church, became a law student, but finally changed over to medicine. He was awarded his degree at the age of thirty-two for a paper 'concerning the influence of the planets on the human body'. This dissertation contained the first mention of his views on animal magnetism, a theory which he was to amplify later in a famous set of twenty-seven propositions. In essence, these contained the main points of his teaching. According to them:

A responsive influence exists between the heavenly bodies, the earth, and animated bodies; a fluid, universally diffused, is the means of this influence. Experiments show that there is a diffusion of matter subtle enough to penetrate all bodies without any considerable loss of energy; its action takes place at a remote distance, without the aid of any intermediary substance. It is, like light, increased and reflected by mirrors. Properties are displayed, analogous to those of the magnet, particularly in the human body. This magnetic virtue may be accumulated, concentrated, and transported. These facts show, in accordance with the practical rules I am about to establish, that this principle will cure nervous diseases directly, and other diseases indirectly. By its aid, the physician is enlightened as to the use of medicine, and may render its action more perfect and direct salutary crises so as to completely control them.

Thus, animal magnetism was held to be a kind of impalpable gas or fluid and its distribution and action were supposed to be under the control of the human will. Not only could this strange fluid be reflected by mirrors, but it was also supposed to be capable of being seen. Trained somnambulists were supposed to behold it streaming forth from the eyes and hands of the magnetizer, though they appear to have disagreed as to whether its colour was white, red, yellow, or blue! To the modern mind all this, of course, seems nothing but a rigmarole of nonsense, but one positive assertion will be noted, namely Mesmer's allegation 'that these principles will cure nervous diseases'. There appears to be little doubt that Mesmer did, in fact, produce what were considered to be miraculous cures. Here, for instance, is a publicly sworn statement by Charles du Hussey, a Major of Infantry and Knight of the Royal Military Order of St Louis.

After four years of useless treatment by other doctors, I consulted Mesmer. My head was constantly shaking and my neck was bent forward. My eyes protruded and were considerably inflamed. My back was almost completely paralysed and I could only speak with difficulty. I laughed involuntarily and for no obvious reasons. My breathing was difficult and I suffered from severe pain between the shoulders and from constant tremors. I staggered when I walked.

Du Hussey was then treated by Mesmer and went through a series of strong emotional crises, 'ice coming from my limbs, followed by great heat and foetid perspiration'. He concludes his statement, 'Now, after four months, I am completely cured'.

Mesmer's methods were certainly unorthodox, and his interest in occult matters generally did not endear him to the medical profession in Vienna. He took the precaution of marrying a rich widow twelve years older than himself, thus ensuring that his experiments would not be disrupted by lack of money. However, his undoubted successes in curing patients whom medical opinion had considered incurable increased the detestation in which he was held by orthodox physicians, and finally, when he was on the point of curing the blindness of a very highly placed young girl who had been given up by the great specialists of the time, orthodoxy succeeded in having him excommunicated from Vienna and he went to Paris.

He was now forty-five years of age, and almost from the beginning of his residence achieved a remarkable triumph. It became fashionable to have 'nervous complaints' and to have these treated by Mesmer, very much in the same way that it has become fashionable in the United States nowadays to have some form of neurosis and be psychoanalysed. (The average upper-middle-class inhabitant of New York, Boston, Los Angeles, or Kansas City would be considered as much out of things if he were unable to talk about his 'psychoanalyst' as would his Parisian counterpart who could not boast a mistress. The American habit is probably no less expensive, certainly more virtuous, but rather less pleasurable, than the French. It probably does little harm, on the whole, but equally it probably does little good.)

Indeed, pressure of work became such that Mesmer was forced to introduce group therapy, very much in the way that modern psychiatry has been forced in a similar direction. His clinic appears to have been a remarkable place indeed. Treatment was given in a large hall which was darkened by covering up the windows. In the centre of this room stood the famous *baque*, a large open tub about a foot high and large enough to permit thirty patients to stand around it. It was filled with water, in which had been placed iron filings, ground glass, and a variety of bottles arranged in a symmetrical pattern. The tub was covered with wooden slats provided with openings through which jointed iron rods projected. The patients applied these rods to their various ailing parts, thus allowing the healing forces of animal magnetism to act. Patients were enjoined to maintain absolute silence, and throughout the session plaintive music was played by an orchestra hidden from view. At the psychological moment, Mesmer himself would appear in a brilliant silk robe. He would move among the patients, fixing them with his eyes, passing his hands over their bodies, and touching them with a long iron wand.

There can be no doubt that very many patients considered this treatment as beneficial, and claimed to have been cured by Mesmer, again very much as modern patients treated by psychoanalysis sometimes claim to have been benefited by that technique. It is difficult nowadays to tell whether Mesmer was a conscious charlatan who exploited the suggestibility of his patients, or whether he seriously believed in the scientific truth of his hypothesis. Bernheim speaks about the discredit which the interested charlatanism of Mesmer threw upon his practices, but Moll, who is perhaps the best-known and best-informed writer of the history of hypnosis, is less severe. This is what he has to say:

I do not wish to join the contemptible group of Mesmer's professional slanderers. He is dead, and can no longer defend himself from those who disparage him without taking into consideration the circumstances or the time in which he lived. Against the universal opinion that he was avaricious, I remark that in Vienna, as well as later in Mörsburg and Paris, he always helped the poor without reward. I believe that he erred in his teaching, but think it is just to attack this only, and not his personal character. Let us consider, however – for I deem it right to uphold the honour of one who is dead – more closely in what his alleged great crime consisted. He believed in the beginning that he could heal by means of a magnet, and later that he could do so by a personal indwelling force that he could transfer to the *baque*. This was evidently his firm conviction and he never made a secret of it. Others believed that a patient's mere imagination played a part, or that Mesmer produced his effects by some concealed means. Then, by degrees, arose the legend that Mesmer possessed some secret by means of which he was able to produce effects on people, but that he would not reveal it. In reality the question was not at all a secret purposely kept back by him, since he imagined that he exercised some individual force. Finally, if he used this supposititious force for the purpose of earning money, he did nothing worse than do modern physicians and proprietors of institutions who likewise do not follow their calling from pure love of their neighbour, but seek to earn their own living, as they are quite justified in doing. Mesmer did not behave worse than those who nowadays discover a new drug, and regard the manufacture of it as a means of enriching themselves. Let us be just and cease to slander Mesmer, who did only what is done by the people just mentioned, against whose procedure no one raises a word of protest, even when the drugs they extol possess no therapeutic properties whatever.

Six years after his arrival in Paris, a dispute arose between Mesmer and some of his disciples about the right to give public lectures, revealing his supposed secret, and the French Government intervened by appointing a Commission to investigate the truth of his claims. They were particularly interested in the so-called 'Mesmeric crises', an example of which we have already encountered in connexion with Major du Hussey. They ran a series of controlled experiments of the kind which Mesmer himself should have carried out before making any claims. This is part of their report:

The commissioners were particularly struck by the fact that the crises did not occur unless the subjects were aware that they were being magnetized. For instance, in the experiments performed by Jumelin, they observed the following fact. A woman, who appeared to be a very sensitive subject, was sensible of heat as soon as Jumelin's hand approached her body. Her eyes were bandaged, she was informed that she was being magnetized, and she experienced the same sensation, but when she was magnetized without being informed of it, she experienced nothing. Several other patients were likewise strongly affected when no operation was taking place, and experienced nothing when the operation was going on.

No wonder the commissioners came to the conclusion that they had 'demonstrated by decisive experiments that imagination apart from magnetism produces convulsions, and that magnetism without imagination produces nothing. They have come to the unanimous conclusion with respect to the existence and utility of magnetism, that there is nothing to prove the existence of the animal magnetic fluid; that this fluid, since it is non-existent, has no beneficial effect; that the violent effects observed in patients under public treatment are due to contact, to the excitement of the imagination, and to the mechanical imitation which involuntarily impels us to repeat that which strikes our senses.'

At about the same time the Royal Society of Medicine made a very similar report to the effect that 'from a curative point of view animal magnetism is nothing but the art of making sensitive people fall into convulsions'. These reports finished Mesmer's career as a mental healer and he left France shortly afterwards.

There is much in Mesmer's story which has interesting parallels to the present time. I shall not take these up, however, until we have learned a little more about the nature of hypnosis, and will instead go on to point out one fact which has not even been commented on, although it is rather curious. The terms 'mesmerize' and 'hypnotize' have become quite synonymous, and most people think of Mesmer as the father of hypnosis, or at least as its discoverer and first conscious exponent. Oddly enough, the truth appears to be that while hypnotic phenomena had been known for many thousands of years, Mesmer did not, in fact, hypnotize his subjects at all. Some of his patients appeared to have had spontaneous hysterical convulsions and similar emotional upheavals and abreactions, but there is no account in his work or that of his followers of genuine hypnotic phenomena.

We thus start with the somewhat unusual finding that the father of hypnosis never, in fact, hypnotized anybody, was not familiar with the phenomena of hypnosis, and would have had no place for them in his theoretical system. It is something of a mystery why popular belief should have firmly credited him with a discovery which in fact was made by others.

The first to have induced the sleeping trance, which constitutes the essential part of hypnosis, appears to have been a pupil of Mesmer, the Marquis de Puységur. In trying to induce Mesmer's usual hysterical convulsion in a young shepherd, Victor, by the use of the magnetizing method, the Marquis found that Victor had fallen into a quiet sleeping trance from which he did not awake for quite a long time, and which he was unable to recall after he had woken up. This sleeping or trance condition, with the amnesia or forgetting of all that occurred during the trance state following it, attracted a good deal of attention, and very soon others reported a variety of hypnotic phenomena, such as positive hallucinations, i.e. seeing things not in fact there; negative hallucinations, i.e. being blind to things actually present; and anaesthesia, or failure to feel a touch on the skin; analgesia, i.e. an insensitivity to pain; and post-hypnotic suggestion, or the tendency to carry out suggestions made under hypnosis even after the hypnosis was terminated. We shall discuss these phenomena in some detail a little later. First of all, let us consider the method of producing the hypnotic trance.

There are many methods of producing hypnosis; indeed, almost every experienced hypnotist employs variations differing slightly from those of others. Perhaps the most common method is something along these lines. The hypnotist tries to obtain his subject's co-operation by pointing out to him the advantages to be secured by the hypnosis, such as, for instance, the help in curing a nervous illness to be derived from the patient's remembering in the trance certain events which otherwise are inaccessible to his memory. The patient is reassured about any possible dangers he might suspect to be present in hypnosis, and he may also be told (quite truthfully) that it is not a sign of instability or weakness to be capable of being put in a hypnotic trance, but that, quite on the contrary, a certain amount of intelligence and concentration on the part of the subject is absolutely essential.

Next, the subject is asked to lie down on a couch, or sit in an easy-chair. External stimulation is reduced to a minimum by drawing the curtains and excluding, as far as possible, all disruptive noises. It is sometimes helpful to concentrate the subject's attention on some small bright object dangled just above eye-level, thus forcing him to look slightly upwards. This leads quickly to a fatigue of the eye-muscles, and thus facilitates his acceptance of the suggestion that he is feeling tired and that his eyes are closing. The hypnotist now begins to talk to the subject in a soft tone of voice, repeating endlessly suggestions to the effect that the subject is feeling drowsy, getting tired, that his eyes are closing, that he is falling into a deep sleep, that he cannot hear anything except the hypnotist's voice, and so on and so forth. In a susceptible subject, a light trance is thus induced after a few minutes, and the hypnotist now begins to deepen this trance and to test the reactions of the subject by giving suggestions which are more and more difficult of execution. Thus, he will ask the subject to clasp his hands together, and tell him that it is impossible for him to separate his hands again. The subject, try as he may, finds, to his astonishment, that he cannot in actual fact pull his hands apart. Successful suggestions of this kind are instrumental in deepening the hypnotic trance until, finally, in particularly good subjects, all the phenomena which will be discussed presently can be elicited.

This, very briefly, is the routine method of establishing a trance. It is very difficult to know just which of the elements mentioned are really important. I have established a deep hypnotic trance in a subject by quietly and soothingly saying to him, 'Monday, Tuesday, Wednesday, Thursday, Friday, Saturday' in endless repetition. During the war, a friend of mine had to hypnotize a French soldier who was suffering from shell-shock. As the soldier spoke no English, it was necessary to convey the suggestions in French. Unfortunately, the hypnotist was no great linguist and, to my horror, he kept telling the subject, not that his eyes were closing, but that his nostrils were! However, this made no difference to the subject, who was soon in a deep trance, regardless of what must, to him, have been a very odd type of suggestion indeed. It does not seem, therefore, that the content of the suggestion is as important as one might have thought at first glance.

On the other hand, the content of the suggestion does appear to be of some relevance. Here is an example quoted by one of the best-known American hypnotists, who found great difficulty in producing a deep trance in one of his subjects. After several hours of intensive effort on the part of the hypnotist, the subject timidly inquired if she might be allowed to advise on technique, even though she had no previous experience with a hypnotist. This is the advice she gave: 'You are talking too fast on that point; you should say that very slowly and emphatically and keep repeating it. Say that very rapidly and wait a while and then repeat it slowly, and please pause now and then to let me rest, and please don't split your infinitives.' When the advice was taken the deep trance was produced quite rapidly. This, of course, is merely anecdotal evidence, but unfortunately very little experimental work has been done on the form and content of suggestions made in inducing a trance, and consequently nothing better than guesswork is possible on this important point at the moment.

Nor, apparently, are the isolation, the quiet, and the darkness important. Successful hypnoses have been carried out under noisy conditions, in broad daylight, and even, as is well known, on the stage in the presence of thousands of people. Some hypnotists, in fact, claim that these conditions are more favourable to the induction of a hypnosis than those of absolute quiet and segregation. No experimental work, again, has been done on this question, but it may be

B

surmised that different conditions suit different people, and that whereas extraverts and hysterics may be more easily hypnotized under conditions of noise, excitement, and while in the limelight, introverted and anxious people might prefer the quiet of the consulting-room. This, however, has by no means been established as a fact.

Contrary to popular superstition, there is little difficulty in awakening the subject once the experimenter decides to end the trance. He usually suggests to the subject that when he, the experimenter, counts up to ten, the subject will awaken from his sleep, that he will forget everything that has happened during the hypnotic trance, that he will feel well and refreshed, and that he will feel all the better for his experience. There are no records of any difficulties in awakening subjects along these lines, and even if the hypnotist should, for some reason, be unable to break off the hypnosis, all that would be likely to happen would be for the subject to fall into an ordinary sleep and wake after a few hours with no evil after-effects.

Having induced a reasonably deep hypnotic trance in our subject, what types of phenomena can be elicited? The first and most obvious one, which, indeed, may be responsible in large measure for all the others, is a tremendous increase in the subject's suggestibility. He will take up any suggestion the hypnotist puts forward and act on it to the best of his ability. Suggest to him that he is a dog, and he will go down on all fours and rush around the room barking and yelping. Suggest to him that he is Hitler, and he will throw his arms about and produce an impassioned harangue in an imitation of the raucous tones of the Führer! This tremendous increase in suggestibility is often exploited on the stage to induce people to do foolish and ridiculous acts. Such practices are not to be encouraged because they go counter to the ideal of human dignity and are not the kind of way in which hypnosis ought to be used; nevertheless, they must be mentioned because it is probably phenomena such as these which are most familiar to people from vaudeville acts, from reading the papers, and so forth.

It would not be true to say, however, that all suggestions are accepted, even in the very deepest trance. This is particularly true when a suggestion is made which is contrary to the ethical and moral conceptions held by the subject. A well-known story may be quoted to illustrate this. Charcot, the great French neurologist, whose classes at one time were attended by Freud, was lecturing on hypnosis and was demonstrating the phenomena of the hypnotic trance on a young girl of eighteen. When she had been hypnotized deeply he was called away, and handed over the demonstration to one of his assistants. This young man, lacking the seriousness of purpose so desirable in students of medicine, even French ones, suggested to the young lady that she should remove her clothes. She immediately awakened from her trance, slapped his face, and flounced out of the room, very much to his discomfiture.

Occasionally, failure to obey a suggestion is quite unaccountable, and does not seem to be based on any kind of ethical or moral scruples. In one of my early experiments I was concerned with the ability of hypnotized people to judge the passage of time. One subject in particular seemed to give very accurate estimates of the number of seconds which had passed between two signals given by the experimenter, and in an attempt to make him improve on this performance it was suggested to him that he was a clock. For some obscure reason he did not take at all kindly to this idea and repeated, in a sort of agitated way, that he was not a clock and that he did not see how he could be a clock. To make the suggestion more acceptable, he was then told that of course he was a clock – couldn't he hear himself tick? This seemed to pacify him for a little while, but he kept listening carefully, and finally, in great agitation, denied that he could hear himself tick. He grew so annoyed that it became necessary to abandon the idea and reassure him that he was not a clock at all. As he had shown no objection to being a great variety of other things more objectionable than clocks, this sudden refusal was rather mysterious, and to this day its exact significance escapes me. Generally, it is not at all unusual to find the hypnotized person taking exception to certain suggestions which, to the hypnotist, appear quite innocuous. Possibly, in these cases, there is some hidden significance peculiar to the subject which would require an elaborate experiment to unearth.

The next phenomenon frequently observed is known as that of positive hallucinations. Here the subject will see, hear, and feel the presence of objects which, objectively, are not present at all. Tell him that his fiancée is sitting in the chair opposite and he will greet her, go across and kiss her, and generally behave as if his fiancée were actually there. Tell him that a lion has just come in through the window and he will show all signs of cringing fear, and may rush out of the room in terror.

The converse of positive hallucinations are negative hallucinations, which can also be easily induced. Here the subject fails to see, feel, or hear objects and persons which are, in fact, actually present. Suggest to him that he and the hypnotist are alone in the room and he will pay no attention to other people and behave as if they were not there. Suggest to him that he cannot feel any touch on his skin, or that he cannot hear a certain sound and he will, in fact, behave as if that were true. Positive and negative hallucinations of this kind are relatively easy to produce in susceptible subjects, but the criticism is often made that we may be dealing with a simple desire on the part of the hypnotized person to please the experimenter and that all these manifestations are faked in some way. Alternatively, it is suggested that hypnotized people are in reality in the pay of the hypnotist and merely pretend to go through the hoop in response to favours received. This criticism may sound reasonable to anyone who has not, in actual fact, seen the difference in behaviour between a person merely pretending to be hypnotized and a person in a trance. Nor does it account for phenomena such as this. A stage hypnotist had hypnotized a rather pompous, well-dressed young man on the stage, and had got him to take off his trousers and to ride around the stage on a broom-stick. The public were shrieking with laughter at this sight, but when the hypnotist wakened the subject from the trance, the latter took one look at his rather undignified appearance, picked up the broom, and knocked the hypnotist flat. It is difficult to consider this as part of the act!

Probably more convincing is the fact that certain hallucinations can be produced by hypnosis which give rise to acts impossible to imitate in the normal state. Take a glass full of soapy water and suggest to a hypnotized person that it is bubbling champagne. He will drink it down with every sign of enjoyment. This is a very difficult feat to encompass in the normal state. The reader who doubts it might like to carry out the experiment on himself! Similarly, it is possible for a normal person to pretend to feel afraid of the non-existing lion who comes through the window, but he would find it very difficult indeed to produce all the autonomic and physiological signs of fear which are not under voluntary control, and which nevertheless can be shown to be present in the hypnotized person. In general it might be said that while a certain amount of faking undoubtedly does occur in stage performances, it would be very difficult, if not impossible, for such fakes not to be detected in the psychological laboratory.

The unique nature of hypnotic phenomena becomes even more apparent when we turn to another field which has been extensively investigated. In connexion with negative hallucinations I mentioned the possibility of producing anaesthesia, i.e. a failure to feel a touch applied to the skin of the subject. It is similarly possible to produce a complete insensitivity to pain, usually referred to as hypnotic analgesia. For many years this phenomenon has been the subject of doubt and derision, possibly because most of the phenomena described so far might just have been capable of simulation and faking. Too much is known, however, about people's response to pain to leave one in any doubt that if the phenomena described by hypnotists are, in fact, accurate, then we are dealing in hypnosis with something quite beyond the usual.

Let us start with a simple demonstration. The deeply hypnotized subject is told that a needle will be pushed through his hand and that he will not feel any pain whatsoever. He is also told that there will be no bleeding. The hypnotist then pushes a needle through the subject's hand; the latter does not even look at it and goes on talking as if nothing had happened. There is no bleeding, or else very little. Again the reader who believes that hypnotic phenomena can be faked might like to try the experiment on himself!

The pushing of a needle through the hand is one thing; major operations are quite another. Yet there is no doubt that in literally thousands of cases, major amputations have been carried out under hypnosis without pain, and without the usual accompaniment of shock, and other traumatic physiological indices. Much of the credit for the introduction of hypnosis into this field goes to Elliotson, a young physician at one of London's major hospitals during the middle of the last century, and to Esdaile, a physician working in India. Anaesthetics had not been discovered then, and any kind of operation, particularly a major one, was a very bloody affair, in the true sense of that term. Elliotson's experiments with hypnosis were not well received by his colleagues, who resented his crusading vigour and did not like the odd and unorthodox nature of the method. Esdaile perfected the technique, and finally his claims were investigated by a special commission, which, though incredulous at first, was forced to report that he had in fact succeeded in carrying out major operations without any evidence of pain or shock on the part of the persons operated upon. This caused considerable and acrimonious controversy, but the discovery of anaesthetics around this time caused medical people to sink back with thankfulness into lethargic uninterestedness in hypnosis and similar oddities, and rest content with the more physical type of anaesthetic, such as ether and chloroform, which they felt they could understand more easily. Nowadays hypnosis is very little used in medical treatment for the purpose of the suppression of pain, although it is superior in many ways to the best available anaesthetics. Occasionally promising results are reported in childbirth, and more recently in connexion with the extraction of teeth. Hypnodontics, as this new method is somewhat oddly called, has already produced a large number of reports of bloodless and painless extractions of teeth, and a few years ago a public exhibition was given in the United States in which, before a large group of dentists, two upper bicuspids and one lower bicuspid, all on the right side, were extracted without the use of drugs or chemical anaesthetics. The periosteum was lifted away and the three teeth extracted without the slightest indication of pain, and without bleeding, while the patient remained in a deep trance. Post-hypnotically there was no sign of bleeding or recollection of pain.

Another phenomenon which appears spontaneously, and has been remarked on from the earliest days of hypnosis, is that of *rapport*. By this is meant a special relationship obtaining between the hypnotist and his subject, such that the latter takes orders, accepts suggestions, and so on, only from the former and not from anyone else. The Freudian concept of transference, i.e. the existence of a special relation between patient and therapist, is in many ways a watered-down version of the notion of *rapport*. It is quite likely, in fact, that the underlying rationale of these two phenomena, when carefully examined, will be found to be somewhat similar. Although psychoanalysts have always protested against this notion, there seems to be little doubt that suggestion, although not necessarily of a hypnotic kind, plays a very important part in their treatment.

Rapport, once it is established, can be transferred to other people at the command of the hypnotist. He may tell the hypnotized subject, 'This is Mr Smith. I want you to carry out everything he tells you, just as you would carry out everything that I tell you.' Such a command establishes *rapport* between the subject and Mr Smith, and in this way *rapport* can be handed on through a whole series of people. In the absence of such a voluntary transfer, the hypnotized subject would not be at all suggestible to anything Mr Smith, or anybody else, might say to him; his *rapport* is entirely with the person who carried out the original hypnosis.

Post-hypnotic amnesia, or a complete forgetting of everything that happened under hypnosis, is a very frequent concomitant of the hypnotic trance. It was first encountered in the case of Victor, the young shepherd hypnotized by the Marquis de Puységur, whom we have already mentioned. When he awoke from the hypnosis he had no recollection of anything that happened during that period. Such amnesias are common in deep states of trance, and do not require to be suggested to the subject. They are apparently a spontaneous outgrowth of the deep hypnotic trance. When the trance is less deep it may be necessary for the hypnotist to suggest that the subject should forget everything that happened; such commands are usually obeyed without difficulty, except in the very slightest stages of hypnosis, where they may be ineffective.

There is thus a continuity between the last moment before the subject sinks into the hypnotic trance and the first moment when he is awakened, with a complete amnesia for everything that happened in between. This may be illustrated by an experiment carried out on a rather boastful and arrogant young man who came to the laboratory loudly protesting to everyone within earshot that he did not believe in hypnosis, that he knew nobody could hypnotize him, and that he would soon show the experimenters up for a bunch of incompetent fools. He kept on talking in this fashion while the hypnotic suggestions were repeated to him, which were to the effect that he would fall into a deep sleep when the experimenter knocked on the table with a reflex hammer held in his hand. The young man was just saying, "... and furthermore, I don't believe for a minute that anybody with as strong a will-power ...", when the experimenter rapped on the table. The subject's eyes closed immediately, he stopped talking, and fell into a reasonably deep trance. For slightly over two hours a series of experiments were conducted with him, which showed him to be a very good subject indeed. At the end of that period the suggestion was made to him that he would awake without remembering anything about this hypnotic period. The moment the experimenter again rapped on the table with a reflex hammer he continued talking, saying, '... as I can possibly be hypnotized'. He was quite incredulous when told of what had happened and only an agitated reference to his watch led him finally to believe that he had actually been hypnotized.

If after awakening the subject we hypnotize him again, then his second hypnotic state is in contact through memory with the first, but whatever happened between the two hypnotic states is not recollected. However, these amnesias can be removed by suggestion. If it is suggested to the subject at the end of the hypnotic trance that he will recall everything that has happened during the trance, there is usually little difficulty in making him conscious of and remember what would normally be unconscious and forgotten.

One of the most striking ways in which post-hypnotic amnesia is found to work is in the case of another hypnotic phenomenon, which has excited considerable interest from the very day of its discovery. This is the phenomenon of post-hypnotic suggestion. If, under hypnosis, the subject is given a suggestion to be carried out at a given time, or after receiving a certain signal, he will carry out this suggestion, although he may at the time not be in a hypnotic trance at all, but may have returned to the waking state. Here is a typical case record to illustrate this. The subject is hypnotized and told that he will be awakened after ten minutes. He is further told that some time after this the hypnotist will blow his nose three times. Upon the receipt of this signal, the subject will get up, go out into the hall, pick up the third umbrella from the left on the rack, go back into the room, and put up the umbrella there. After a little while the subject is then awakened; he talks animatedly, has forgotten all about his experience, and when questioned as to whether he has been asked to do anything, seems astonished at the idea, and certainly cannot recall anything of the kind.

When the experimenter blows his nose three times, the subject becomes vaguely restless and uneasy; finally, he gets up, leaves the room, picks up the designated umbrella, brings it back into the room and puts it up. When questioned as to the reasons for his actions, he cannot, of course, give the true reason because he is unconscious of it. Instead he will make up as good a reason as he can. Thus, he may say, 'Well, you know the old superstition about putting up umbrellas in a building. We were talking just now about superstition and I wanted to show you that I was not superstitious myself.' Many of these rationalizations are quite remarkable in their ingenuity, and intelligent people in particular can usually find a good reason for doing almost anything that has been suggested to them under hypnosis. What is more, they apparently believe their own rationalizations implicitly. The tendency of human beings to rationalize their actions and to believe in their own rationalizations implicitly is, unfortunately, a phenomenon too widespread and too well known to have escaped the notice of philosophers and psychologists from the very beginning of interest in human actions. What is important in this demonstration is the way in which it becomes possible to control the situation in such a way that the true cause of a person's conduct is known to the experimenter, but not to the person himself. Oddly enough, this very powerful method of investigating the process of rationalization has not been used to any considerable extent for experimental purposes; it has largely remained an amusing demonstration and an after-dinner game.

There is no doubt about the great strength of post-hypnotic suggestion and its capacity to produce action. An illustration may serve to make this clear. The subject of the experiment was a well-known psychologist, deeply interested in the phenomena of hypnosis, and himself an experimentalist of considerable standing in this field. His personality was very stable and strong, with no traces of neurotic weakness. He expressed a desire to experience the phenomena of hypnosis at first hand, and was accordingly hypnotized, falling into a reasonably deep trance. In the trance it was suggested to him that upon a prearranged signal he would get up from his chair, walk across the room, and sit down in another chair. He was awakened from the hypnosis, and after half-an-hour or so the prearranged signal was given. He became a little agitated, began to look across the room at the other chair, and finally said, 'I feel a strong tendency to go across the room and sit on that chair. I am sure you have given me a post-hypnotic suggestion to this effect. Well, I'm damned if I'll do it!'

He continued taking part in the conversation, but became more and more distracted and monosyllabic, until finally he jumped out of his chair, crossed over, sat down in the designated chair, and exclaimed, 'I couldn't stand it any longer!'

What apparently happens is that the post-hypnotic suggestion sets up an encapsulated action tendency in the mind which is relatively independent of voluntary control, and powerfully demands action before it can be reintegrated with the remainder of the subject's mind. In this it very much resembles in miniature the kind of complex so often found in neurotic and otherwise emotionally unstable patients. The cause of this action tendency is unknown to the subject, and even where it is guessed, as in the case of the psychologist just mentioned, this knowledge does not seem capable of counteracting the determining influence of this small 'complex'. When it is remembered that in the particular case just mentioned this single suggestion triumphed over the strength and will-power of a well-integrated, strong-willed, competent person, who, in fact, had guessed what was happening, it will be realized that hypnosis and hypnotic suggestions are no playthings, but carry with them an almost frightening degree of strength and importance.

In view of this, it is small wonder that attempts have been made to use post-hypnotic suggestion as a curative agent. This idea was particularly obvious when it became known that post-hypnotic suggestion could last for very long periods of time. Responsible investigators have claimed that post-hypnotic suggestions have been carried out as much as five years after they were originally given, and periods of several months to a year have been vouched for by a number of trustworthy experimentalists. Yet, in spite of this, results of curative post-hypnotic suggestion have not usually been very positive. Supposing you wish to give up the habit of drugging yourself with alcohol or tobacco. It is possible to give a suggestion to the effect that alcohol will make you sick and that tobacco will taste like aloes. This suggestion certainly works in the hypnotic trance, and even when given as a post-hypnotic suggestion it works for a day or two afterwards, but gradually the strength of the suggestion seems to wane, until within a week or so nothing is left and the subject returns to his original addiction. It is, of course, possible to re-hypnotize him every few days and give post-hypnotic suggestions again and again, but this course is not favoured because many people fear that hypnosis itself will become an addiction and possibly a worse and more expensive one than either alcohol or tobacco. Consequently, at the present time, little use is being made of post-hypnotic suggestion, although it has always seemed to me that if the method could be experimented with in a more whole-hearted and intelligent manner than has been done so far much more positive results might be obtained.

Another phenomenon often observed in hypnosis is the transcendence of normal working capacity. Many absurdly exaggerated claims have been made in this connexion, particularly by some of the earlier writers who were so much impressed with what people could do under hypnosis that they did not bother to find out whether much the same could not be done in the normal state also! However, a kernel of truth does seem to be contained in the view that under hypnosis certain activities are performed more quickly or more accurately than in the waking state. In carrying out such simple tasks as placing dots as rapidly as possible into small squares, multiplying numbers, crossing out certain letters in a given list, adding numbers, counting in threes, tapping as fast as possible, sorting cards into packs, placing rings on a pole, and so forth, it has been found that improvements varying from 30 to 60 per cent can be produced through hypnotic suggestion. A rather smaller amount can be produced by post-hypnotic suggestion, percentages ranging from 20 to 40 per cent approximately.

When a study is made of all the reports on properly planned and executed experiments in this field, it becomes clear that the amount of improvement shown in a given task is not invariable, but appears to be a function of the complexity of the task. As a general rule it may be said that *the simpler the task the greater the improvement,* and, conversely, *the more complex the task the less improvement will there be.* In very complex activities, such as doing an intelligence test, there may not only be no improvement at all, but a slight drop in performance may occur.

It is difficult to know to what causal factors one may ascribe improvements of this type. One hypothesis, which has a certain amount of experimental backing, is that they are related to a decrease in fatigue, which is a well-known concomitant of hypnotic suggestion. This is one of the most noticeable features of hypnosis, and one which is recognized by all workers in the field. The report of an actual experiment may illustrate the difference between the normal and the hypnotic state. The subject is asked to pull a dynamometer in rhythm with a metronome. A dynamometer is an instrument for measuring strength of grip. The subject pulls the handle as strongly as he can; this handle is connected to a steel spring, and the pressure exerted by him against the spring is recorded on a dial. Pulling a dynamometer at frequent intervals is a very tiring business and scores dropped off rapidly. Figure 1 shows the amount of pull exerted by a subject in the normal state (N) and also when hypnotized (H). Under hypnosis it was suggested to him that he was the strongest man in the world and that he would show no fatigue at all.

It will be seen that the suggestion of increased strength produced practically no effect, as the starting points of the two curves are very close together. The effect of the suggestion of 'no fatigue', however, can be seen from the fifth trial onwards. While the curve depicting the strength of pull in the normal state drops until, after the twelfth trial, the subject is incapable of going on at all, under hypnosis it remains at the same level after the fifth trial and the subject goes on for quite a long time after the twelfth trial. This result is

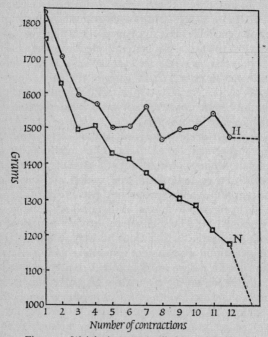

Figure 1: Weight in grams pulled by subject in the normal (N) and in the hypnotized (H) state

quite typical of many others achieved in this field, and as a good number of the tasks on which hypnotized people show superiority over the normal state involve muscular contractions of one kind or another, the possibility cannot be ruled out that improvement is largely due to absence of fatigue in the hypnotized condition.

Another hypothesis which has to be considered relates to the possibility that the improvement in performance is really due to changes in the emotional state of the subject. Many people, when subjected to psychological tests, show a certain amount of anxiety and react emotionally to the whole testing situation. It will be shown in a later chapter that emotion tends to interfere with fine muscular adjustment, and, consequently, it might be thought that the more even emotional tone induced as part of the hypnotic procedure, and the dispersal of anxiety through suggestion, which also forms part of the hypnotist's method, will improve performance through a reduction in the amount of interference by emotion. In many cases this may be a concomitant, but it is unlikely to be the whole explanation. One or two reports have indicated that, under certain circumstances, the removal of anxiety and other disturbing emotions, through hypnosis, may even improve performance on tests of intelligence. It should, however, be emphasized that this appears to be true only in cases of extreme emotional instability, and that for normal people there is little likelihood of their obtaining an improved I.Q. through hypnotic suggestion!

A third hypothesis relates to the question of motivation. In the normal state many subjects may not be very strongly motivated to carry out the simple tasks required of them by the experimenter. Hypnosis may alter the degree of motivation and, in consequence, may produce improvements in output. All these theories may be in part true; while the fact of improvement in simple motor functions under hypnosis is undisputed, its causes are not known for certain.

Another phenomenon of hypnosis which has attracted probably more attention than almost any other, because of its therapeutic promise, is the improvement of memory under hypnosis. It is claimed that under hypnosis a person can remember things which in the normal state he would be quite unable to recall. In fact, it is suggested that under hypnosis a person can be 'regressed' to an earlier age and that in this condition he will experience again the events which were happening at that time, and the emotions which they evoked in him. This claim has led to a considerable amount of critical discussion, particularly because some of the advocates of hypnotic regression have gone to rather extreme lengths in their claims. Thus, not only has it been said that under hypnosis people can be regressed to the moment of birth, but claims have even been made that memory of an intra-uterine existence has been achieved. Absurd claims of this nature have not helped to make the subject popular with critical scientists, but there is some evidence available which is of considerable interest and importance.

First of all, let us look, from a purely descriptive point of view, at the sort of thing that happens when a subject is hypnotized and regressed to an early age. The subject usually employs language such as might be expected of a person of the regressed age. His voice may become child-like, or he may retain a normal tone but use only simple words and phrases. His general behaviour will tend to conform to the suggested age. If regressed to the age of five, say, he will play with toys and react with protests and tears if the toys are taken away. Drawings will be child-like and correspond roughly to the level of a child of the regressed age. The handwriting changes and frequently becomes very like the actual specimens of the subject's childhood writing. In one case it was found that when a twenty-year-old girl was regressed to various ages she changed the chalk to her left hand at the six-year level; she had started writing with the left hand, but had been forced to change over at the age of six.

In another case, a male subject, thirty years old, was seated in a chair arranged in such a way that the release of a latch would cause it to fall back into a horizontal position. (This is a favourite torturing device much used by psychologists to stimulate emotional reactions!) When the man was regressed to a level of about one year of age, the latch was suddenly released so that the chair fell back. An adult, or an older child, would quite involuntarily extend both arms and legs in an effort to maintain balance. The regressed subject, however, screamed in fright, but made no movement of the limbs and fell backward with the chair.

Another reaction, quite unexpected and embarrassing, both to the hypnotist and to the subject, was an accompanying urination which soaked the man's trousers! It is unlikely that such behaviour is simply due to play-acting.

Other types of investigation have been concerned with the behaviour of regressed subjects in tests of intelligence, and in various types of achievement tests. It is usually found that when regressed to a certain level, people tend to behave on tests of this type in a manner roughly appropriate to the given age. Such reactions, of course, could easily be faked, but it has also been shown that when, for instance, the eye movements of subjects are photographed, a considerable lack of ocular co-ordination and stability is found when regression to a relatively young age occurs. Such physiological phenomena are characteristic of young children and are difficult, if not impossible, to produce voluntarily.

A similar effect has been reported in the case of a subject whose eyesight had been defective since early childhood, and who had begun wearing glasses at the age of twelve. Regression to the age of seven produced a definite improvement in both near and far vision, as measured by an optometrist. Even more impressive is another case of a subject who had had a colloid cyst removed from the floor of the third ventricle. Prior to this removal, the subject had been suffering from blindness in the left half of the right eye. After the operation, vision had become normal, but when the subject was regressed to a time shortly before the operation the visual defect again reappeared during the regression.

A rather different type of proof is of a purely neurophysiological nature and concerns the Babinski reflex. In a normal adult, stroking the sole of the foot causes the great toe to turn down. In infants up to approximately seven months of age, however, the reflex response to stroking the sole of the foot is dorsiflection, or the turning up of the toe. If regression were a real phenomenon, then we would expect that, on regressing adults to the age of five or six months, the Babinski reflex, i.e. dorsiflection, should occur. This has actually been found to be so in subjects who could not be expected to have known these rather esoteric details of neurophysiological development.

In discussing some of the evidence, I have not mentioned the many studies in which patients have been asked to remember certain events which happened at a relatively early stage of their lives, and where later checks revealed that these had actually happened. This type of work is too much open to falsification and all sorts of uncontrolled influences to be of much value. The alleged events which the hypnotized person experiences under regression may have been discussed with him by other people long after they had in fact happened; the memories of the witnesses may themselves be affected by the story told by the subject who is being regressed; also, certain confirmative details may be elaborated by the experimenter to the exclusion of items that had not fitted in. Quite recently, however, this unsatisfactory type of evidence has been transformed into a scientifically useful and quite decisive method of experimentation. The idea is so simple, and so lacking in any technical complexity, that the reader might like to exercise his own ingenuity in deciding how he would solve this particular problem. The patient under hypnotic regression tells of certain events and memories of things that happened many years ago. How can the truthfulness of these memories be checked without relying on subjective memories of other people? The answer to this problem is a very simple one, but any reader who can think out the right answer has shown more scientific inventiveness than hundreds of academic and medical hypnotists who have repeated the same type of invalid and useless investigation time and time again.

The solution essentially consists in finding an objective fact which at the time to which the subject is regressed would be well known to him, but which during the course of his life he would certainly forget. Facts of this kind are the day of the week on which his fourth, or eighth, or tenth birthday fell, or the day of the week on which a certain Christmas celebration fell, and so on. The procedure of testing is a very simple one. The subject is asked on what day of the week, say, his sixth birthday fell. Practically no one succeeds in correctly remembering this far-off event, which took place twenty or more years ago. He is then hypnotized and gradually regressed to this particular day. Now birthdays are of the very greatest importance to children, and they know perfectly well *at that time* what day of the week their birthday is. Consequently, having been regressed to the day, the subject is simply asked what day of the week it is. Correct answers have been obtained for 93 per cent of subjects, regressed to the age of ten; 82 per cent of subjects regressed to the age of seven; and 69 per cent of those regressed to the age of four.

Experiments such as those described in some detail above leave little doubt that there is a substantial amount of truth in the hypothesis that age regression does, in fact, take place, and that memories can be recovered which most people would think had been completely lost. This fact may be used for psychotherapeutic purposes, and an illustrative case may show how this can be done. The patient is a married woman of forty-two, intelligent and well-informed. For many years this patient, Mrs Smith, has suffered from recurrent asthmatic attacks. Her work necessitated her entering various hospitals (she was a psychiatric social worker), and in such a situation she always experienced a very strong fear reaction. Other unreasonable fear reactions were produced by the sight of a pair of hairy arms on a man. Knives also produced considerable fear in her, and she sometimes experienced nightmares.

During a self-induced trance one day, she was regressed to an early age, when she experienced a previously completely forgotten incident with unusual clarity. She seemed to be lying on a table under brilliant lights. A man was standing beside her holding a small knife. A vague, threatening object was descending from above her head, and settled down over her face. She was terror-stricken and tried to rise, but two hairy arms grabbed her and roughly forced her back. She continued to struggle, but was violently shaken and slapped repeatedly by someone.

Finally, the object came down over her face and smothered her.

On inquiry, it was found that at the age of sixteen months a mastoidectomy had been performed on her and that she had been very sick afterwards with complications caused by severe shock. Two of the nurses at the hospital had told her mother about the brutality displayed towards the child by the anaesthetist, and they had resigned in protest. For some time afterwards the child experienced nightmares and had been emotionally disturbed. It was following this operation that Mrs Smith's first attacks of asthma had occurred.

The result of this 'Mesmeric crisis' or 'Freudian abreaction' was that Mrs Smith has been entirely free of asthma ever since; she lost her fear of hairy arms, and the phobias of knives and hospitals have completely disappeared.

Two further points may be mentioned next in connexion with our discussion of the phenomena characterizing hypnosis, although they are only indirectly related to this topic. One is the question of whether people can be induced to commit criminal acts under hypnosis; the other how many people are capable of being hypnotized. Both are questions probably more frequently asked than any others in connexion with hypnosis. Taking the question of the production of criminal activity in hypnotized persons first, it may be said that until fairly recently the more sober writers tended to discountenance this possibility. They tended to quote the case of Charcot's young assistant, who failed to induce the young hypnotized girl to take off her clothes, and to infer that, quite generally, a suggestion urging a person to act in ways which were very much counter to his moral and ethical ideas would not be carried out, but would merely lead to his awakening. There are, indeed, many observations of this kind to be found in the experimental literature, and it may be said with a reasonable degree of confidence that in many cases an *explicit suggestion to do something unethical or immoral will not be carried out by the subject.*

More recently, however, a number of experiments have been conducted to show, first, that this conclusion is not universally true, and, secondly, that the whole framework of the type of experiment on which it is based is much too narrow. One example may suffice to show the kind of experimentation involved. The experimenter demonstrated the power of nitric acid to the subject by throwing a penny into it. The penny, of course, was completely disintegrated and the subject began to realize the tremendous destructive power of nitric acid. While the subject's view of the bowl of acid was cut off by the experimenter, an assistant substituted for it a like-sized bowl of methylene-blue water, continuously kept boiling by the presence in it of miniscule droplets of barium peroxide.

The hypnotized subject was then ordered to throw the dish of nitric acid (in actual fact, of course, innocuous water) over the assistant who was present in the same room. Under these conditions it was possible to induce, under hypnosis, various subjects to throw what they considered to be an extremely dangerous acid into the face of a human being. It might be argued that perhaps they had noticed the difference between the acid and the water. Actually, in this particular experiment, the person in charge made what he calls 'a most regrettable mistake in technique' by forgetting to change the nitric acid to the innocuous dish of water, so that in one case the assistant had real nitric acid thrown over him. (Because of the promptness of remedial measures, no scars were left on the face of the assistant.) This touch of realism was not intended, but it does illustrate that even the experimenter and the assistant could not tell the true acid from the fake one.

Another experiment reports how a post-hypnotic suggestion was implanted in a soldier assigned to military duty. The post-hypnotic suggestion was carried out and the soldier deserted his duty, an anti-social act which would undoubtedly have resulted in severe punishment if the circumstances had not been known. It will be seen, therefore, that certain anti-social activities can be produced by hypnosis, although they might not seem to the reader to be of a very serious nature. The difficulty, of course, is that if the misdemeanour is of a serious nature, then the execution of the act would quite rightly result in punishment by the courts for the hypnotist, and perhaps also for the person hypnotized.

However, much more important than these demonstrations that direct suggestion can produce anti-social activities is a rather different line of work which is based on an important theoretical consideration. It is maintained that, by making a direct suggestion to the subject, the hypnotist does not, in fact, make the best use of the known phenomena of hypnosis. We may consider as an example the case, already several times mentioned, of the young girl who refused to take off her clothes. Speculating on her state of mind, we might argue that she would be exposed to a considerable conflict. On the one hand, there is the powerful suggestion to undress; on the other hand, there is the obvious presence of a group of young men, resulting in a conflict between the suggestion and the ethical and moral ideas inculcated in her through a long process of education.

Now, if the hypnotist were serious in his attempt he would, of course, set about it in quite a different way. He would, by means of suggestion, attempt to remove the conflict in the girl's mind. He would do this first of all by inducing negative hallucinations in her to the effect that she was alone in the room, or possibly that only she and a girl friend were in the room, the experimenter casting himself in the role of the girl friend. He would then go on to use positive hallucinations to suggest that they were both in the girl's bedroom, spending quite a while implanting this suggestion in great detail in the subject's mind, and painting very vividly the existence and position of different articles of furniture.

The next suggestion would be, perhaps, to the effect that it was getting late, that the light was fading, that they had to get up early next morning, and that they ought to be going to bed. This kind of suggestion, once accepted, could then rapidly lead to the suggestion that they should now take off their clothes and go to bed. There is little doubt that, under these conditions, there would be no difficulty at all in producing the desired result. (The experiment has not, to my knowledge, been done, but evidence will be quoted below to leave little doubt on this score.)

Essentially, the technique suggested for achieving anti-social results is not so very different from that used by many people in ordinary life. Let us take the case of Sir Pumperdinck Flannel Flannel, the moustachioed cad in a Victorian melodrama. Bent on the seduction of the innocent maiden, what does he do? He obviously does not go up to her and say, 'To bed with you, my proud beauty'. What he does instead is the well-known routine of trying to create the impression in the girl's mind of a situation which, in fact, does not exist. He pretends to eternal love; he pretends to desire to marry her; he makes a large number of vows designed to confuse the issue and make his desires appear in a different light. The result, as is shown by the published statistics on illegitimacy, is often quite favourable, in spite of the absence of hypnosis. When hypnosis is added to the picture there is little doubt about the much greater efficacy of this type of method.

From speculation to experimentation. Here is an experiment on a private soldier, about twenty years of age, who had a very good Army record. He was placed in a trance while several senior Army men were present. A lieutenant-colonel was placed directly in front of the subject, about ten feet away from him, and the subject was then put in a trance and the following suggestions made to him: 'In a minute you will slowly open your eyes. In front of you you will see a dirty Jap soldier. He has a bayonet and is going to kill you unless you kill him first. You will have to strangle him with your bare hands.'

The subject opened his eyes, began to creep forward very slowly, and finally, in a flying tackle, brought the lieutenant-colonel down on the floor, knocked him against the wall, and began strangling him with both his hands. It needed three people to pull him off and break his grip, and he could not be pacified until the experimenter had put him back into a deep, quiet sleep. The attacked man reported that there was no make-believe about the attack and that he might have been killed or injured had assistance not been immediately available. When it is remembered that to attack a commissioned officer is a very serious offence in the Army, it will readily be seen that a skilled hypnotist, by misrepresenting the situation to the subject, could easily provoke an anti-social act of very great severity indeed. When we add to these considerations the fact that the subject may be hypnotized against his will, we can see that the easy belief that not much harm can be done under hypnosis, because of the safeguards latent in the individual's ethical and moral code, is dangerously complacent. Much work will need to be done before we know the possible limitations of hypnotic control over other people, but the dangers inherent in the anti-social use of hypnosis should certainly not be minimized.

The seriousness of these dangers is probably related to the proportion of people in whom a deep hypnotic trance can be induced. This proportion, unfortunately, is not known; indeed, in principle the problem as stated is an insoluble one. We cannot, in the nature of things, say what proportion of the population is tall, or intelligent, or fat, because these are graded qualities and there is no point at which we can say anybody beyond this point is tall, or intelligent, or fat, and anybody who falls short of it is the opposite. Similarly, hypnotic susceptibility forms a graded continuum, different people being susceptible to different degrees, and there is no one point where one could say that anyone beyond it could be called hypnotizable. This continuous nature of hypnotic suggestibility is demonstrated fairly clearly in a number of 'hypnotic scales', which have been drawn up to measure the depth of trance. These scales make use of a number of suggestions of increasing difficulty, recording in each case the success or failure of the hypnotized person with respect to the suggestion employed. The importance of a particular phenomenon is assessed by taking into account its rarity, i.e. the difficulty of eliciting it in a large group of people who are being hypnotized. Table 1 below illustrates the construction of one such scale. The suggestions given are printed on the left; the number of points given to each item indicate the number of instances in which that particular suggestion was successfully employed. Thus, a large number of people accepted the suggestion that their eyes were feeling tired, that they were completely relaxed and incapable of activity. A glove anaesthesia, i.e. the incapacity to feel a touch over an area of skin covered by a glove, was distinctly more difficult to induce. The illusions of bell-ringing and of leg-movement were even more rare. The illusion of an electric bulb lighting up, a post-hypnotic suggestion to the effect that the subject should shake and open a box, and spontaneous amnesia to the whole process were rarest of all. Each individual could be given a score on this scale according to

TABLE I

Eysenck-Furneaux Scale

Items Suggested	Points
Eyes tired	76
Complete relaxation	76
Feels incapable of activity	65
Arm falls irresistibly	63
Eyelids heavy	61
Impossible to raise arm	59
Feels miles away	54
Feels pleasant warmth	53
Glove anaesthesia	46
Eyes closing	45
Both arms stiff and rigid	36
Impossible to raise arm (eyes open)	24
Illusion of bell-ringing	22
Complete catalepsy	21
Cannot hear buzzer	19
Illusion of leg movement	18
Increase of Body Sway (post-hypnotic)	18
Line length suggestibility (post-hypnotic)	16
Amnesia (spontaneous)	15
Shake and open box (post-hypnotic)	13
Illusion of electric bulb lighting up	12

the degree of susceptibility shown by him, and these scores could be shown to form a regular progression or continuum from high to low.

Some authors, instead of using a continuous scale, have preferred to use categories; thus, one author uses the following five categories:

(1) *Insusceptible:* total lack of response to suggestion.

(2) *Hypnoidal:* relaxation, fluttering of the eyelids, closing of the eyes; complete physical relaxation.

(3) *Light Trance:* Catalepsy of the eyes; limb catalepsies; rigid catalepsies; glove anaesthesia.

(4) *Medium Trance:* Partial amnesia; post-hypnotic anaesthesia; personality changes; simple post-hypnotic suggestions.

(5) *Deep Trance:* Ability to open the eyes without affecting the trance; bizarre post-hypnotic suggestions; post-hypnotic hallucinations; positive and negative auditory hallucinations; systematized post-hypnotic amnesias.

It is possible, from the writings of many different experimenters, to give rough percentage figures of people falling into these various categories. About 15 per cent are found to be insusceptible; about 40 per cent are found to fall into a hypnoidal or light trance; some 25 per cent show phenomena characteristic of a medium trance; and some 20 per cent show phenomena characteristic of a deep trance.

These values are representative but, unfortunately, their meaning is not too clear. There are several reasons for this. In the first place, hypnotic behaviour can be learned and practised very much in the same way that other types of behaviour are learned and practised. A person may start out as a rather indifferent subject, but after a certain amount of practice he may develop deeper and deeper stages of hypnosis. If he is classified according to his reactions right at the beginning, he would be considered insusceptible or hypnoidal only; if classified after several hours of practice, he might be classified as capable of a deep trance.

Another difficulty which arises is connected with different methods used by hypnotists; the different capabilities of hypnotists; and the different degrees of practice which they have had. Thus, some people are considerably better than others in inducing a deep hypnotic trance, and consequently the per cent figures obtained by them would be quite different from those obtained by an indifferent hypnotist. Nor can it be said that the hypnotist is necessarily 'good' or 'bad' in absolute terms. A particular hypnotist may succeed with Mr Smith and fail with Mr Brown, while another hypnotist may succeed with Mr Brown and fail with Mr Smith. There are complexities in these personal relationships which very much complicate the picture.

Another complicating feature is the particular technique employed by a given hypnotist on a given occasion, and the length of time he is willing to continue trying. One of the best-known modern hypnotists reports that one of his most capable subjects required less than thirty seconds to develop his first profound trance, while a second, equally competent subject, required 300 hours of systematic labour before a trance could be induced. Few experimenters have spent as much time as this on their less successful subjects; it is quite possible that if they had done so most of these would have been put into a higher category. One report will illustrate the chance element which makes most of the quoted figures somewhat meaningless. A very determined hypnotist spent several hours on a given subject without inducing any kind of hypnotic reaction whatsoever. Finally, at the end of a three-hour session he completely lost his temper and shouted at the subject, 'For —'s sake go to sleep you — —!' The subject immediately fell into a deep trance and was an exemplary subject ever after.

To these many difficulties are added the frequent changes in motivation which undoubtedly play a role in determining a person's reaction to these hypnotic situations. It will be realized that the simple question regarding the proportion of people who were hypnotizable in the population does not admit of any kind of straightforward answer. There are so many qualifying conditions, and so little experimental work to clarify their influence that not even a guess would seem justified. What can be said, however, is that in the hands of a competent hypnotist who is willing to spend at least four hours on each person, and under conditions which make the subject reasonably co-operative rather than hostile, hypnotic phenomena can be induced in something like 85 per cent of the population. It is quite possible that this figure should be higher still, and, indeed, it might easily go up to 100 per cent. Thus, hypnosis is not a rare and isolated phenomenon, but one which is relevant to the great majority of people, and possibly to everyone.

We have now covered the main events characterizing the hypnotic state; we may next turn to some of the theories advanced by various people to account for these phenomena. Mesmer's theory of 'animal magnetism' was taken over by some of his followers, who became interested in hypnotic phenomena. It should hardly be necessary to argue against this ancient doctrine, but we may note some of the people who were instrumental in proposing alternative theories. Mainly involved in this liberation from the absurdities of Mesmer's views were James Braid, an English physician, and a group of French investigators. Braid, who became interested in hypnotic phenomena through seeing a public demonstration of them, was at first sceptical, but later became convinced of the reality of the phenomena displayed. He conducted a series of researches, and these very soon caused him to reject the view that hypnotic phenomena were due to a fluid passing from the body of the hypnotist to that of the subject.

Braid also coined the word 'hypnotism', introduced the method of hypnotism described early in this chapter, and still most widely used, and also utilized the trance for painless surgical operations. In addition, he was one of the first to realize that suggestion played the major role in hypnosis, a conclusion which had already been adumbrated by the Royal Commission, whose report on Mesmer's work has been quoted earlier on.

While these things are to Braid's credit, it should be noted that much of his experimental work was thoroughly bad and gave rise to beliefs hardly less absurd than those of Mesmer. Braid was a firm believer in phrenology, that curious view which teaches that human beings are possessed of certain faculties; that these faculties are located in certain parts of the brain; that the degree of development of a given faculty is indicated by the physical development of the corresponding part of the brain; and that this physical development is mirrored in the contours of the skull. Phrenologists accordingly feel the bumps of the skull in order to arrive at their analysis of a person's temperament and abilities. Braid contributed to this view by teaching that if pressure was applied to the various areas of the heads of hypnotized persons, then behaviour characteristic of the corresponding phrenological faculty would be elicited. Thus, he writes that when he pressed the bump, or 'organ', of veneration on the head of the patient, 'an altered expression of countenance took place, and a movement of arms and hands, which later became clasped in addition, and the patient ... arose from the seat and knelt down as if engaged in prayer'. It is only fair to say that Braid gradually improved the standards of his experimentation and that he finally gave up his belief in phrenology. The fact, however, that such an able and completely honest person as Braid committed these very elementary errors suggests both the difficulty of experimental work in this field, and also the very undeveloped state of psychological experimentation. There will be occasion later on to return to this point.

In France a comparable development took place, largely due to the work of a humble physician in Nancy, who practised hypnotism on the poor peasants who came to his house. This man, Liébeault, has rightly become famous, not only for his contribution to the study of hypnosis, but also because of his unselfish generosity. He refused to accept fees for his hypnotic treatments, and the lovable nature of the man may be seen from a description of his clinic given by Bramwell, a well-known British historian of hypnosis:

His clinique, invariably thronged, was held in two rooms in the corner of this garden. ... The patients told to go to sleep apparently fell at once into a quiet slumber, then received their dose of curative suggestions, and when told to awake, either walked quietly away or sat for a little to chat with their friends, the whole process rarely lasting longer than ten minutes. ... No drugs were given, and Liébeault took special pains to explain to his patients that he neither exercised nor possessed any mysterious powers, and that all he did was simple and capable of scientific explanation. ... A little girl, about five years old, dressed shabbily, but evidently in her best, with a crown of paper laurel leaves on her head and carrying a little book in her hand, toddled into the sanctum, fearlessly interrupted the doctor in the midst of his work by pulling his coat, and said, 'You promised me a penny if I got a prize'. This, accompanied by kindly words, was smilingly given, incitement to work having been evoked in a pleasing, if not scientific way. Two little girls about six or seven years of age, no doubt brought in the first instance by friends, walked in and sat down on a sofa behind the doctor. He, stopping for a moment in his work, made a pass in the direction of one of them, and said, 'Sleep, my little kitten', repeated the same for the other, and in an instant they were both asleep. He rapidly gave them their dose of suggestion and then evidently forgot all about them. In about twenty minutes one awoke, and wishing to go, essayed by shaking and pulling to awaken her companion – her amused expression of face, when she failed to do so, being very comic. In about five minutes more the second one awoke, and, hand in hand, they trotted laughingly away.

After many years of hard work, Liébeault put his views into a book, the main teachings of which were similar to those of Braid. However, as was perhaps inevitable in one so self-effacing, only one copy of this book was sold, and it was not until twenty years later, when Bernheim, a Professor in the medical school at Nancy, became acquainted with Liébeault, that the attention of the medical profession was directed towards Liébeault's great successes in treating various types of disorders by means of hypnosis, and to his theories attributing these effects to suggestion.

It might have been thought that when serious scientists had exorcised the devil of 'animal magnetism' in this thoroughgoing fashion, and when so much experimental work was available to show the influences that were really operating, a period of patient, quiet research would follow, untroubled by arguments about the ancient Mesmeric doctrines. However, this was not to be, and the person responsible for the revival of the doctrine of animal magnetism was a well-known French anatomist and neurologist named Charcot. It is one of the tragedies of science that Charcot, who was an extremely able experimenter in physiology, is known to posterity largely because of the egregious errors committed in his experimental studies of hypnosis. The story of how this came about is a fascinating one, and also instructive, as it shows clearly that competence in physiological experimentation does not, by any means, guarantee competence in psychological work, and may in fact blind the person in question to sources of error of a purely psychological nature.

Charcot was very much afraid of being deceived by his subjects, and determined that his experiments should be as rigorous and ultra-scientific as his physiological work. Consequently, he sought diligently in the behaviour of his subjects for signs of hypnotic trance behaviour which could not be simulated and which were of a completely objective nature. He concluded from his studies that hypnotism showed three definite stages: lethargy, catalepsy, and somnambulism. The lethargic stage, which was induced by closing the subject's eyes, was characterized by an inability on the part of the subject to hear or to speak. Also contractures of a specified nature resulted when certain nerves were pressed. The cataleptic stage was produced by opening the subject's eyes while he was in the lethargic stage. Now limbs would remain in any position in which they were placed by the experimenter, and the subject was still unable to hear or speak. The somnambulistic stage could then be induced by applying friction to the top of the head, and it is this somnambulistic condition which appeared similar to what we would now call an ordinary hypnotic trance.

Another phenomenon much stressed by Charcot was that

of *transference*. Sometimes he found that the contractures, catalepsies, and so on, would appear on only one side of the body. If now a large magnet was brought close to the limbs in question, the symptoms could be displaced at once to the other side of the body.

Bernheim and Liébeault reported that these alleged stages of hypnosis were never found in their own work *unless the subjects had been taught to expect to go through them*. In other words, Charcot's allegedly 'objective' signs of hypnosis had, in fact, been suggested by him in some form or other to his subjects and had no necessary connexion of any kind with hypnosis. Thus, by neglecting the psychological effects of suggestion, Charcot's demonstrations lost the reality of scientific experiment for the appearance. An acrimonious controversy ensued, but there is no doubt whatever that Charcot was completely mistaken in his beliefs.

He was also wrong in another theory he put forward to the effect that hypnosis could be induced only in abnormal and neurotic subjects, particularly in hysterics, and that hysteria was causally related to hypnosis. Bernheim retorted that in his work, and in that of Liébeault, many hundreds and thousands of entirely normal individuals had been successfully hypnotized, and that consequently there was no special relation of any kind between hypnosis and mental abnormality. Again the so-called 'Nancy' school was right and Charcot was wrong; all modern workers are agreed that the hypnotic trance can be produced at least as well in mentally normal as in mentally abnormal individuals.

When we turn to modern theories of hypnosis, it cannot be said that we leave the realm of absurdity behind. Some, at least, of the more recent theories of hypnosis are equally implausible as Mesmer's original notions, or Charcot's views. A brief mention of some of the better-known ones may serve to show the reader how very little agreement there is between different authorities.

One of the older and more respectable theories sees in it a modified form of sleep. The very term 'hypnosis' shows that originally the sleep-like characteristic of the hypnotic trance suggested an identification of the two states, and Pavlov comes foremost in claiming that sleep and hypnosis are similar, involving a spread of cerebral inhibition in both cases. This theory is almost certainly false. The physiological reaction of the organism under hypnosis is quite different from that which is observed in sleep. Thus, certain reflexes are abolished in sleep, but not under hypnosis. Electroencephalogram recordings, or 'brain waves', show different characteristics in the two states. The evidence is very strong in opposing an identification of these two states.

A more acceptable hypothesis would regard hypnosis as a conditioned response. Such a view might in due course be elaborated into a proper theory, but at the moment it fails completely to account for many of the phenomena associated with hypnosis. How, one might ask, could conditioning account for spontaneous post-hypnotic amnesias? While conditioning cannot be completely rejected as a likely part of a true theory of hypnosis, certainly by itself it is not sufficient.

Much the same might be said of dissociation as an explanation of hypnotic phenomena. It is well known that parts of the cortex and the central nervous system can be dissociated from the remainder, and many hypnotic phenomena seem to be of this character. However, it will be difficult to account for hypnosis in terms of dissociation because very little is, in fact, known about association, so that we would merely be explaining one unknown by another.

A similar objection might be presented against another view which looks upon hypnosis as an exaggerated form of suggestibility. While, undoubtedly, there is a considerably increased degree of suggestibility in hypnosis, it is idle to seek for an explanatory principle in the laws of suggestibility, because very little is known about suggestibility itself. Again we would merely be attempting to explain one unknown by another.

Among the more esoteric theories is a Freudian one, according to which susceptibility to hypnosis depends on the extent of 'transference' formed between the subject and the hypnotist. This 'transference' is a special relationship which

C

revives attitudes originally present in the parent–child relationship. Added to this are various erotic components which are supposed to be present in hypnosis, which is considered to be a manifestation of the Oedipus complex, of masochistic tendencies, and so on.

Weirdest of all is a theory which states essentially 'that the phenomena of hypnosis result from the subject's motive to behave like a hypnotized person, as defined by the hypnotist, and as understood by the subject'. This is perhaps the most question-begging of all, because it leaves unanswered the two crucial questions as to why the subject should want to behave in this fashion, and how he manages to do this. It is all very well to say a person wants to behave like a hypnotized subject, but how does that help him to produce an analgesia to an operation?

Most promising perhaps is a theory of ideo-motor action. There is ample experimental evidence to show that ideas of certain movements are closely related to the execution of these movements. If electrodes and an amplifier are connected to the muscles of the arm, and the subject is told to lie quite still on a couch, but to imagine that he is lifting that arm, then a barrage of nervous impulses is recorded as passing through the nerves and into the muscles which would have been used had the movement, in fact, been executed. Thus, nerve transmission and mental images or ideas are closely related, and, indeed, it appears that the one is never found without the other. Without going into the question of which causes which, the mutual interdependence of mental and physical phenomena does not seem to be in doubt. Under these conditions, the possibility of achieving changes in a person's behaviour through verbal means, as in hypnosis, appears possible. At best, this is only a partial theory and it stands very much in need of considerable amplification. If it could be combined with some such form of inhibition theory as will be discussed in a later chapter, we might here have the beginning of a true theory of hypnosis. At the moment such a theory cannot be said to exist, and all that we can do is to note the experimental facts, which are reasonably well established, and hope that a greater interest in these important discoveries will eventually lead to greater knowledge.

It is interesting to speculate why the development of a scientific study of hypnotic phenomena has been so slow. The main point undoubtedly has been the following. The quotation is from Clark L. Hull, whose book on *Hypnosis and Suggestibility* appeared in 1933, and which may be said to mark the end of the pre-scientific and the beginning of a truly scientific investigation of the subject. This is what he has to say:

All sciences alike have descended from magic and superstition, but none has been so slow as hypnosis in shaking off the evil associations of its origin. None has been so slow in taking on a truly experimental and genuinely scientific character.... The tardy development of the science of hypnotism, moreover, is especially striking when it is recalled that practically from the beginning hypnosis has been definitely an experimental phenomenon. Not only this, but experimentation has been continuous and widespread during a period in which other fields of science have made the greatest advances ever known. The paradox in this case, as in all others, disappears with full knowledge of the attendant circumstances ... the dominant motive throughout the entire history of hypnotism has been clinical, that of curing human ills. A worse method for the establishment of scientific principles among highly elusive phenomena could hardly have been devised.... The physician's task is to effect a cure in the quickest manner possible, using more or less simultaneously any and all means at his disposal. General laws which call for the varying of a single factor at a time do not readily emerge from such situations.

The essential point emphasized again and again by Hull is that what is lacking in most of the early work on hypnosis is a notion of a controlled experiment. This notion is of almost universal application in science, and the method underlying it has been formally stated by John Stuart Mill in the following words:

If an instance in which the phenomenon under investigation occurs, and an instance in which it does not occur, have every circumstance in common save one, that one occurring only in the former; the circumstance in which alone the two instances differ is the effect, or the cause, or an indispensable part of the cause, of the phenomenon.

As an example of the need for controlled experiments, let us take the problem of the effectiveness of psychotherapy. What most investigators have done in order to find out whether psychoanalysis and other types of psychotherapy are effective in producing a remission of neurotic symptoms has been to take a group of seriously ill people, submit them to the particular type of therapy in question, and state at the end of a period of treatment, extending over several years, how many of the patients have been cured, how many have improved, how many remain in pretty much the original state, and how many have actually deteriorated. This has been the universal practice, but quite obviously it is not in any sense conclusive. Suppose we find that 70 per cent of our patients are cured after four years of treatment. This improvement in their condition might be due to the treatment, but it might also be due to any number of other causes. We can only be sure that it is the treatment which has been effective by having a control group, i.e. another group of patients, similarly afflicted, who do not obtain psychotherapy of the type administered to the experimental group. If this control group fails to improve to the same extent as the experimental group, then, indeed, we have reason to believe that psychotherapy has been effective.

In *Uses and Abuses of Psychology* I pointed out two facts. The first was that no experiment along these lines had ever been carried out, and that, of the fifty or so papers published on the effectiveness of psychotherapy, not one had made use of a control group. I also pointed out that it was possible from certain reports in the literature to demonstrate that, without any form of psychotherapy, considerable improvement occurred in the condition of neurotic patients with the simple passage of time. Indeed, this improvement can be put in terms of a formula. If we let X stand for the per cent of improvement achieved, and N for the number of weeks elapsing without treatment of a psychotherapeutic kind, then

$$X = 100(1 - 10^{-0.00435N}).$$

Using these figures it was found that the improvement claimed by psychotherapists after treatment was no more and no less extensive than that found without any treatment at all.

Since that time a proper experiment has been recorded from California in which matched groups of neurotic subjects were respectively treated by psychotherapy and not treated at all. The outcome of the experiment was very much in line with my previous conclusion. The treated group improved to a considerable extent, but the untreated group improved equally. Without the existence of such a control group the erroneous impression would have been given that psychotherapy was responsible for the improvement. It cannot be emphasized too strongly that erroneous conclusions of this kind have arisen so frequently in work on hypnosis, on psychotherapy, and so forth, because of the clinical inclination of the experimenters concerned. The desire to help the unfortunate patient suffering from neurotic and other symptoms has been stronger than the desire for scientific knowledge, which alone can enable us to give effective help. There are, admittedly, ethical problems involved in withholding treatment from people in trouble, but it should not be forgotten that there are also ethical problems involved in administering treatments the efficacy of which is unknown, unproven, and suspect. Is the psychotherapist justified in demanding from his patient the considerable expenditure of time, energy, and money, which is involved in psychoanalysis when he has no evidence of any kind to show that this treatment will be more effective than doing nothing at all? Whatever the correct answer may be to this problem, the reader may like to ponder the many parallels and similarities between the development of Mesmerism and that of psychoanalysis. In both cases there is a strong personality as the founder of the cult; there is a large congregation of pupils, fanatically devoted to the furtherance of the master's teaching; there are the splits and the formation of different schools; there is a formulation of unusual, unorthodox, and unlikely theories on the basis of highly questionable evidence. In both cases there are reports of cures achieved, and in both cases there is an absence of the controlled experiment which alone could verify the claims made. Only the future can tell whether the Freudian libido will join animal magnetism on the heap of discarded hypotheses for which science has no use.

2

LIE DETECTORS AND TRUTH DRUGS

IF it be true that there are more things in heaven and earth than are dreamed of in our philosophy, it is surely equally true that things are dreamed of in our philosophy which do not appear in heaven or on earth. Among these figments of the imagination appear such varied objects as the philosopher's stone, which was supposed to transmute base metals into gold, the Oedipus complex, which was supposed to transmute a normal person into a gibbering neurotic, the houris, whose beauty and voluptuous sensuality were supposed to console the Mohammedan warrior who lost his life fighting for the faith of the Prophet, and the Jungian archetypes, which are supposed to haunt our modern minds with mystical reminders of the inherited wisdom, or otherwise, of our race.

A little nearer to a scientifically ascertainable fact than these lie certain rather odd phenomena, which have received a good deal of study in recent years under the general title of psychosomatic disorders. What is meant by this somewhat ill-conceived phrase is simply that certain disorders of the body, or soma, may be caused by psychological events, such as strong emotions, and that the cure for the somatic disorder may thus be achieved by first accomplishing a psychological purge. This insistence on the close relationship between body and mind, and the interplay between the two, is regarded as a very modern trend, and Freud and the psychoanalysts generally are often credited with the discovery of what many people have considered a vital new truth in medicine.

This is a very unhistorical way of looking at the facts. The general theory of psychosomatic interaction is at least as old as human thinking about mind and matter, and there is little in these modern theories that cannot be found in the Greek philosophers or even earlier. Nor is the specific application of the principles involved to medical diagnosis and treatment anything novel. To quote just one example, we may consider a story told in the fifteenth century in a well-known Persian work, the *Akhlaq-i-Jalali*. The author tells how the great physician Rhazes was summoned to Transoxiana to attend the Amir Mansur, who was suffering from a rheumatic affection of the joints which none of his medical attendants could cure. When he came to the river Oxus, Rhazes refused to cross the river in the boat provided because it was too small and fragile. The King's messengers bound him hand and foot, threw him into the boat, and carried him across by force. Rhazes explained the motive of his resistance to them. He knew, he said, that every year many thousands of people crossed the Oxus safely, but if he had chanced to be drowned, people would have said what a fool he was to expose himself to this risk of his own free will, but had he perished while being carried across by force, people would have pitied, not blamed him.

Having reached Bukhara, Rhazes tried various methods of treatment without success. Finally, he said to the Amir, 'Tomorrow I shall try a new treatment, but it will cost you the best horse and best mule in your stables'. The animals having been placed at his disposal, Rhazes took the Amir to a hot bath outside the city, tied up the horse and the mule, saddled and bridled, outside, and entered the hot room of the bath alone with his patient. He then took out a knife and began reviling the Amir, reminding him of the indignity he had undergone in being carried across the Oxus by force, and threatened now to take his life in revenge. 'The Amir was furious and, partly from anger, partly from fear, sprang to his feet.' Rhazes at once ran outside to where his servant was awaiting him with the horse and the mule, rode off at full speed, and did not stop in his flight until he had crossed the Oxus and had reached Merv, whence he wrote to the Amir as follows: 'May the life of the king be prolonged in health and authority! Agreeably to my undertaking, I treated you to the best of my ability. There was, however, a deficiency in the natural caloric, and this treatment would have been unduly protracted, so I abandoned it in favour of psychotherapy, and, when the peccant humours had undergone sufficient coction in the bath, I deliberately provoked you in order to increase the natural caloric, which thus gained sufficient strength to dissolve the already softened humours. But henceforth it is inexpedient that we should meet.'

This example of 'psychotherapy' actually was designated thus in the original tome, and turned out to be no less rewarding on the material plane than modern psychotherapy has been found to be. The Amir, delighted to find himself restored to health and freedom of movement, awarded Rhazes a robe of honour, a cloak, a turban, arms, a male and female slave of beauteous countenance, a horse, fully caparisoned, and further assigned to him a yearly donation of 2,000 gold dinars and 200 ass-loads of corn.

Rather similar in principle is a story told by the greatest of Mohammedan physicians, Avicenna, who was born around the year 980. It comes from his rare and unpublished *Book of the Origin and the Return*. The patient here is a woman in the King's household who, while bending down to lay the table, is attacked by a sudden rheumatic swelling of the joints and is unable to assume an erect posture. The King's physician, commanded to cure her, but having no medicaments at hand, has recourse to psychotherapy (again so called by the author). He calls to his aid the emotion of shame and begins to remove her clothes, starting with her veil and going on to her skirt. Thus, in the author's words, 'A flush of heat was produced within her which dissolved the rheumatic humour', and she stood upright completely cured.

Many other stories in a similar vein could be quoted from historical writings of many countries. They all suggest that a knowledge of certain principles governing the relation between body and mind have been quite well understood from time immemorial. One of these principles forms the basis of our modern techniques of lie detection, and again we must note that what appears to be a very modern development can, in fact, be traced back hundreds and even thousands of years to people whom we would regard as untutored savages. One such application, vouched for by modern anthropologists, goes back beyond the reach of human memory. An example may illustrate the method used: A chief of the tribe has been slain and five men to whom he had done injuries in the past are suspected of having taken revenge on him. How can the guilty one be found? The tribe is drawn up in the form of a huge semi-circle by the bank of the river; the five accused stand facing the tribe and with their backs to the river. The witch doctor, gruesomely attired and painted, is jumping about to the sound of rhythmic drum-beats. The tension is growing steadily as the moment of truth approaches. Finally, the dance comes to an end and the witch doctor ceremoniously heaps rice from a bowl on to five plates made of palm leaves. He then harangues the tribe at great length about the iniquity of the murder of a chieftain and about the magic which will discover the murderer. Those who are innocent, he explains, will eat the rice without difficulty; the guilty one, whose crime is so repellent to nature that the very animals and plants will have nothing to do with him, will find it impossible to swallow even a mouthful and will thus stand revealed in all his iniquity. Being a good practical psychologist, as most witch doctors are (they would not survive long if they were not!), he rams this suggestion home time and time again, reciting previous trials where this infallible method had been found to detect the culprit and produce a confession. He then dramatically presents the five accused with their platefuls of rice. Lo and behold, four of them proceed to eat it, if not with outward signs of enjoyment, at least without any apparent trouble. The fifth, however, ashen-faced, and hardly able to stand upright on trembling legs, is moving his jaws desperately in a vain attempt to swallow at least some of the rice, but without success. The picture of guilt could not be clearer, and as he is dragged away at the orders of the witch doctor, he bawls out his confession before being thrown to the crocodiles.

The psychological processes at work here are reasonably

obvious. We all know the dry mouth of fear; strong emotion inhibits digestion and also salivary secretion, which is so intimately connected with digestion. Without saliva, however, the mastication and swallowing of food become difficult, if not impossible. We can thus easily reconstruct what is happening to the unfortunate victim in the trial scene described above. Knowing his guilt, and superstitiously afraid of the power of the witch doctor and his ability to ferret out the truth, he implicitly believes all that the latter is saying about the difficulties the guilty person will experience in eating the rice. Thus, fear of the consequences of what appears an inevitable discovery dries out his mouth, and the conscious awareness of this change that is taking place further increases his fear and his certainty of being discovered. When finally the rice is actually produced he is in no fit state to eat, and again his subjective awareness of the difficulties he has in swallowing increases his fear, and thereby enmeshes him further in the vicious circle of his own emotional reactions. Barbaric as this story may sound, there is nothing, in principle, in modern methods of lie detection that is not clearly contained in this account. We will find certain technical improvements in recording the effects of emotion, but, on the other hand, our modern procedures produce much less emotion than the witch doctor was capable of generating and, on balance, it is not certain that the advantage lies with our modern techniques.

Salivation, as an index of emotion, is not used at all by modern lie-detector experts. Nowadays we concentrate more on the circulation of the blood, respiration, and certain electrical phenomena of the skin, which will be described in due course. A rather less gruesome story than the one about the witch doctor may illustrate that these methods also were well known a thousand years ago. It also concerns Avicenna and is quoted in his own masterpiece, the *Qanun*, in the section devoted to love, which he classes under cerebral or mental diseases, together with somnolence, insomnia, amnesia, mania, hydrophobia, melancholia, and the like. When Mahmud of Ghazna was trying to kidnap him (kings and rulers in general went to extreme lengths at that time to obtain the services of a good consultant!), Avicenna fled and came incognito to the town of Hyrcania by the Caspian Sea. A relative of the ruler of that province was sick with a disease which had baffled all the local doctors. Avicenna was asked to give his opinion. Having examined the patient carefully, he requested the collaboration of someone who knew all the districts and towns of the province, and repeated their names while Avicenna kept his finger on the patient's pulse. At the mention of a certain town he felt a flutter in the pulse. 'Now', said he, 'I need someone who knows all the houses, streets, and quarters of this town.' Again, when a certain street was mentioned there was a flutter in the pulse, and once again when the names of the inhabitants of a certain household were enumerated. Then Avicenna said, 'It is finished. This lad is in love with such-and-such a girl, who lives in such-and-such a house, in such-and-such a street, in such-and-such a quarter of such-and-such a town; and the girl's face is the patient's cure.' So the marriage was solemnized at a fortunate hour chosen by Avicenna, and thus the cure was completed.

Here, then, we again have an example of an involuntary emotional response giving away a secret which, for some reason or other, the subject of the experiment wants to keep to himself, and again this involuntary response is one of the well-known concomitants of strong emotion. This close relationship between the emotions felt by human beings and the physiological changes taking place in their bodies is the basis of our lie-detection techniques, and it has been dealt with both on the experimental and on the theoretical level by many psychologists and physiologists. Probably the most famous is the American psychologist, William James, brother of the novelist Henry James, who, together with a Norwegian physiologist called Lange, gave his name to a law which forms the basis, in one form or another, of most modern work on emotions. This James–Lange law inverts what we might consider the normal sequence of events. What, in everyday opinion, happens when we feel an emotion? We are sad and, therefore, we cry; we are afraid and our heart beats faster; we are enraged and adrenal glands pump adrenalin into our blood-stream. In other words, emotion, as felt consciously by ourselves, comes first, the physiological concomitants come second. James and Lange maintain that this is putting the cart before the horse. In response to a certain situation, the adrenal glands pour adrenalin into our blood-stream, and therefore we feel anger; in a certain situation our heart beats faster, and this causes us to feel the emotion of fear; a certain situation causes us to cry, and our subjective feeling response to the crying is to feel sad. In other words, the external stimulus situation (S) produces certain physiological responses (fears, adrenalin, increase in heart-beat) which we may designate PR. These physiological responses in turn produce the felt emotion (E). Thus, the James–Lange formula is $S \rightarrow PR \rightarrow E$, whereas normally we conceive of the sequence as being rather like this: $S \rightarrow E \rightarrow PR$.

There has been much discussion of this theory and much experimentation. Unfortunately, little of what has been done can be said to throw much light on this problem, which, in a nutshell, is a problem of the relation between body and mind generally. We can only decide which causes which – the emotion the physiological response, or the physiological response the emotion – by finding out which comes first, but this, unfortunately, we cannot do. Emotions are subjective, and for timing we would have to rely on the introspective reports of our subjects, which could not be expected to be very accurate, particularly when it is a matter of split seconds. On the other hand, the physiological response is not a sudden, all-or-none, affair; it also requires some time to build up. These difficulties suggest that while a decision may not perhaps be impossible, it is certainly impossible at the present time. Consequently, we need not concern ourselves too much with this question. Let us merely note that emotional experiences, as felt by the individual, and certain types of physiological disturbances, as detected by specialized electronic recording equipment, are always found to go together, and that consequently we may use evidence for the occurrence of the one as evidence for the occurrence of the other. This essentially is the principle on which lie detection is based, and there is no doubt that it is a perfectly sound and respectable scientific principle. We will have occasion to consider the difficulties which may arise in using this principle a little later.

First of all, let us inquire what precisely are the physiological reactions which denote the presence of an emotion. Largely, these reactions can be identified because they are transmitted by a special part of the nervous system. Speaking quite broadly and generally, we may say that human beings (and the higher animals as well, of course) have two nervous systems. One, the so-called central nervous system, is responsible for the transmission of impulses to the skeletal musculature, which is responsible for carrying out voluntary movements. Kicking a ball, writing a sonnet, jumping in the lake, or putting a cross against a candidate's name, these are all voluntary activities carried out by our skeleton, the bones of which are being moved by muscles receiving their orders from the cortex through the central nervous system.

There is, however, another system more ancient and relatively independent of the central nervous system. This has been called the autonomic, or vegetative, nervous system, and deals essentially with certain vital but unconscious activities, which maintain our body in good trim. Thus, we breathe, our heart beats, digestion takes place, hormones are pouring into our blood-stream, the amount of blood passing through different parts of the body is finely regulated in response to temperature, our pupil dilatates and contracts in response to differences in brightness – all without any kind of conscious adjustment. It is these autonomic, or vegetative, responses which are so closely related to emotion. Some of the major autonomic changes accompanying emotion are familiar to everyone, and do not require instrumentation for their detection. These changes include flushing, or pallor, of the face, excessive sweating, increase in heart rate, the drying out of the mouth, many vague visceral sensations, and so forth. Under laboratory conditions many other more subtle physiological changes can be observed, such as a rise in blood pressure; increased oxygen consumption; dilatation of the bronchioles of the lungs; increase in the number of red cells and platelets in the circulating blood; liberation of glucose into the blood-stream; secretion of adrenalin; reduction in the electrical responses of the skin; inhibition of peristalsis in the gastro-intestinal tract; increase in blood-sugar; and many hundreds of others which could be mentioned.

Most of these changes appear to have an adaptive purpose; the major emotions, like fear and anger, are usually the precursors of violent activity, which might be fight or flight. For both a powerful supply of blood is needed. Consequently, the heart beats faster to supply the anticipated needs; blood is withdrawn from the stomach, thus stopping digestion; some of the energy stored up by the body is released into the blood, which makes the organism more capable of exertion. Cannon, in his book on *The Wisdom of the Body*, has traced in great detail the wonderful adaptability shown by our bodies in responding to urgent situations of this kind; an adaptability which owes nothing to conscious thought and everything to an inherited response pattern developed in millions of years of evolution.

Unfortunately, many of the emotional responses so produced are maladaptive in modern society. In civilized society, neither fight nor flight are responses having survival value. This generalization does not apply in exceptional circumstances, and in war-time particularly the responses which were useful to our forefathers when they lived in the jungle may become useful again. But even that becomes less and less true as wars become depersonalized, and as hand-to-hand combat is replaced by machine warfare. There is no evidence to suggest that the bomb-aimer who releases the unspeakable horror of the atom or hydrogen bomb by a push of his finger on a button is enabled to do so with greater precision because of strong emotion and vehement autonomic activity. Quite on the contrary, it appears that fine mental and muscular co-ordination, such as is required in skilled tasks of this kind, is actually impeded by strong emotion. Most people will have introspective evidence of this from their own experiences. Clever argumentation becomes disrupted by strong emotion; we cannot think as cogently and as logically when we are annoyed as we do when we consider the issues in an unemotional way. In playing a game, strong emotion may actually make us more powerful and less liable to feel injuries or succumb to exhaustion, but it will also make us less skilful and less intellectual in our approach; we may hit the ball harder, but accuracy will suffer.

On the whole, then, strong emotions may prepare us for the primitive type of battle in which brute strength and endurance and speed of flight determine survival, but they will not only fail to be of advantage to us in most circumstances in the type of world we have created in the last few hundred years – they will frequently be an actual handicap. A struggle in the Board Room for control of a large enterprise, or a fight between rival politicians in an election; a battle with the income-tax inspector for a change in one's code number, or a negotiation with one's employers for an increase in salary – all these are modern forms of combat which have replaced the more physical types prevalent during the course of human evolution. In all of them emotion is a handicap rather than a help, and we have the unfortunate position of having to reverse the evolutionary process and try to respond to a challenge with an intellectual rather than with an emotional response. It might not be too fanciful to consider that our success in thus reversing the course of evolution may determine our survival on this planet.

If this reversal were ever accomplished, human beings would certainly make better liars. From many points of view, of course, that would not altogether be an advantage, and one of the socially useful functions of an emotion is certainly that of making lie detection possible. In a sense, of course, the term 'lie detection' in this connexion is a misnomer. What we, in fact, detect is the presence of some kind of emotional response; we interpret this as evidence of lying because we arrange the whole interrogation situation in such a way that other sources of emotion are excluded as far as possible. In this way, the fear of being found out, associated with the telling of a lie, provides an emotional response peculiar to the guilty person and is absent when the truth is being told. Consequently, 'emotion detection' becomes 'lie detection' in certain specially arranged circumstances, but the jump from the one to the other still remains a jump, and great care has to be taken, as we shall see presently, to make certain that this jump is, in truth, justified and that wrong deductions are not made from the truth as revealed by the so-called lie detector. An example may make clearer some of the difficulties encountered. Supposing that in the case of the witch doctor's attempt to discover the guilty person all five had been innocent, but one had known that the witch doctor held a grudge against him and was going to throw the blame for murder on him. Under those circumstances he might, quite reasonably, be expected to show the same kind of fear reaction as the guilty person, and, consequently, his failure to swallow the rice might be wrongly interpreted as an indication of his guilt. There are several possible ways of avoiding such pitfalls, and these will be discussed in the remainder of this chapter.

We must now turn to the instrument used in modern work on lie detection. Popularly, the lie detector is often thought of as an instrument which rings a bell or flashes a light whenever a lie is told by the person who is undergoing investigation. Unfortunately, nothing as certain and dramatic as this is available. Lie detection depends on deduction, on circumstantial evidence, and on the fitting together of a large number of disparate facts. It obtains its most dependable information from a continuous and simultaneous recording of changes in blood pressure, pulse, and respiration occurring during the interrogation of the suspect. These recordings are made on an instrument, or polygraph, which provides a progressive record of these various physiological responses. The polygraph itself essentially consists of a long roll of paper which is pulled across a surface at a uniform speed, and on which a number of recording pens leave a permanent record of their movements. The movement of the recording pens in turn is governed by various instruments attached to the person of the subject who is being investigated. The instruments are connected to the recording pens either electronically or mechanically.

Typical of the kind of instrument used is the so-called pneumograph, which is used for recording breathing. The pneumograph tube, which is tied round the subject's chest, consists of a closely wound spring covered with a thin rubber tubing; one end of the tube is sealed, while the other end is connected to the polygraph itself by means of a small rubber tube. During the test the circumference of the subject's chest increases as he breathes in and decreases as he breathes out. With each inspiration, therefore, the pneumograph tube stretches, and with each exhalation it contracts. This movement of the tube produces pressure changes inside it, and these are transmitted to the polygraph and recorded there.

In an actual investigation our first task will be to obtain a quiet, private examination room, to attach the various parts of the instrument to the subject, and to inform him of the general nature of the test. He is shown the instrument and told that it is capable of determining whether or not a given person is telling the truth. It is explained to him that the instrument records certain bodily changes which are indicative of lying, but that it will, in no circumstances, cause any kind of physical pain except for a slight and temporary discomfort caused by the blood-pressure cuff. To reduce nervousness and tension, he is told that if he is telling the truth he has nothing to worry about because the instrument will indicate that he is telling the truth. Further, he is told that he will not be questioned about any of his personal affairs, or about anything except the offence which is being investigated. Everything is now ready for the test to begin.

The first part of the test serves very much the same purpose as the long harangue by the witch doctor, describing previous successes achieved by the use of his particular technique. The modern equivalent to the witch doctor is handicapped by the fact that his listeners would be very much more sceptical and less liable to unreasoning fears and beliefs in his omnipotence than would primitive savages. Consequently, instead of telling his subject what a wonderful instrument this is, the modern operator would give an actual demonstration. This is usually done in the following way. The operator picks up seven or eight playing-cards and asks the subject to pick out one, look at it, and return it to the pack. He then tells the subject that he will show him each of the seven or eight cards in turn and that he wants him each time to answer 'No' to the question, 'Is this the card you picked out?' He emphasizes particularly that even when the right card comes along the subject should tell a lie and say 'No'. He then goes through the procedure of showing the subject one card or another, eliciting a 'No' response to each, all the time carefully watching the movements of the recording pens on the polygraph. In ninety-five cases out of a hundred a revealing over-reaction of the subject's autonomic system is apparent in the recording when he answers 'No' to the card which he had seen before. To make quite sure, the operator goes through the whole procedure again, and then tells the subject which was the card he had looked at. He also – and this is considerably more impressive to subjects used to seeing this kind of thing done by sleight of hand in the Music Hall – points out the actual changes taking place in the polygraph recording when the lie is told. Thus, the subject can see with his own eyes that reactions over which he has no control can give him away completely, and that the lie detector can be a very deadly instrument indeed for anyone who is trying to give a false impression on any matter of fact.

The subject, suitably impressed by now, is then asked a series of questions relevant to the crime under investigation. Depending on external circumstances, one of two rather different techniques may be used. The first of these is the so-called relevant–irrelevant question technique. In this, the questions which are irrelevant to the point at issue, like 'Is your name John Smith?', or 'Were you born in Liverpool?', are asked in alternation with questions which are relevant to the crime, such as 'Did you steal the diamond ring?', or, 'Did you shoot Lord Edgware?' This technique is rather similar to that employed with the playing-cards, where the card which the subject had looked at played the part of the relevant questions, and the other cards would play the part of the irrelevant questions. What is indicative of lying is a difference in physiological reaction as we pass from the irrelevant to the relevant questions.

What are the main changes which are indicative of deception? The most reliable index is a simultaneous occurrence of a suppression in respiration and an increase in blood pressure immediately after the subject's answer. However, even if only one of these two reactions occurs it is a fairly safe guide to the examiner. Occasionally, deception may be indicated by a decrease in blood pressure, occurring several seconds after the subject has made his untruthful reply to the question. Heavier breathing fifteen to twenty seconds after a reply to a relevant question has been given is also frequently indicative of lying; it is the physiological concomitant of a feeling of relief that this dangerous point has been passed with apparent safety, and it may also occur at the end of the questioning period when the subject is told that he will not be asked any more questions. A last deception criterion is a slowing up of a subject's pulse-beat immediately after his reply to a question.

Certain rules must be followed in interpreting these reactions, however, the main rule being that in order to be considered as evidence of lying, *a physiological response to a relevant question must be quite different to the physiological response to an irrelevant question*. Many people, although innocent of the crime under investigation, have a bad conscience in general, which makes them nervous and jittery altogether, or are emotionally over-reactive. Such people show considerable physiological reactivity, even after irrelevant questions, and might be considered to be lying if this fact were not taken into account. The answer pattern on the irrelevant questions provides us for each subject with a base line indicative of his response pattern when he is speaking the truth; lying can be diagnosed only when marked differences from this normal response pattern are apparent in connexion with relevant questions.

Another safeguard which should always be employed is that no single response is taken as evidence of lying. The same question, or a similar one, should always be asked several times, and only if there is considerable consistency in the subject's response pattern indicating his guilt should this be regarded as suggestive. This is a very important safeguard indeed. Accidental factors, such as a sudden cramp, a sneeze, or a sudden loud noise, may produce effects indistinguishable from the emotional concomitants of lying, and these irrelevant factors can only be excluded by repeating the whole procedure several times.

In certain circumstances a rather different form of questioning can be used, which has great advantages. This has been called the 'peak of tension', or 'guilty knowledge' technique, and is dependent for its usefulness on the fact that a guilty person may possess knowledge which no innocent person would have. Any question regarding this knowledge, or any reference to it, would produce emotional reactions in the guilty person which would not be present in an innocent one. An example from my own experience may make this point clearer. At a certain hospital, bed-sheets were collected once a week and put into large laundry bins on each floor of the hospital. For several weeks running the sheets in one of these bins were found mysteriously mutilated, and as the patients had no access to the bins, suspicion centred on about a dozen nurses working on that floor. No mention had been made to them of these acts of vandalism and none of them except the guilty one could therefore have known of what had happened. This set the stage for the inquiry. The nurses were told that they would be expected to take part in a psychological experiment in which certain words would be read out to them, and they had to say the first thing that came into their minds. Among the hundred words used in the experiment were a few which had some relevance to the 'crime'. Among these were bed-sheet, linen, cut, and bin. After the records had been taken, these 'guilty' words were compared with the 'innocent' ones for each of the nurses. Only one of them showed a very marked increase in autonomic activity for the guilty words, and in her case this reaction appeared to every one of the guilty words. On being confronted with the record, she confessed and disclosed her motives, which were essentially those of revenge against the matron, who she thought had treated her badly.

In this particular case the type of physiological reaction used was not one of those mentioned so far, but the so-called psychogalvanic reflex. This is a rather mysterious phenomenon involving the measurement of the resistance of the skin to the passage of an electric current. Electrodes are fixed to the palm and the back of the hand, and a current so slight as to be quite imperceptible is then set up. The resistance offered by the hand to the passage of this current is measured, and it has been universally found that any sudden shock or emotion produces a characteristic fall in this resistance. This fall occurs after a latency period of about a second or so after the stimulus has been applied and appears to be proportional, roughly, to the amount of disturbance caused. There is no universally accepted explanation of this phenomenon, although there is some reason to believe that it is connected with the activity of the sweat-glands of the hand. Emotion is known to produce activity in these sweat-glands, and sweat, being slightly salty, is a good conductor of electricity. However, this is hardly the whole explanation, and other possibilities have still to be considered. Fortunately, the usefulness of this method of registering emotion does not depend entirely on a knowledge of the mechanisms which produce it and, in certain circumstances, the psychogalvanic reflex is a better indicator of deception than any of those mentioned previously.

Curiously enough, the P.G.R. is hardly ever used in actual police work. Apparently it provides too responsive a measure of even slight emotional changes, so that in the highly charged atmosphere of the police laboratory, responses to relevant and irrelevant stimuli may both show so much evidence of emotion that differentiation becomes impossible. The P.G.R. comes into its own more in relation to the parlour trick kind of investigation, as when the operator wants to find out which of several cards the subject has looked at, and under those conditions it is almost infallible. It was used in the investigation described above because, to the nurses, the whole experiment appeared as a kind of parlour trick and was not in their minds associated with the question of crime, guilt, and lying at all. This may explain the good results obtained here. For the interest of the reader who may be unfamiliar with tracings of this kind, a record is shown of the actual reactions given by the guilty subject and by one innocent subject to the guilty words, and some representative neutral words. In looking at this record, it should be remembered that a dip in the curve is the equivalent to a decrease in the resistance of the skin to the passage of the superimposed electric current. There is little need to comment on this record; it is literally true to say that 'it speaks for itself' (Figure 2).

This, then, is a rough picture of the kind of procedure employed in the lie-detector test and the kind of criteria used for establishing the presence or absence of emotion accompanying a reply. How valid is the lie-detector test, and how much reliance can be placed on it? These are difficult questions, and before answering them we must consider certain factors which affect the interpretation of scores. One of the main difficulties in tests of this kind is the nervousness shown by many a truthful or innocent person under the conditions of police interrogation. Such nervousness is usually manifested in the record by the general erratic character of the tracings, and by the failure of the larger reactions to be related specifically to the pertinent questions; thus, the physiological disturbances associated with nervousness appear on the lie-detector record without any consistent relationship to any particular question or questions. They are no greater when pertinent questions are asked than when neutral questions are asked for control purposes. Sometimes, changes or

disturbances of a similar size to those appearing in the record
are even found during rest periods when no questions are
being asked at all. The best way of counteracting the presence of nervousness in a subject is by reassurance and by
repetition. Repeating the whole procedure five, or even ten,
times acts very much like a sedative because the subject,

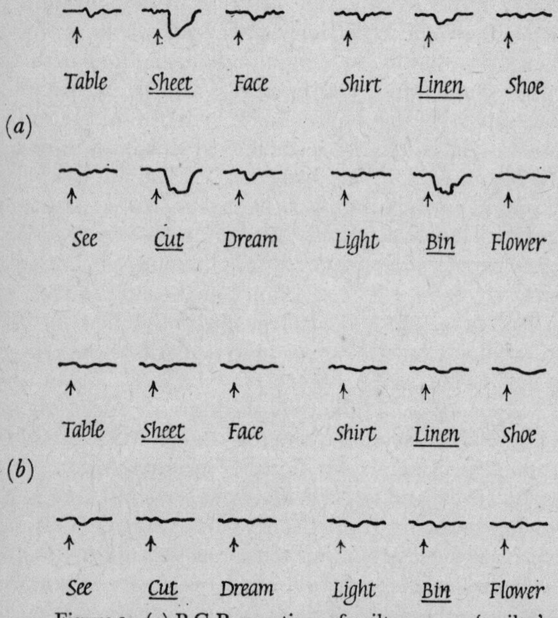

Figure 2: (*a*) P.G.R. reactions of guilty person; 'guilty'
words underlined. Arrow indicates when this stimulus
word was pronounced. (*b*) P.G.R. reactions of innocent
person; 'guilty' words underlined

who may originally have been afraid of all sorts of things
(many people when they are being strapped into the machine express fear of receiving electric shocks, for instance),
now gets used to the procedure and realizes that there is
little in it of which to be afraid. Also, frequent repetition, as
mentioned before, enables the examiner to look for consistency of exaggerated responses to the same question, or ques-

tions which are regarded as relevant, and this consistency is far more important than individual isolated reactions can ever be.

Nervousness is relatively easily diagnosed (it does not usually require an inspection of the lie-detector record to tell whether or not the person is extremely nervous!), and it does not present an insuperable difficulty. Other factors are more difficult to deal with. Mental deficiency, for instance, makes a subject almost useless for a lie-detector test. A very stupid person, who may not be able to distinguish between truth and falsehood, or understand the social obligation of telling the truth, or who has no fear of detection, will not give useful results which can be interpreted in any way. Much the same is true of young children, who also are not fit subjects for lie-detector tests. Obviously innocent persons frequently give records so abnormal and erratic that no interpretation is possible. Again, these various conditions do not present insuperable difficulties. Mental deficiency and mental abnormality sufficient to invalidate the lie-detector test are easily recognized, and other methods of arriving at the truth substituted for the lie detector.

Much greater difficulties are caused by certain people who are relatively unresponsive to the conditions of testing. A person who refuses to believe in the efficacy of the test, and who therefore is not worried at all about giving himself away, will tend to show less emotion when telling a lie and therefore produce less easily interpretable records on the polygraph. Some people show a quite extreme absence of emotion, and such people, while actually guilty, might easily be pronounced innocent in terms of their reaction in the lie-detection test. Again, some people are able to control their mental associations and processes sufficiently to avoid give-away responses. An excellent example of this technique occurred in connexion with the trial of Jerry Thompson, who was executed for the rape-murder of Mildred Hallmark. His lie-detector records were rather indefinite and could not be interpreted. However, quite independently of the lie-detector test, he confessed, and several days before his execution was interviewed by the lie-detector expert, who was interested to learn how Thompson had been able to beat the test. Thompson stated that whenever he was asked during the test whether he 'raped and killed Mildred' he would concentrate upon, and enact in his own mind, various abnormal sexual experiences he had had with another girl of the same name. He stated that by doing this each time the question was asked he was able to dismiss for the time being the rape and murder of Mildred Hallmark from his mind. Fortunately, only few people seem to be able to control their minds to the extent required in order to 'beat the machine', but it should be remembered that some people do possess this ability, and that their number seems to be particularly large among hardened criminals.

Among persons knowing the physiological basis of the lie detector, other tricks may sometimes be employed to make detection impossible. It will be remembered that lie detection depends very much on a comparison between items which are relevant and items which are irrelevant. If the subject is capable of causing physiological reactions to irrelevant items, then the comparison will become useless and the record will not be capable of revealing damaging information. Causing physiological responses to innocent items may be done in various ways. One subject, a physiologist, who had pushed his wife down into the Grand Canyon, produced autonomic reactions when being asked irrelevant questions by stepping on his left foot with the heel of his shoe, the resulting pain producing a reaction sufficiently like those of lying to make the record unusable. Other people have been known to indulge in sexual fantasies when answering innocent questions, thus producing physiological responses to the fantasies which the investigator would attribute to the next question. It is not categorically possible to say that such tricks may not work occasionally, but in most cases the experienced examiner will notice what the accused person is doing and will draw his own conclusions.

We are now in a position to assess the practical utility of lie-detector tests. By and large, it is difficult to disagree with

Inbau, a very experienced expert in this field, when he writes that

> Lie-detector tests, when conducted by competent and experienced operators, are of considerable practical utility. In the first place, with the aid of a lie-detector, it is possible to detect deception with much greater accuracy than is otherwise attainable. Secondly, the instrument, the tests, and the accompanying procedures have a decided psychological effect in inducing admissions and confessions from guilty individuals.

Unfortunately, exact figures as to the accuracy of lie-detector results are almost impossible to obtain. In actual police work, confirmatory or contradictory evidence cannot always be obtained, so that we may never know in certain cases what the truth of the matter really was. For this reason, many investigators have given figures purporting to demonstrate the accuracy of lie-detector tests which are based on experiments conducted in the laboratory. In these experiments no actual crime is committed, but the task of the investigator is to find out, as in the example already quoted, which of several cards an individual has looked at, or, alternatively, which of several individuals has read a certain letter. In such laboratory tests the actual truth is known and the success of the lie-detector tests can be checked against it. Reports of accuracy varying from 80 to 100 per cent have been published, and it would probably be a fair estimate to say that, when properly conducted, such tests are accurate in about 95 per cent of the cases.

Unfortunately, we cannot extrapolate from experimental investigations of this type to the kind of work going on in the police laboratory. It has already been pointed out that whereas in the psychological laboratory the psychogalvanic reflex type of response is particularly effective, it is by no means so useful in the interrogation by the police of actual suspects. Why this should be so is not too clear at the present moment, but the fact must be faced that the accuracy of police work cannot be gauged adequately by reference to work in the psychological laboratory.

The most convincing estimate of the accuracy of lie-detection techniques comes from Inbau, and is based on some twelve years experience in the Scientific Crime Detection Laboratory in Chicago. According to his estimate, out of 100 cases the examiner can make a definite and accurate deception diagnosis in about 70. In twenty cases the records will be too indefinite in their indications to permit a competent and cautious examiner to make a definite diagnosis. Doubt in these cases may be due either to the inconsistency and the rapid nature of responses in the record, or else to the general unresponsiveness of the subject. As regards the remaining ten cases, here even the most experienced examiner is likely to make a definitely erroneous diagnosis. The chief source of error in these cases lies in the failure of the examiner to detect deception in a guilty individual rather than in his misinterpretation of the record of the innocent subject.

This is a conservative estimate, and it should be said that some experts have published claims for their methods of 97, 98, or 99 per cent accuracy, or even in one case for 100 per cent efficiency. These are undoubtedly exaggerations, and the disappointment inevitably following expectations based on such claims has probably been responsible for some of the distrust of lie-detector techniques, which can be observed among some members of the police force.

At first sight the degree of accuracy achieved by the lie detector in competent hands may not seem impressive. If we leave out the 20 per cent of cases where the experts cannot come to a decision, we find that in seven out of eight cases the expert is right, leaving a margin of error of something like 12 per cent. To anyone desirous of 100 per cent accuracy – and in science this degree of accuracy must be the goal, however much we may in practice fall short of it – a margin of error of 12 per cent may appear discouragingly high. However, while it limits the usefulness of the lie detector, it certainly cannot be said to render it useless.

In the first place, one of the most valuable by-products of the lie-detection technique is that it helps to obtain a confession in cases where other methods have failed, and where a considerable amount of work would be required if the confession had not been forthcoming. To be confronted with the objective evidence of his lying on the tracing paper of the polygraph is a very disconcerting experience for most criminals, and experience has shown that confessions are produced in a very large number of cases. Indeed, there have been innumerable instances of confessions made as a result simply of the proposal to have a suspect submit to a lie-detector test. On many occasions suspects have confessed their guilt while waiting to be tested. Others, again, have confessed immediately after the operator had set up the test and adjusted the instruments.

Confessions so obtained still have to be checked, of course, against objective evidence; a confession alone, whether obtained with or without the use of the lie detector, would not be regarded by most courts as sufficient. However, included in the confession are usually details which make it possible to obtain an objective verification of the claims of the guilty subject, and it should certainly be stressed that so far no case has come to light where false confessions have been produced because of the psychological effect of the instrument or the techniques used in administering it. In this there is a very marked difference between lie-detection techniques, and the use of the 'third degree', which has caused many subjects to confess to crimes they have not committed in order to escape from an intolerable situation.

This ability of the lie detector to induce confessions in guilty persons is, to many people, its main claim to practical usefulness. However, in spite of its liability to error in a small portion of the cases, we cannot ignore the contribution which, in fact, is made by the lie detector, even in cases where no confession is obtained. To have a guide to the truth, even if it be only a 90 per cent reliable guide, is certainly better than to have no guide at all. In many cases, the lie detector test record enables the police to abandon a line of inquiry because of the obvious innocence of the subject under suspicion. In other cases, the suspicion of his guilt, strongly supported by the lie detector test record, may enable the police to concentrate efforts on the most promising suspects. In many cases, details of the examination may be helpful in suggesting certain clues to the police, such as the names of likely confederates, or the place where money or murder weapons were hidden, and so forth. In all this, of course, it is important to realize that conviction is not based directly on the record of the lie detector. This record is only one item which is taken into account in arriving at a conclusion; one item of evidence among other items, none of which can be said to be perfectly reliable, but all of which together point to the guilt or innocence of a given suspect.

People who criticize the use of lie-detection techniques on the basis of this lack of perfect reliability often overlook the fact that all other techniques at present in use for determining the truth or falsity of a suspect's story are at least equally fallible, and in many instances more so. The question that should be asked is not whether a new departure, such as the lie-detection technique, is completely accurate, but rather whether it is more accurate than the techniques which it would replace, and whether, in fact, its employment would, or would not, improve the degree of success obtainable at the present moment. On these grounds there is little doubt that the lie-detection technique emerges with flying colours.

To these considerations, arguing in favour of the use of lie-detection techniques, there should also be added another. The only possible way in which imperfect techniques can be improved is by experimentation and use. To say that lie-detection techniques should not be used because they are not perfectly reliable at the same time means that the only path leading towards an improvement of the lie-detection technique is blocked. It is possible, up to a point, to conduct experiments in the psychological laboratory, but for the practical development of a technique such as that of lie detection, actual use in practice is indispensable. Only by such use can the most effective and efficient method of interrogation be worked out; only in this way can competent personnel be trained; and only thus can theoretical research be directed along the most promising paths.

To say that lie-detection techniques should be used in
police work is rather a vague statement. There are many
ways in which a technique such as this can be used, and it is
important to be more precise in one's recommendations.
Before making these recommendations we may perhaps look
at the present legal studies of the lie detector. I have been
unable to find any legal decisions regarding its use in Great
Britain, and we must therefore perforce turn to the United
States, where several courts have considered this issue. The
first appellate court decision upon the admissibility of lie-
detector evidence was given in 1923 by a Federal court. The
accused, on trial for murder, offered as evidence the results
of a lie-detector test. The reasons why this offer was refused
were very clearly stated: 'Just when a scientific principle or
discovery crosses the line between the experimental and demonstrable stages is difficult to define. Somewhere in this
twilight zone the evidential force of the principle must be
recognized, and while courts will go a long way in admitting
expert testimony deduced from a well-recognized scientific
principle or discovery, the thing from which the deduction
is made must be sufficiently established to have gained
general acceptance in the particular field in which it belongs. We think the systolic blood pressure deception test
has not yet gained such standing and scientific recognition
among physiological and psychological authorities as would
justify the courts in admitting expert testimony deduced
from the discovery, development, and experiments thus far
made.' Several other cases have come up in more recent
years, all agreeing in refusing to admit the evidence of lie-
detector tests. Consequently, evidence of this kind has practically no judicial recognition at the present time in the
United States, and it is probably safe to say that the position
in Britain would not be different.

Are these decisions reasonable, or are they simply evidence of an 'old-fogey' mentality, so frequently found in
traditional pursuits like the law? Here again there is little
doubt that we must agree with Inbau, the expert whose
estimate about the reliability of lie-detection results we

quoted before. This is his conclusion from considering the evidence:

It is generally recognized that our present legal methods and procedures for ascertaining the truth and administering justice are far from perfect and that therefore we should forever remain alert and eager for corrective measures and improvements. At the same time, however, we should not be too hasty in our acceptance of proposed innovations. In the case of the lie-detector technique such a cautious attitude will operate not only in the best interests of the administration of justice but also to the ultimate advantage of the technique itself. A premature acceptance of the test results as legal evidence would undoubtedly occasion such a series of abuses and miscarriages of justice as to stigmatize forever the technique in the field of law as well as of science. It seems much wiser, therefore, to await a further development and improvement of the technique, and to let it first stand the acid test of a truly scientific inquiry into its accuracy and reliability.

Inbau bases this conclusion on two main arguments. A technique, in order to be admissible, must possess 'a reasonable measure of precision in its indications'. The percentage of errors admitted to be in the neighbourhood of 10 per cent is no greater, and in many cases no less, than that possessed by some forms of scientific testimony actually admitted by the courts. However, it should be remembered that if lie-detector test results were to be admitted as legal evidence, they would be offered and treated as proof of some important phase of the case, or even of the validity of the entire claim or contention of one of the parties. In other words, a decision on the truth or falsity of a statement given in answer to the question, 'Did you shoot X?' would completely decide the case. This is not so with most forms of scientific testimony. A ballistics expert might be prepared to give evidence, saying that a given bullet had been fired by a given gun, but this single fact would not, in itself, decide the issue. Quite generally, scientific testimony is not ordinarily conclusive regarding the entire issue under litigation, and consequently there is not so much likelihood of injustice resulting from erroneous expert testimony. Lie-detector evidence, however, usually relates to the crux of the whole matter, and consequently, if it were admitted, an error would be extremely serious. The words, 'a reasonable measure of precision', therefore have to be interpreted in the context of the importance of the decision; what might be a reasonable measure of precision in a small matter might be quite unreasonably lacking in precision, when it is a matter of life and death. As it is in the latter kind of case that appeal is made to the lie-detector test, its precision and accuracy require to be greater rather than less than those of other forms of scientific evidence.

When it comes to the second prerequisite as to the admissibility as legal evidence, namely, the acceptance of a technique in the fields of science to which it belongs, we find that while the principles underlying lie-detection techniques are recognized by physiologists and psychologists, this particular form of application of the principle is not so widely accepted. In part, this is due to ignorance; few psychologists and physiologists have taken an interest in this matter, and consequently, quite rightly, are not prepared to commit themselves on a subject-matter in which they are not themselves experts. In addition, the exaggerated and sensational claims made by a few lie-detector operators have made scientifically minded people very chary indeed of accepting any claims at all in this field.

In addition, the lie-detection techniques at present in use have not been adequately standardized with respect to instrumentation, the manner in which a test should be conducted, the interpretation of the recordings, or the training of competent examiners. In such circumstances, incompetent or dishonest persons might represent themselves as 'lie-detector experts' and be allowed to give inaccurate or perjured testimony for the party by whom they are employed.

There is one exception to this rule of inadmissibility of lie-detector test results in court. If the lawyers representing the prosecution and the defence agree on admitting lie-detector test results as evidence, and also agree on a particular expert

D

to carry out the investigation, such evidence has been recognized, at least in the United States, by a number of trial courts. This exception is justified for two reasons. In the first place, it may be assumed that when both the opposing litigants and their lawyers are willing to resort to the use of lie-detector tests, the case must be a doubtful one, i.e. one where the evidence on either side is unconvincing and incapable of circumstantial corroboration. (Sexual crimes often fall into this category, as in most cases none but the two persons involved are present, and physical evidence as to precisely what happened is rarely forthcoming.) In those circumstances, where any decision reached on the basis of the available evidence would be little more than guess-work, there is little doubt that the utilization of lie-detector test results would substantially increase the accuracy of the final decision over what it would have been had it been based merely on the guess or hunch of judge and jury deciding in the absence of lie-detector evidence. There is also the point that, where both the parties agree on the selection of the test expert, he is likely to be both honest and competent and not in any way influenced by an attachment to one or the other party.

It may appear to the reader that in what we have said so far there is a glaring contradiction. On the one hand, it has been maintained that the present practice of not making the lie-detector test results legally admissible evidence is a reasonable one, and that at present there are no grounds for altering this position; on the other hand, it has been suggested that official use should be made by the police of the lie detector. How can these apparently two contradictory recommendations be reconciled? The answer, in effect, has already been given when it was pointed out that one of the main advantages of the use of the lie detector was the procurement by its use of confessions in cases where the more usual types of police interrogation had failed. Confessions, admissions, and other evidence obtained in consequence of the use of a lie detector are admissible in court and have legal status, at least in the United States; the legal admissibility of such evidence in Great Britain has not so far been tested, but it seems likely that the position here would not be very different from that obtaining in the United States. A legal decision on this point was made by the Supreme Court of Pennsylvania in 1939 in a case in which the defendant confessed to having committed a murder. This confession followed the administration of a lie-detector test, and the defendant's counsel objected to the admissibility of a confession. The objections were based on the fact that a lie detector had been used, and the fact that the investigating officers had told the suspect that 'You can lie to us, but you cannot lie to this machine'. The Pennsylvania Supreme Court upheld the trial court's ruling that the confession was admissible. They stated that since no promises, force, or threats had been employed in obtaining the confession, the mere use of the instrument did not render it inadmissible. Nor would it regard the officers' comments about the impossibility of lying to the machine as invalidating the confession. Even though these words might be considered a trick, that fact alone would not invalidate the confession, because of the general legal rule in the United States which makes admissible confessions procured 'by a trick or artifice not calculated to produce an untruth'.

Another argument sometimes used by lawyers appearing for the defence is that the use of the lie detector constitutes a 'third-degree' practice. This argument has not recommended itself to most competent observers or legal authorities. Some slight discomfort of a purely temporary nature is produced by the blood-pressure cuff, but this is much too slight to be considered painful in any sense. Furthermore, the test procedure is not of a kind which would encourage or compel a person to make a confession merely in order to escape from an intolerable situation. It is interesting to note in this connexion that there are several cases in which a suspect, having withstood the rigour of third degree interviewing without confessing, has finally admitted his guilt after a brief session with the lie detector. The use of the third degree, apart from being uncivilized and non-humanitarian, is also inefficient, and a substitution of the lie-detector test in its place in American police interrogations would considerably improve the efficiency and accuracy of crime detection there.

This whole question of using tricks in order to obtain a confession or admission from a criminal raises many thorny legal problems. It is not at all certain that to say 'You can lie to us, but you cannot lie to this machine' is a mere trick, because, in fact, the statement is substantially correct. Of course, in a sense this might be regarded as a quibble because the statement becomes true only by being made in the first place, and by being believed by the suspect. However that may be, many people, particularly those of a humanitarian cast of mind, and with a high degree of religious or ethical responsibility, have argued against the use of lie-detection techniques because of a feeling that it weights the scale somewhat unfairly against the accused and makes use, if not of trickery exactly, then of something very closely approaching it. With this general view, which, in fact, was responsible for the elaboration of the rules of evidence which the police are obliged to follow in Great Britain, one cannot but have much sympathy. To make sure that the underdog is fully protected against society, and that injustice is not inflicted on him because he cannot stand alone against the forces representing the law, this is one of the most important features of democratic life, and one which few people would be willing to give up in the interests of greater efficiency.

However, if the underdog is to be protected from society, particularly in its monolithic modern form, society also has to be protected from the vicious criminal, and one's sympathy should go, not only to the wrongdoer, but also to his actual or prospective victim. Take the case of Jerry Thompson, whose trial for rape-murder caused quite a sensation a few years ago. Thompson had a long history of assault and rape. In this particular case Thompson had choked and slugged his victim in a fit of passion, as he had done many times before in connexion with other girls. In this particular instance, however, his victim failed to recover consciousness soon enough and, assuming her to be dead, he threw her body from his automobile. Apparently she was still alive when thrown from the moving car and only died from the impact her body made on the road.

A lie-detector interrogation technique was used on Thompson, who later confessed. Few people, surely, would consider that morality would have been satisfied more by allowing him to go free and pursue his career of assault and rape for several more years rather than make him submit himself to a lie-detector test and be made to suffer the consequences of his actions. This may be an extreme example, but it may counteract our sentimental tendencies to see vicious and brutal killers and murderers as essentially kind-hearted underdogs who never had a fair chance.

Essentially, surely, the position is this. The lie-detector test in itself is legally neutral. Its efficacy at the present time is reasonably well known, and its value in producing true confessions is without doubt. It does not in any way partake of 'third-degree' methods; it does not cause physical pain to the accused; and it does not, when it fails, fail by implicating the innocent person. Its failure rather is a failure to detect the person who has lied. Lastly, in many cases it serves as a shield to the innocent person, who, without fault of his own, is enmeshed in a mass of circumstantial evidence, but the truth of whose protestations of innocence is verified by the lie detector. It would be foolish to accept testimony so secured without reservation, to admit it to the status of legal evidence, and to employ the technique in every single case. It would be equally foolish to refuse to recognize its potential usefulness, to refuse to employ it in carefully selected cases where it would show to maximum advantage, and to refuse to use it with strict safeguards in the furtherance of the ends of justice.

The whole position was put in a nutshell by none other than Daniel Defoe, who in 1730 published a pamphlet called *An Effectual Scheme for the Immediate Preventing of Street Robberies and Suppressing all Other Disorders of the Night*. As the following quotation will show, Defoe not only discovered the basis of the modern lie-detector technique, but also dealt with the ethical objections to its application very much in the way that modern writers do.

Guilt carries Fear always about with it; there is a Tremor in the Blood of a Thief, that, if attended to, would effectually discover him; and if charged as a suspicious Fellow, on that Suspicion only I would always feel his Pulse, and I would recommend it to Practice. The innocent Man which knows himself clear and has no Surprise upon him; when they cry, *Stop Thief*, he does not start; or strive to get out of the Way; much less does he tremble and shake, change Countenance or look pale, and less still does he run for it and endeavour to escape.

It is true some are so harden'd in Crime that they will boldly hold their Faces to it, carry it off with an Air of Contempt, and outface even a Pursuer; but take hold of his Wrist and feel his Pulse, there you shall find his Guilt; a fluttering Heart, an unequal Pulse, a sudden Palpitation shall evidently confess he is the Man, in spite of a bold Countenance or a false Tongue: This they cannot conceal; 'tis in vain to counterfeit there; a conscious Heart will discover itself by a faltering Pulse; the greatest Stock of Brass in the Face cannot hide it, or the most Firm Resolution of a harden'd Offender conceal and cover it: The Experiment perhaps has not been try'd, and some may think it is not a fair Way, even with a Thief, because 'tis making the Man an Evidence against himself: As for that, I shall not enter into the Enquiry farther than this; if it is agreeable to Justice to apprehend a Man upon Suspicion, if the Particulars are probable and well grounded; it cannot than [*sic*] be unlawful by any Stratagem that is not injurious in itself, to seek out collateral Grounds of Suspicion, and see how one thing concurs with another.

It may be true, that this Discovery by the Pulsation of the Blood, cannot be brought to a Certainty, and therefore it is not to be brought into Evidence; but I insist, if it be duly and skilfully observ'd, it may be brought to be allow'd for a just Addition to other Circumstances, especially if concurring with other just Grounds of Suspicion.

In concentrating in this chapter so much on the lie detector, and in devoting only a few words to the discussion of 'truth drugs', we may be said to give an accurate presentation of the importance of these two types of development and their prospective usefulness. The lie detector is based on a well-established scientific theory; it is of acknowledged usefulness, and its value is vouched for by impeccable scientific research. Truth drugs, on the other hand, are in quite a different category. Their value is exceedingly problematical; their use is based on no well-thought-out scientific theory. Only in one respect do they resemble the lie-detector test, and that is in having a very long history, stretching back into primitive times. Even among ancient Romans the tendency of alcoholic beverages to cause people to reveal what they would much rather have kept secret was well known, and the proverb *in vino veritas* has its analogue in every civilized tongue.

Modern truth drugs are similar to alcohol in this, that they depress the activity of the higher centres of the brain, thus temporarily releasing the lower centres from surveillance. It is in these unguarded moments, when the ever-wakeful censor is, as it were, drugged, that certain statements may slip out which otherwise would have been severely blue-pencilled. The balance, however, is difficult to achieve. A little too much and the lower centres also become paralysed, and the subject goes to sleep; too little and the higher levels retain their censorship functions and little worth-while is revealed. Even when the proper balance is struck, however, and conditions are optimal, it is doubtful if the truth is really revealed. By this, I mean that an individual conscious of a certain fact, and having strong motives for not admitting such knowledge, could not, in effect, be made to reveal it by any of these so-called truth drugs at present available. This was shown dramatically in an experiment carried out on a variety of normal and neurotic subjects. They were told a story and also told that they must not reveal any details of this story to a person who would come and question them about it. Injections of pentothal (one of the truth drugs) were then administered, and an attempt made to elicit details of the story from the subjects. The effort ended in failure. Normal people did not, in fact, divulge any information at all; the neurotic ones did spill details of the story, but they introduced so much imaginary material that it was quite impossible to reconstruct the truth from their outpourings. On the whole, then, there is no good evidence to suggest that a conscious determination not to divulge a secret can be overcome by the use of drugs at present known to medical science. The possibility that there may be secret drugs available to certain Eastern governments and unknown here cannot, of course, be ruled out, but in the absence of any evidence it would require a considerable amount of credulity to take such hypotheses very seriously.

There is, however, one use of the so-called truth drugs which does lend some point to the use of that term. Neurotic patients are often unconscious of certain events in their past lives, and such events are frequently of great emotional importance and closely related to the particular disability from which the patient suffers. Thus, a soldier suffering from a hysterical paralysis may have acquired this symptom as a direct outcome of being buried as an effect of an exploding shell; he may have completely forgotten this episode and have no memory of it at all. When questioned under one of the truth drugs, he frequently will not only remember the episode, but may actually relive it all, cowering in the corner of the room, shouting with fear, and finally subsiding into unconsciousness. The therapeutic use of such a drug to induce recollections cannot easily be assessed, but the fact that factually true statements are made under such conditions of events which the subject does not recollect in the normal state cannot be doubted.

An example may make clear the difference between the recovery of repressed material of this kind of which the subject is himself unconscious, and the discovery of certain facts which are well known to the subject, but which he is not willing to disclose. During the war a middle-aged soldier was picked up by the military police, wandering about London. He claimed an almost complete amnesia, could not recall his name, his civilian address, or, in fact, anything about his circumstances at all. He carried no marks of identification, and it proved impossible to discover anything about his true identity. After an injection of pentothal he still failed completely to remember anything at all, and this roused considerable suspicion, as a true neurotic amnesia could have been expected to show some signs, at least, of breaking down under the drug. However, about the same time he fell in love with a young female patient at the hospital, and they were about to get married when, one day, going down the local High Street, he encountered a woman accompanied by seven children who claimed to be his wife and would not let him go back to the hospital. Her story turned out to be true, and after some questioning the man finally admitted to having made up the whole story of his amnesia in order to get away from his wife.

From the point of view of police interrogation and getting the truth from someone determined not to reveal it, truth drugs are of little value. It is possible, but not very likely, that new discoveries in the near future will improve the situation. Until more is known about the physiological basis on which these drugs work, it is doubtful if very much useful experimentation can be done in this field. Possibilities exist, of course, of combining truth drugs and lie-detector techniques, but unfortunately the truth drugs themselves have a direct influence on the autonomic nervous system, thus counteracting the smooth running of the lie-detection technique. For the moment, at least, we may dismiss the idea of a 'truth drug', properly so called, from our minds and concentrate for all practical purposes on the development of the lie detector.

3

TELEPATHY AND CLAIRVOYANCE

ACCORDING to T. H. Huxley it is a customary fate of new truths to begin as heresies and to end as superstitions. While many people would not be willing to regard psychical phenomena in any sense as 'truths', they certainly have begun as superstitions, and belief in them at the moment is regarded as a heresy in scientific circles. Thus, in this as in so many other ways, telepathy and clairvoyance seem to be intent on standing the ordinary, accepted, and understandable course of nature on its head.

The types of phenomena with which psychical research deals have been known for many thousands of years. They include such things as premonitions, fire-walking, water-divining, haunted houses, poltergeists, survival after death, and telepathic messages. In the words of an official description of the aims of the Society for Psychical Research, it is the object of the research worker in this field 'To examine without prejudice or prepossession and in a scientific spirit those faculties of man, real or supposed, which appear to be inexplicable on any generally recognized hypothesis.' This definition is a little sweeping. We have no recognized hypothesis to account for the apparent interaction of mind and matter in a simple act of consciousness, nor is there any official hypothesis to account for the phenomena of hypnosis or of memory. Yet consciousness, hypnosis, and memory are not generally included in psychical research.

We will not attempt here any general definition of psychical phenomena, but will merely indicate the nature of those phenomena which will be dealt with in this chapter. These are often subsumed under the general term 'extra-sensory perception', or E.S.P. for short. By this is meant the acquisition of knowledge through channels other than those of the senses. Two main types of extra-sensory perception are recognized, namely, clairvoyance and telepathy. Clairvoyance is supposed to occur when a person experiences a certain mental pattern which corresponds wholly, or in part, with the sensory aspects of a past, present, or future physical object or event, in such a way that the observed correspondence cannot be accounted for by sense perception or inference based on sense perception or by chance coincidence. A further requirement, the necessity for which we shall see a little later, is that this physical object or event is never at any time perceived by anyone. (This added requirement may seem to make it quite impossible to check up on the occurrence of clairvoyance, but it will be seen later that ingenious methods of experimentation have succeeded in overcoming the apparent difficulties involved in this condition.)

Telepathy is supposed to occur when a person experiences a mental pattern which wholly, or in part, corresponds to a past, present, or future mental pattern of another person, whether living or dead, under conditions when the correspondence cannot be accounted for by sense perception or inference based on sense perception or by chance coincidence. A further requirement is that the possibility of clairvoyance should have been eliminated. In the great majority of studies which have been reported, it is impossible to decide whether the E.S.P. faculty supposedly demonstrated is telepathic or clairvoyant, because the facts, if they be accepted as such for the moment, can be accounted for equally easily in terms of either. Consequently, for the most part, we shall be concerned with the generalized extrasensory perception faculty rather than with any demarcation between clairvoyance and telepathy. There are, however, one or two specialized studies which have attempted rigorous discrimination between these two faculties, and these will be introduced in their appropriate place.

One further phenomenon will be dealt with briefly, and that is a faculty or ability called psycho-kinesis, often shortened to PK effect. As telepathy and clairvoyance derive from ancient claims of sorcerers, mediums, and medicine men, so psycho-kinesis derives from poltergeists and the beliefs of gamblers that they can influence the fall of dice by willing them to fall in a certain way. The alleged ability of human beings to influence the behaviour of physical objects without the transfer of any known form of energy is the subject-matter of psycho-kinetic studies, and although only little is known about it, it cannot be wholly omitted in a chapter such as this.

The notion of investigating claims of this kind will be repugnant to many people. The very possibility of extra-sensory perception, or psycho-kinesis, appears contrary to modern scientific logic, and many people have shown considerable reluctance even to look at the evidence that has been produced in favour of these alleged abilities. Many laymen have a kind of stereotyped view of the scientist as an inhuman, completely objective and rational sort of person, who only takes into account facts and is not swayed by emotions and feelings in his judgement. Unfortunately, there is little truth in such a picture. Scientists, especially when they leave the particular field in which they have specialized, are just as ordinary, pig-headed, and unreasonable as anybody else, and their unusually high intelligence only makes their prejudices all the more dangerous because it enables them to cover these up with an unusually glib and smooth flow of high-sounding talk. We shall encounter a good deal of such talk in the course of our exploration.

How, it might be asked, did this type of research originate? The answer is that it originated in much the same way as any other kind of scientific research. Certain phenomena having been reported consistently for thousands of years, certain obvious problems are being raised. At face value they seem to contradict certain widely held beliefs; yet it seems difficult to dismiss these phenomena as being simply due to chance, to misconception, or to fraudulence. In other words, we seem to have a problem here, and a particularly important and interesting one, because it touches on the root of our modern scientific outlook on life. Small wonder that scientists with an open mind began to apply the methods of science to this field in order to throw some light on these interesting and unlikely events.

Let us take just a few well-known examples from ancient and modern times to illustrate the kind of phenomena which aroused this type of interest. St Augustine, who must be regarded as a reasonably trustworthy witness, relates that one of his pupils asked Albicerius, a Carthaginian medium and diviner, to say what he, the pupil, was thinking about. Albicerius replied that the pupil was thinking of a line of Virgil, and although he was a man of little education, actually recited the passage. This correct perception on the part of Albicerius of what was in the mind of another person would suggest the reality of telepathy, although, of course, there may be more acceptable ways of accounting for the coincidence.

Another example is the case of Sosipatra, a feminine don and philosopher in ancient Greece, who interrupted a lecture she was giving to describe in detail an accident that was happening at that very moment to her kinsman Philometor, who was riding in his carriage many miles away. Her description appears to have been correct in most of its details, and again an explanation in terms of clairvoyance or telepathy is the most obvious, although, of course, not a necessary explanation of this event. Better known, perhaps, than either of these stories is that of King Croesus, as told by Herodotus. Croesus sought the help of a medium to discover the strength of his enemies. Being experimentally minded, he first of all decided to find out which was the most reliable of the many oracles. Accordingly, he sent his representatives to the seven most famous ones, instructing them to make their visits all on the same day and to put to all the oracles the same question: 'What is the King of Lydia doing at this moment?' When the specified day arrived, the king went through the most improbable performance he could think of. He cut up a tortoise and a lamb and boiled them in a brass cauldron. Only the famous oracle at Delphi was able to give the correct answer. When the King then asked what would happen if he attacked the Persians, he was told that a mighty empire would be destroyed. He accepted this as an encouragement, and, indeed, the prediction was fulfilled in the event, but it was his own empire that was destroyed. We hardly need extra-sensory perception of the precognitive kind to account for the success of the oracle at Delphi's prediction because, in a war, one or the other side must, after all, win, but the divination of what the king was doing is rather more difficult to explain.

It is, of course, possible in all these stories that rumour, and the constant retelling, have added many details which make the whole thing more miraculous than it might have been to begin with, and it is difficult to rule out coincidence and trickery completely. It would be more difficult, however, to use such interpretations of certain more modern events. Here, for instance, is a story told by Dr J. F. Laubscher, a psychiatrist working in South Africa. He describes how he made a friend of a native witch doctor who was believed to have E.S.P. abilities. On one occasion, without mentioning his plans to anyone, Laubscher secretly hid a cheap purse in the ground and then went at once by car to the witch doctor's kraal some 60 miles away. In the course of a séance dance, the witch doctor was able to describe correctly, in minute detail, the hidden article, down to the colour of the wrappings and the nature of the locality where it was buried.

Stories of this type are not, of course, acceptable as proof, however miraculous they may seem. They pose a problem of explanation, but no scientist would rate their value any higher than that. There are too many uncontrolled features about them, and these make it unsafe to take them very seriously. However, for several years after the founding of the Society for Psychical Research in London, an event which took place in 1882, the main energies of the investigators were concerned with the collection of stories of this type, as well as the actual investigation of cases of psychical phenomena reported to them. Interesting as much of this early work is, it again fails to satisfy the demand for proof. Too much attention is paid to human testimony, and relatively uncontrolled conditions are accepted too readily. Human testimony, unfortunately, is so unreliable, and the human being is an observer so much given to inaccuracies and downright falsifications, that little credence attaches to anything reported by human beings having nothing to aid them but their senses. That this is not too harsh a verdict has been shown in any number of experimental investigations. These have mostly been concerned with the fallibility of testimony given before courts of law, but their results are very relevant here also. In the usual experiment, a group of students is assembled, receives a lecture on the inaccuracy of testimony, and then some kind of complex and exciting event is stage-managed. An intruder may come in, brandish a revolver, threaten to shoot the lecturer, and then be frog-marched out by two of the students. Written accounts are then called for of what has happened, and few people who have not participated in experiments of this type would credit the variety of inaccuracies appearing in these reports. The revolver becomes a knife, or a gun, or a stick; the intruder becomes a woman, an old man with a beard, a Negro, or a lunatic. His words are completely garbled and he may, in the stories, either run away by himself or be marched out by dozens of students.

A good example of this technique of investigating the reliability of reports is an experiment reported by S. J. Davey. He was interested in the kind of phenomena reported during séances and, using quite simple trickery, which he had planned in advance, he reproduced some of the effects popular among the mediums of the day. His audiences were asked to write down accounts of what they had witnessed, and these observations were then compared with what actually happened. Here is a report written by one witness of such a séance. 'On entering the dining-room where the séance was held', so the report runs, 'every article of furniture was searched and Mr Davey turned out his pockets. The door was locked and sealed, the gas turned out, and they all sat round the table holding hands, including Mr Davey. A musical box on the table played and floated about. Knockings were heard and bright lights seen. The head of a woman appeared, came close and dematerialized. A half-figure of a man was seen a few seconds later. He bowed and then disappeared through the ceiling with a scraping noise.'

Another witness also described the searching of the room, the sealing of the door, and the disposition of the medium and sitters round the table. She alleged that a female head appeared in a strong light and afterwards a bearded man reading a book, who disappeared through the ceiling. All the while Mr Davey's hands were held tightly by the sitters on either side, and when the gas was relit the door was still locked and the seal unbroken.

A third witness's account was even more sensational. He reported that 'nothing was prepared beforehand, the séance was quite casual'. Having described the locking and sealing of the door, he went on to say that he was touched by a cold, clammy hand and heard various raps. After that he saw a bluish-white light which hovered over the heads of the sitters and gradually developed into an apparition that was 'frightful in its ugliness, but so distinct that everyone could see it.... The features were distinct ... a kind of hood covered the head, and the whole resembled the head of a mummy'. After this an even more wonderful spirit appeared. It began with a streak of light and developed by degrees into a bearded man of Oriental appearance. His eyes were stony and fixed, with a vacant, listless expression. At the end of the séance the door was still locked and the seal was intact.

So much for some of the reports. Now for the reality. The séance was not a casual affair at all, but had been carefully rehearsed beforehand. At the beginning, Mr Davey went through the motion of apparently locking the door, but he turned the key back again so that the door was actually left unlocked. The 'props' for the materializations had been stowed away in a cupboard underneath a bookshelf; this was not looked into by the witnesses who searched the room because, just as they were about to do so, Mr Davey diverted their attention by emptying his pockets to show that he had nothing hidden on his person. The phenomena were produced by a confederate who came in by the unlocked door after the lights had been turned out, and while the musical box was playing loudly to drown the noise of his entry. The 'apparition of frightful ugliness' was a mask draped in muslin with a cardboard collar coated with luminous paint. The second spirit was the confederate himself, standing on the back of Mr Davey's chair, his face faintly illuminated by phosphorescent light from the pages of a book he was holding. The rasping noise made when the spirits seemed to disappear through the ceiling was caused accidentally, but interpreted by the witnesses according to their conception of what was happening. When the light was turned on the gummed paper that had been used to seal the door had fallen off, but Mr Davey quickly pressed it back into position and then called the witnesses' attention to the fact that it was 'still intact'. Mr Davey's performances were so convincing that some leading investigators, including the biologist A. R. Wallace, F.R.S., refused to believe him when he said that he had no mediumistic powers and it had all been done by trickery. In effect the conjurer was challenged to prove that he was *not* a medium!

More recently other investigations of a similar kind have been reported, and they all agree that, from the point of view of proof, human testimony in the absence of careful controls is quite useless. This conclusion will hardly surprise anyone who has ever seen a good conjurer at work on the stage. Few of the happenings in séances are anything like as miraculous as what happens on the brightly lit stage in front of thousands of people. A few hours' instruction in elementary conjuring should enable any reasonably adept person to produce most of the alleged psychical phenomena seen at séances.

It should be stated quite emphatically that the witnesses who were misled in these experiments were not particularly foolish or particularly credulous people. It is very doubtful if, under conditions of this kind, even the most eminent scientist would have been any more likely to give a correct account. It is generally recognized in science that instruments are required to supplement available human observation, and that years of training in the use of such instruments are essential before reports can be accepted as representing the truth of what actually happened during the experiment. The notion that psychical phenomena could be investigated without such safeguards is a slightly absurd one because, if anything, the conditions surrounding these observations (darkness, excitement, etc.) are such as to make the usual safeguards more rather than less necessary and desirable.

Another difficulty which must be taken into account is the fact that even when a highly intelligent and apparently trustworthy witness is speaking about events which have happened to himself, he may be giving an account which is far from true. A good example of such fabrication is the case of Sir Edmund Hornby. Sir Edmund Hornby was Chief Judge of the Supreme Consular Court of China and Japan. According to his story, which was published by the Society of Psychical Research in 1884, he stated that a certain newspaper editor and reporter used to call at his house in the evening and collect his written judgements for the day so that they could be printed in the next morning's paper. One night Sir Edmund was roused by a tap on the door, and in walked the reporter. Looking deadly pale, he approached the foot of the bed, and in a polite but desperately insistent manner pleaded with Sir Edmund to give him verbally a summary of the judgements. Sir Edmund complied, and the reporter thanked him and left the room. Sir Edmund looked at the clock, which showed the hour to have been half past one. Lady Hornby woke up and was told what had happened.

The next day, Sir Edmund heard that the reporter had died in the night. He had been seen writing at a quarter to one, and at half past one his wife found him dead. Beside his body was his shorthand notebook with the heading for the judgements the last item in it. He had apparently died of heart disease, and it was absolutely impossible for him to have left home during the night.

Here, then, is a highly impressive story, told by a witness of unimpeachable integrity. Yet it emerged later that the editor in question had died between eight and nine o'clock in the morning on a day following one on which no judgements had been made in court, and three months before Sir Edmund had married. On hearing these facts, which proved indisputable, Sir Edmund admitted that his memory must have played him an extraordinary trick. It is unlikely that he would have invented the story and allowed it to be published, knowing all the while that it was false and apt to be exposed. It appears more likely that he did have a vision of the dead reporter, but that the various striking details were added to the occurrence bit by bit, until finally his memory of the event had become almost completely changed. Such falsification is liable to occur in one's recollection of any highly emotional scene, and again it should not be assumed that Sir Edmund Hornby reacted in any way differently from how other people might have reacted. Testimony of a single person, however authoritative he may be, must never be accepted as evidence for a psychic experience.

Must we, then, reject all these earlier accounts of mediums, séances, and telepathic and clairvoyant performances? The answer is that the great majority are suggestive but could never be used to convince the sceptic, and in a new field such as this, the scientist must almost by definition assume the role of sceptic. If any alternative explanation to extra-sensory perception is possible, then that alternative explanation, however unlikely it may be, must be accepted. Thus, as long as there is any possibility of fraud, trickery, collusion, coincidence, memory falsification, or anything else of this sort, the investigator may regard the reported events as interesting, and may use them to suggest hypotheses to him, but he must not, under any circumstances, regard them as evidence in favour of the occurrence of either telepathy or clairvoyance.

There are, however, a few events which are rather difficult to explain away, even by the most sceptical. As an example, let us take the case of Mrs Piper, a young married woman of Boston, Massachusetts. Her abilities were investigated by Professor William James, one of the really great names in psychology. Knowing the quality of most mediums,

James was inclined to scoff when two of his female relatives were greatly impressed by Mrs Piper. He went to see for himself and quickly changed his mind. She became his 'one white crow', and throughout her career she was constantly being investigated by highly critical and able experimenters. James himself was joined in this work by Dr Richard Hodgson, Secretary to the American Society for Psychical Research. Hodgson had quite a reputation for exposing fraudulent mediums, and he went so far as to set detectives to watch Mrs Piper and her family to find out if she made secret inquiries about her sitters' private affairs. Neither the detectives nor any of the investigators ever discovered Mrs Piper in a dishonest act.

Mrs Piper's forte was to tell strangers things about their private affairs which she could not normally have known. In order to make ignorance even more certain, Mrs Piper was invited to England so that she could meet foreign sitters, about whose personal affairs she could not possibly have any prior information. Here is an example of the type of work she did. She was staying at the time with Sir Oliver Lodge, Professor of Physics at Liverpool University, in his own house. All the servants were new and ignorant of the family connexions, and Lodge, very sceptical at this stage, took such precautions as locking up the photograph albums and family Bibles, and searching Mrs Piper's luggage. Strangers were asked to call and were introduced to Mrs Piper under assumed names. Mrs Piper herself was quite uninquisitive and seemed somewhat self-absorbed.

Lodge tried an experiment with Mrs Piper. He wrote to an uncle to ask for a relic of the uncle's twin brother who had died about twenty years previously. He was sent an old watch, which he gave to Mrs Piper while she was in a trance. She said, almost at once, that the watch belonged to an uncle, and after a lot of stumbling she produced the name of 'Jerry'. Lodge encouraged 'Uncle Jerry' to recall boyhood incidents that his surviving brother would remember. Several such incidents were mentioned, including the swimming of a creek, being nearly drowned, killing a cat in

Smith's field, and possessing a long peculiar skin, like a snakeskin. The uncle with whom Lodge was in correspondence did not recollect all these points, but on writing to yet another brother, Frank, verification was received for every one of the items mentioned by Mrs Piper.

Lodge sent an inquiry agent to Uncle Jerry's home village to see how much information could be obtained by questioning the old men of the place about Smith's field and the rest. The result was almost nil. It is particularly interesting in this connexion to note that Lodge himself did not know anything about Uncle Jerry's boyhood and therefore could not say until after he had made inquiries whether or not the medium's statements were correct. Here, it seems, we have a case reliably reported by several people of integrity and intelligence where explanations not involving extra-sensory perception are rather difficult to come by unless, indeed, we explain it simply in terms of coincidence. Yet coincidence would not often result in such startling revelations, and it should be remembered that Mrs Piper did not produce this as an isolated event, but kept on producing 'coincidences', for some twenty-five years, day in and day out. There are one or two other mediums whose performances rival those of Mrs Piper, and while scientists will always tend to have a rather odd feeling at the very mention of the term 'medium', this does not justify us in rejecting the performances so carefully studied and investigated.

Yet however unlikely 'coincidence' may sound as an explanation of the events ascribed to Mrs Piper and other mediums, we cannot set an actual probability level to the likelihood of such events as the name of Lodge's uncle being correctly produced by Mrs Piper. What appears unlikely to one person may not appear so unlikely to another, and science does not deal with subjective estimates of this kind. We must have some firm statistical estimate of the probability of correct guesses, as well as the total number of guesses produced, before we can make any rational and scientifically acceptable statement about matters of this kind. The odd and uncontrolled events of séances, of prophetic dreams, of the utterances of mediums – all these may be lively and interesting and intriguing, but they cannot easily be subjected to the processes of counting, of measurement, and of statistical probability theory.

The main contribution of psychology to the study of psychical phenomena has been two-fold. In the first place, the circumstances in which these phenomena are produced have been placed under the control of the experimenter, and in the second place the phenomena have been made amenable to measurement and statistical calculation. This two-fold process of tightening up conditions of the experiment and of obtaining an exact statement of the probability of 'coincidence' as an explanation has made it possible to achieve a degree of rigour which makes the acceptance or the rejection of the evidence no longer a matter of individual belief. While this change in emphasis has been all to the good and has, indeed, been absolutely essential for making the alleged phenomena acceptable to scientists, it has also had one rather unfortunate effect. Gone are the miraculous stories and the interesting personalities, the mediums, the conjurers, the oracles. Gone are the impassioned arguments about trustworthiness and about the effects of chance. Gone are the serious, long-bearded Victorians, crowding into small rooms to watch ectoplasm emerge from the mouths of mediums. Instead of all this colour and glamour and amusement we now have clean-shaven young scientists repeating hundreds of thousands of times simple card-guessing games; we have calculating machines churning out probabilities in terms of highly complex formulas which only the initiated can comprehend. The whole colourful story is boiling down to simple statements, such as that Mr A, in five million calls, in which by chance he should have been correct once in fifty-two cases in calling the right card, was correct once in fifty cases, the probabilities against this happening by chance being said to be astronomical.

There is little point in regretting the passing of the Victorian era of psychical research; nothing we can do will bring it back. But the reader will soon notice that the improvement in methodology has to be bought at a price, and this price, to many people, has been the unmitigated boredom produced by having to read through countless reports, all as similar as two peas, of people doing exactly the same thing under exactly the same conditions, getting results slightly better than chance would allow. However, fortunately, even in this bleak field there are items of interest and moments of excitement. Before turning to these, let us consider quite briefly the statistical basis of modern research on extra-sensory perception. Let the reader take a pack of fifty-two playing cards, shuffle it thoroughly, cut it, and look at the top card. As he is looking at the card, let him press an electric key which gives a signal to a person in another room to write down his guess at the suite of the card. The pack is then shuffled again after the card has been replaced, and card after card is drawn, looked at, and replaced in the same manner. Let us make 1,200 guesses in this way. Now it will be clear that the probability of a guess being right by chance is one in four. Consequently, if nothing but chance were operating in our experiment, then the probability of a correct guess should be one-quarter of 1,200, or 300 in all. Of course, in any actual experiment it is unlikely that the number of guesses would be precisely 300. We would have sometimes a few more and sometimes a few less. If we had 100 experiments, each consisting of 1,200 trials, and recorded the mean number of successes for each of these experiments, we would find that the scores, i.e. the number of successes, would vary around the 300 mark from about 270 to 330. Very occasionally we would get more extreme scores, but the very great majority, on the hypothesis that chance only was operating, would be within that range.

Suppose, now, that we are testing a subject in this manner whose score over the 1,200 trials is 400. Can we dismiss that as a simple coincidence? The answer is not simply 'Yes' or 'No'. What we do is to calculate the probability of such an extreme deviation occurring by chance. In our case this probability would be less than a million to one and we would certainly be justified in thinking that chance was a pretty poor explanation. If the chances of a horse winning the Derby were a million to one against, few people would be willing to bet on that horse, and similarly, if the chances against the 'coincidence' hypothesis are a million to one, as in this case, few scientists would be willing to back it. Thus, we would be able to conclude that something was probably acting here other than chance to produce the observed results.

If we were very strongly opposed to a belief in telepathy or clairvoyance, we might say that the odds against it were so strong that no single experiment could be considered convincing. We would then simply have to duplicate the experiment; if we obtained another run of 400, the probabilities against chance being active would be something like a million times a million. We could go on piling probabilities on probabilities, but for most people a reasonable level like a million to one would probably be acceptable enough, provided the experiment was technically satisfactory in other respects. Of course, the reader might insist on adopting Pascal's logic to this problem. Pascal, it will be remembered, was a very gifted mathematician, as well as a very bigoted Catholic. As befits one of the founders of modern probability theory, he used his theory to prove that we should believe in God. His argument runs as follows: The felicity of Paradise is infinite. Therefore, however low the probability be that God exists, if you multiply this probability by infinity it becomes certainty. Consequently, we ought to believe in God. Pascal's argument appealed neither to the mathematicians nor to his co-religionists, and has remained somewhat of a historical curiosity. Its inverse, which states that psychical phenomena are infinitely unlikely and that, therefore, no finite set of probabilities can prove them, has received somewhat wider acclaim, although its logical basis is equally fallacious.

Many people, of course, believe that you can prove anything by statistics and are, consequently, neither impressed nor surprised by these modern findings. This is rather too drastic a view to take, because the greater part of modern science is based on statistical methodology and the calculus of probability; to relinquish all of modern science in order to get rid of the necessity of having to admit psychical phenomena is like throwing out the baby with the bath-water. It may be possible to prove anything by statistics, but only to people who are foolish or ignorant; the methodology of modern statistics is so widely accepted by scientists that few people who know anything about it would imagine that they could get away with any kind of fallacious proof simply because the proof rested on a statistical basis.

The essence of modern work in psychical research, then, consists in arranging the experiment in such a way that the probability of any given result occurring by chance can be calculated, thus giving us an estimate of the likelihood of 'coincidence' having been responsible for our findings. Even if 'coincidence' is to be ruled out as a likely cause of our findings, this does not, of course, by itself prove the existence of extra-sensory perception. There may be weaknesses in the experimental design itself which are responsible for the extra-chance results we obtained. Before we can turn to statistics as the arbiter, we must ensure that not even the most persistent and sceptical critic can find anything to cavil at in our experimental design. Only then does the statistical argument become of crucial importance.

The first experimenter whose work should be mentioned here was an American psychologist, Coover, who was strongly opposed to the theory of extra-sensory perception. He used two people for each of his experiments, the 'sender' or 'agent', who looks at the cards one by one, and the 'receiver' or 'recipient' who records his guesses. Coover used altogether 105 guessers and ninety-seven senders. He sat with the sender in one room while the subject being tested sat in an adjoining room. The purpose of having two rooms, of course, is to make it absolutely impossible for the receiver to catch any glimpse of the cards, and to prevent the sender giving him any signal, intentional or unintentional, which might enable him to identify the card by normal means.

Altogether, 10,000 guesses were recorded, using packs of playing cards from which the twelve picture cards had been removed, so that each pack contained forty cards. Having shuffled and cut the pack, Coover threw a die for 'odds' or 'evens' in order to decide whether or not the sender should look at the face of the card drawn. Coover intended those trials in which no one saw the card to act as an empirical control on the trials in which the agent concentrated on the cards, but nowadays we could consider them rather as clairvoyance trials, as opposed to the telepathy trials.

Coover reported that neither the telepathy trials nor the 'control' trials showed any significant deviations from mean chance expectation, and he accordingly concluded that there was no evidence for telepathy. However, out of a grand total of 10,000 calls, 294 were correct as compared with an expectation of 250, and it can be shown that the odds against this happening by chance are roughly of the order of 160 to 1. Odds of 20 to 1 are usually considered significant in psychological work, and odds of 100 to 1 very significant. If this had been any ordinary kind of psychological experiment, the experimenter would undoubtedly have concluded that the experiment had been successful in proving the existence of extra-sensory perception. The results certainly do not bear out Coover's contention that there is no evidence for telepathy or clairvoyance in his work, but, on the other hand, we cannot either accept it as positive proof. The main weakness is an experimental one. As S. G. Soal and F. Bateman have pointed out in *Modern Experiments in Telepathy*, Coover's method of obtaining a series of call cards that was approximately random by means of hand-shuffling a solitary pack of cards was not very efficient. A pack of cards tends to cut more easily at certain places than at others, and if the card situated in such a place happened to be a popular one, such as the nine of diamonds or the ace of spades, this card would turn up more frequently than the others, and would also be guessed more frequently, thus increasing the number of correct guesses.

As far as it goes, then, Coover's pioneer experiment, while

technically faulty, did produce evidence in favour of extra-sensory perception, the odds being something like 160 to 1. Strangely enough, he is still often quoted as having 'disproved' the existence of extra-sensory perception. This is an interesting case of wishful thinking and suppression of evidence, and unfortunately many other such cases can be found in the literature of the subject.

A rather different type of experimental set-up was used by three Dutch investigators, Heymans, Brugmans, and Wynberg. The guesser sat blindfolded by himself in front of a large chess-board containing forty-eight squares instead of the usual sixty-four. There were six rows numbered 1 to 6 and eight columns with the letters *A* to *H*, so that any of the forty-eight squares could be located by the letter and the number, as in the Continental system of chess notation. The experimenters were in a room immediately above that in which the guesser was seated, and watched him through a thick pane of glass let into the floor. They selected one of the forty-eight squares by drawing a card from each of two shuffled packs, one containing the numbers 1 to 6 and the other the letters *A* to *H*. The subject was then observed to make his choice, and the choice was written down and compared with the correct position. Their best subject, a young man called van Dam, was right sixty times in 187 trials, as compared with a chance expectation of about four successes. This, again, is far beyond any reasonable level of statistical significance for the acceptance of chance as a likely explanation, but, again, there are certain criticisms of the experimental method. Conditions of observations were unfavourable for the experimenters, and they may well have made mistakes by counting near successes as successes. Again, the observers, who knew the correct square, watched the subject while he was groping over the board, and it is not entirely impossible that they became excited when his hand was in the region of the right square and by some slight movement they might have produced auditory cues for him to pick up. The reader may consider these objections as trifling and unlikely, but there is ample evidence in the history of the subject that a very small auditory and visual cue can provide a suitably acute subject with all the information needed.

Two examples may be quoted. The first one is the case of the Elberfeld horses. These horses, which have enjoyed a considerable degree of renown, worked out the answers to arithmetical problems given to them by spectators, and apparently showed an uncommonly high degree of intelligence, even for horses. Although many investigators were convinced that the phenomena produced were genuine, it was finally established that the horses were responding to slight movements made by their trainer, probably quite unconsciously. Many stage magicians who find hidden objects rely on unconscious movements made by the spectators who know the place where the object is hidden, and by responding to these movements succeed in their search.

A classic example in the use of subliminal hearing cues is the case of a Latvian peasant child, Ilga, who was supposed to be able to read by telepathy any book that her mother was looking at. The mother was always in the background, encouraging her, while the girl read falteringly almost syllable by syllable. By taking sound recordings of the mother's interjections of encouragement, and by playing these back to Ilgar, it was discovered that the girl was responding to very slight auditory cues picked up from her mother. These cues were not noticed by quite a large number of investigators, who were taken in by Ilgar's performance.

Again, some performers make use of signal cues, as in the case of the blindfolded 'clairvoyant' who sits on the stage while his confederate goes round the auditorium asking for articles of various kinds to be handed to him, which his colleague then guesses. These guesses are based on various types of auditory cues elaborated into a system by the performers, which completely escape the notice of the spectators. There is some evidence that quite a few successful bridge partnerships have been based on the same principle!

It might be argued that Heymans and the other experimenters were highly competent psychologists and would be on the look-out for this kind of thing. This, of course, is perfectly true, but it is not really a relevant argument. An experiment, to be acceptable as decisive in a matter of this kind, must not depend on one's faith or belief in the professional competence of anyone. The design must be completely foolproof in order to be acceptable. If there is the slightest possibility, however unlikely, that the subject might have succeeded by means other than extra-sensory ones, then the experiment fails to prove the case. How necessary this general rule is will be realized when it is remembered that both the Elberfeld horses and Ilga were investigated and accepted as genuine cases of telepathy by scientists of a standing equal to that of the Dutch investigators, whose work we are now considering.

The next to investigate telepathy was G. H. Estabrooks, who used an ordinary pack of playing-cards. He took the precaution of having sender and receiver and guesser separated in the two halves of a relatively sound-proof room, separated by a partition with double doors which were closed during the experiment. He also carried out long-distance experiments in which the sender and the guesser were in two rooms sixty feet distant from each other. His results were significant at the 1,000 to 1 level, but the number of trials was relatively small because Estabrooks seems to have become discouraged by the fact that subjects who start out by making positive scores later on make negative ones. This has been found in many investigations since and appears to be an almost universal psychological fact. It is a pity that Estabrooks did not continue his work because, technically, it appears to be the best until it was superseded by more recent investigations, and the results, while promising, do not reach a level of significance which would make the acceptance of extra-sensory perception mandatory.

We now come to the work carried out by J. B. Rhine at Duke University in North Carolina. The countless studies carried out by this investigator, his wife, and numerous colleagues and students, have probably done more than anybody else's to put parapsychology 'on the map'. At the same time, Rhine's experiments are so well known that any detailed recounting of them would not have very much point. I shall, therefore, recount them in less detail than their importance would obviously deserve.

Rhine's main innovation in technique was the introduction of a new type of experimental material. Where previously playing-cards and numbers had been used, he now introduced the so-called Zener cards, which had inscribed on them one of five symbols – a circle, square, five-pointed star, wavy lines, or plus sign. The cards were made up into packs of twenty-five, each pack containing five cards of each symbol.

This may seem a very slight change, but for many reasons it is a very important one. Playing-cards and numbers, like human beings, have their favourites and their wall-flowers. Among cards, the ace of spades and the nine of diamonds are much more likely to be called than the four of clubs or the ace of hearts. Among numbers, seven is much more likely to be called than two. Playing-cards and numbers, therefore, have associated values which interfere with the calculation of chance agreements, and which upset an experiment based on the equivalence in the minds of the subjects of all the symbols which are available. In choosing five relatively innocuous symbols, as Rhine had done, most of these difficulties were eliminated, although even this method does not completely get rid of them.

Rhine tried out various techniques with these cards in an attempt to separate out telepathy from clairvoyance. Sometimes in telepathy tests the sender would look at each card in turn and 'transmit' that to the receiver and then put them down. Sometimes in clairvoyant tests the sender would just lift each card in turn without looking at it, and then put it down again, to be checked later against the receiver's guesses. In the so-called 'down-through' technique, the sender would just look at a pack of Zener cards and the receiver would try to guess the sequence of cards without their being touched at all.

With these various conditions, Rhine reported astonishing

successes which set the odds against chance soaring into the millions. However, the results were much criticized on various grounds. Some of these are statistical and are related to the fact that each pack contained exactly five cards bearing each of the five symbols. This is not strictly a chance arrangement and requires a slight modification in the usual formula for calculating probabilities. The correction required is very small, however, and could not possibly account for Rhine's results. In later work the correct formula has been used, or else the sequence of the symbols has been established on the basis of a table of random numbers, a procedure which is perhaps preferable. In any case, the statistical criticisms which have been brought forward against Rhine, with this one exception, are not valid, and there is no doubt that if modern experiments on telepathy are vulnerable to criticism, it must be on the grounds of experimental rather than of statistical inadequacies. A lot of nonsense is talked on this point, even by people who should know better, and it should be emphasized that the highest authorities on mathematical statistics have explicitly given their blessings to the methods of analysis currently used.

Another criticism made is that of inadequate shuffling. As most card-players know, the ordinary process of shuffling and cutting does not destroy completely sequences of cards, and if in telepathy experiments the habits of the guesser happen to fit in with the sequence of cards, then it is possible that these sequences may persist through several processes of shuffling, thus producing slightly inflated scores. While it is perfectly true that successive arrangements obtained by repeated shufflings of a pack of Zener cards are not perfectly random cards drawn from the 623,360,743,125,120 possible arrangements of the twenty-five cards, yet there is ample experimental evidence that high scores made by good subjects cannot be accounted for by such differences. The method of proof, which is a very simple one, is that of matching guessing sequences of a given person against runs of cards for which they were not intended. Thus we might compare the set of guesses made by

Mr Smith with the set of cards shown on another occasion to Miss Doolittle, and the set of guesses made by Miss Doolittle with the run of cards but before Mr Smith. In half a million such matchings the average score was found to be 4·9743 as opposed to the chance value of 5·00. Thus, this criticism cannot account for the average scores of 7, 8, or more scored by successful subjects.

Optional stopping has been another alleged cause of high scores. As by chance people's scores will be equal often above and below the chance level of 5 successes per 25 calls, it is suggested that a high score can be built up by simply going on with each subject until he reaches a point where he has an above-average score. The run is then stopped before the subject can go down into his next negative swing. By accumulating a large number of subjects and following the same procedure with each, we would then arrive at the large number of positive deviations which, when added together, will give high odds against chance. This is an interesting and, at first sight, plausible theory, which in a slightly adapted form has led many people to lose millions of francs at the roulette wheels of Monte Carlo. As Soal and Bateman point out the main difficulty with the argument is this. Some people start out with a negative score and go on having negative scores on the average. To convert these into positive scores requires so many runs that the over-all significance of the total results is reduced to practically zero because of the large number of runs required to produce the positive total. It is possible, by means of optional stopping, to increase the chance score slightly above 5, but this can be taken into account by suitable statistical formulas and it cannot, under any circumstances, produce the persistent high scoring observed in some subjects.

Unconscious whispering has also been suggested as a possible explanation of some of the findings, and we have already seen that this cannot be ruled out too quickly. However, experiments have been conducted with a distance of several miles between sender and recipient, and it can hardly be suggested that an unconscious, or subliminal, whisper would carry that far! In the clairvoyant tests the sender himself had no notion of the sequence of cards, and thus could hardly give them away by whispering. The same is true of the calls made by means of the down-through technique.

Errors in recording and checking have been considered as possibly accounting for some of the extra-chance results, the hypothesis being that the investigator would tend to make errors in favour of his preconceived notion, counting as co-incidences guesses where, in fact, card and guess were different. This again is not a likely explanation. Repeated checking has shown that errors are almost negligible and that where they do occur they tend much more frequently to indicate a correct matching missed rather than an incorrect matching scored as correct. Considerable care is taken in modern experiments to make duplicates of all card and guess sequences, and these are usually independently checked by several people.

Improper selection of data is the last of the main criticisms brought against Rhine. It is suggested that perhaps groups of data giving only chance results were rejected and only those giving positive results reported. As an alternative, it is suggested that perhaps the positive results reported by some investigators are counterbalanced by the more numerous negative results which may have been obtained by others, but not reported because of their negative nature. The first of these arguments impugns the integrity of the investigator, and there is no evidence that Rhine fell into this error. The fact that many other previously hostile investigators who were fully aware of this difficulty confirmed his positive results tends to disarm this line of criticism. As regards the second version of this argument, it can be shown that it would require quite impossibly large series of negative instances to reduce the obtained positive results to insignificance. This argument too, therefore, must be rejected.

One further criticism must be mentioned because much has been made of this. It is suggested that certain irregularities on the backs of the cards may have given the subjects certain cues; that occasionally the symbols may have been

E

printed so heavily that they could be seen through the back of the cards; and that it was not always impossible for the subjects to see directly the bottom card of the pack, or the card where the cut was made. These possibilities cannot be ruled out for some of the early Rhine experiments, but they certainly do not obtain in most of this work. The cards were usually screened from the receiver, or the receiver and sender were in different rooms. Usually the subject did not know when he had scored a success and when not, so that he had no opportunity for associating the back of the card with the symbol on the face of it.

It is important to realize in considering the storm of criticism that broke over Rhine's head that, at least in part, he was responsible for much of it. There are, roughly speaking, two ways of carrying out work in this field. One method – namely, that adopted by Rhine – is to start out with very unstandardized and loose conditions which give the subject a more positive, co-operative type of attitude. This attitude, apparently, is an important psychological factor in successful work, and it tends to be destroyed by the imposition of stringent controls. Gradually, Rhine would tighten up his controls, always trying to retain the positive attitude on the part of the subject, until finally he would reach a point where controls were completely stringent and where yet positive scores were still obtained from the subject. An alternative method would have been to start right away with the more stringent controls, but it is quite possible that under those conditions co-operation would have suffered and less significant scores would have been obtained.

Rhine's method is probably the superior one, but it is doubtful whether he was right in publishing the results from his less rigidly controlled experiments. The criticisms rightly levelled against these have prejudiced many people against accepting the more rigidly controlled experimental investigations which followed, and it would probably have been better to have restricted the account only to a small number of cast-iron experiments which left no loophole at all.

One of these highly impressive experiments was carried

out on Hubert Pearce, one of Rhine's star subjects. Subject and sender were in different buildings at Duke University while the experiment was being carried on, there being no telephonic communication between the two buildings. According to a prearranged timing schedule, Dr Pratt, who carried out the experiment, lifted out the top card from the shuffled pack at a specified time and laid it face downwards on the centre of the table. Thirty seconds later, Pearce wrote down his guess, and after another thirty seconds, Pratt lifted off the next card. Thus, they worked at the rate of one card a minute, with fifty guesses at each sitting. Pratt and Pearce would then seal up their record sheets and deliver them independently to Rhine, who checked the results. An average over 750 trials of 8·7 hits per 25 cards was scored, giving odds against chance of something like 10^{20} to 1. The reader may like to try out the various criticisms made and evaluated above and see for himself how little they can account for the effects observed in this study.

During the years in which Rhine tightened up his controls there seems to have come about a definite change in outlook. At first, it used to be believed that almost anyone had parapsychology powers, if only to a slight extent, and that experiments involving large numbers of people would, on the whole, tend to give positive results. It is not inconceivable that the positive results achieved under those conditions were, wholly or in part, due to laxity of experimental conditions. In more recent years attention has shifted rather to a small number of highly gifted individuals who can be relied on to give high scores over long periods. Large-scale experiments involving many people tend to give only chance results, although they may be useful in discovering the rare gifted person who can then be studied further.

It would not be very interesting to recount in detail the many confirmatory experiments carried out by Rhine and by others who have followed in his footsteps over the years. Unless there is a gigantic conspiracy involving some thirty University departments all over the world, and several hundred highly respected scientists in various fields, many of them originally hostile to the claims of the psychical researchers, the only conclusion the unbiased observer can come to must be that there does exist a small number of people who obtain knowledge existing either in other people's minds, or in the outer world, by means as yet unknown to science. This should not be interpreted as giving any support to such notions as survival after death, philosophical idealism, or anything else; the interpretation of this fact must await a more thorough knowledge of the conditions under which such results can be obtained and the means through which extra-sensory knowledge is transmitted.

Rhine and his associates tried out various methods to discover the correlates of this extra-sensory ability. In particular, they were concerned with the question of which kind of personality was most likely to give positive E.S.P. results. Intelligence, although the most obvious candidate, was soon ruled out because there appears to be no good cause to suspect extra-sensory perception to occur more frequently among people of high, medium, or low intelligence. Attention was therefore directed towards the non-cognitive side of personality. One of the first to work along these lines was Humphrey, who made use of a drawing test. This test, originated by Elkisch, makes use of the types of drawings produced by experimental subjects, contrasting the 'expansive type', which shows imagination, vitality, and freedom of expression, with the 'compressive type', which shows inhibition, lack of imagination, and timidity.

Humphrey got her subjects to make a sketch aimed at a drawing contained in an opaque sealed envelope in the hope that there would be some relation between the expansive–compressive quality of the sketch and the clairvoyant ability of the person to respond to the drawing in the envelope. A complex scoring system was elaborated, and Humphrey found that the 'expansives' scored on the average above chance expectation, while the 'compressives' scored below the chance level, the difference being highly significant with the odds against chance in the neighbourhood of 300,000 to one. With the total score of the expansives showing a positive deviation, and the total score of the compressives showing a negative deviation, the combined total score did not significantly deviate from chance, the total score thus showing no evidence of extra-sensory perception.

In a further experiment telepathy was used rather than clairvoyance by having the sender look at the pictures in a distant room, and the guessers drawing sketches in another room. This time the relationship was reversed, the compressives scoring above-chance level and expansives scoring below. In conformity with this finding, another investigator found that expansive subjects, selected because they had produced high scores in clairvoyance tests, scored significantly below chance expectation when they were made to do telepathy tests. Conversely, compressive subjects who had scored below chance expectation in clairvoyance tests obtained large above-chance scores with telepathy. Repetition of these experiments in Great Britain has not succeeded in duplicating the results reported from America, and it should be noted in any case that the Elkisch technique is not a very reliable one, as one and the same person may make compressive drawings on one occasion and expansive ones on another. Altogether, it is probably a safe rule here, as in other fields of psychology, to insist that a finding, before it can be accepted, should be duplicated in several different departments. Until this is done we can hardly accept Humphrey's results as being anything but suggestive.

Much the same is true of experiments carried out by Schmeidler. She divided her subjects into two groups, whom she called sheep and goats respectively. The goats had expressed the conviction that telepathy was impossible under the conditions of the experiments, while the sheep considered that it might occur. On the average, the sheep tended to score little above five and the goats a little below. On 185,725 guesses the average scores were 5·15 and 4·92 respectively.

Next Schmeidler went on to use the Rorschach ink-blot test on her subjects as a measure of emotional adjustment or stability. She then divided her subjects into four groups: well adjusted and poorly adjusted sheep, and well adjusted and poorly adjusted goats. Her hunch was that well adjusted sheep would get higher scores than poorly adjusted sheep, and that well-adjusted goats would get larger negative deviations than poorly-adjusted goats. Thus, in her view, poor adjustment might inhibit both the positive and the negative scoring ability of subjects. On the whole, her surmise appears to have worked out, but the differences are very small throughout. In addition, it should be noted that in her calculations she did not employ the correct formula, although the results would probably still have been significant if she had done so.

For various reasons, these results are difficult to accept. We know so little about telepathy and clairvoyance that one might be inclined to say that anything is possible and that these results are no more miraculous than others which we have considered previously. However, we do know something about the Rorschach test, and, as we shall see in a later chapter, this test is very unreliable and almost completely lacking in validity as far as the measurement of good or poor adjustment and emotional stability are concerned. Under those conditions, it seems exceedingly unlikely that such a test should succeed in picking out good and poor subjects respectively. Until these results are repeated we certainly should be extremely chary of accepting the implications contained therein. To show how necessary such scepticism is, we may perhaps recall that the particular version of the Rorschach used by Schmeidler had early on been used by another investigator to predict success at college with considerable accuracy. When the study was repeated elsewhere, however, results never went beyond chance. Repetition of experiments is our only safeguard against accepting false conclusions. On the whole, therefore, we must say that nothing is definitely known with respect to the personality traits which correlate with parapsychological ability, although a few promising leads may be contained in some of the work briefly summarized above.

We must now turn to quite a different aspect of telepathy and clairvoyance, which in a sense is much more miraculous and hard to accept than anything that has been mentioned so far. Throughout the older literature there is apparent a belief in the existence of precognition, i.e. the ability to look into the future and predict what will happen. Dreams which foretell the future have often been reported and will be considered in our next chapter, but the experimental investigation of prediction and precognition had to await the experimental work of Rhine, Tyrrell, and Soal. In Rhine's work what essentially happened was that the receiver called out the sequence of cards in a Zener pack, before that pack had been shuffled; these calls were then matched with the subsequent order of cards. Scoring was above chance, but only very little so, and as certain alternative hypotheses may account for his findings they are not considered completely convincing by certain critics.

Tyrrell's work is noteworthy because it is based on a machine which effectively gets rid of the human element in shuffling, recording, and so forth. This apparatus consisted of a row of five boxes, each of which contained a small electric lamp. The lamps were connected by wires to five keys which were operated by the experimenter from a desk situated a few feet away. The lids of these boxes could be lifted by the subject, who sat behind a large screen. When a key was pressed by the experimenter, the corresponding lamp was lighted, and the subject, at a signal from an electric buzzer, lifted the lid of what she thought to be the correct box. (The lamp was not allowed to light up before the lid was lifted, as otherwise the subject might have obtained slight cues from the heat of the box or the light which might have emanated from it.) The opening of any box automatically drew a line upon a roll of paper, and success was recorded by a double line. A commutator in the circuit changed the connexions between lamps and keys all the time, so that the experimenter did not know which lamp he was lighting when he pressed a given key. Alternatively, the keys could be dispensed with and a rotating switch with a single arm brought into play to act as a mechanical selector.

Under all these conditions, telepathy was ruled out, as Tyrrell himself would not know which was the correct box. Tyrrell's main subject, a Miss Johnson, was extremely successful in trials of clairvoyance, but she also succeeded in trials of precognitive clairvoyance, which makes her successes very much more interesting. In these trials, Miss Johnson opened a box about half a second before the experimenter pressed the key. There were 2,255 such trials with 539 hits, which is in excess of 88 above chance expectation, with odds against chance of about 270,000 to one. Inspection of the automatic recording on the paper showed that in the case of every hit the box had really been opened before the key was pressed. It would be very difficult indeed to explain these results away.

Most impressive perhaps of all the studies in precognition, however, is the work of S. G. Soal, a British mathematician who started out as a sceptic and for many years failed to produce positive results. Encouraged by another investigator who claimed to have found evidence of precognition, Soal went back over a large portion of his data to seek for what are now called 'displacement' effects. According to the theory, a person aiming at the card which is his target for the moment may actually miss it and displace his guess to the card immediately preceding or immediately following the one shown. Soal found, indeed, that two of his subjects, Basil Shackleton and Gloria Stewart, had given highly significant scores on the cards, one behind and one ahead of the target at which they were aiming. Shackleton in particular was found in subsequent investigations persistently to displace his aim to the card one ahead. Shackleton could, when specially pressed, shelve his guessing to the target card, but found it more congenial and natural to guess the card not yet exposed. When the rate of calling the cards was speeded up, Shackleton's guess would shift to a card two ahead so as to preserve his usual time relation.

These experiments do not necessarily prove the existence of precognition. The target sequence was predetermined by a list of random numbers, and if the subject could obtain knowledge of this list by telepathy he could then deduce the card one or two ahead without using precognition. However, Soal tested this hypothesis by arranging for the target order at certain sessions to be determined on the spot by drawing counters from a bowl. An assistant would pick up a counter and show it to the sender, who would instantly look at the card corresponding to the number shown on the counter. Still the pre-intuitive effect continued at much the same level of significance.

Taking together the work of Rhine, Tyrrell, Soal, and other investigators, such as Carington, who used the technique of getting people to draw pictures of objects which he was trying to 'send', there appears to be little possibility of denying the existence of precognition. However much such a conclusion may go against our ingrained habits of thought, the experimental rigour and the statistical adequacy of the experiments are such as to make criticism impotent. Unless, again, all these people and the many independent scorers and colleagues involved in this work are actively fraudulent, the conclusion is inescapable that certain people possess a faculty which enables them to foretell events in the immediate future.

Displacement effect is one of many secondary effects found in parapsychological research. Other such secondary effects have been known for quite a long time. Thus, it is known that many subjects tend to show a decline in their ability as time goes on; few subjects retain their abilities over more than two or three years. Even on a given occasion there tends to be a decline from the calls made in the first ten minutes of a three-hour session, say, to those made towards the end of that session. It is sometimes possible to depress the rate of calling below a chance level, so that people who start out giving highly positive scores decline until they give significantly negative ones at the end. If this happened just once or twice it might, of course, be just a chance effect, but it has been found to happen consistently with many subjects and in many different experiments. Another secondary effect has been labelled salience and relates to the observation that within a given run of twenty-five cards, most hits will be made at the beginning rather than in the middle of the series. The fact that secondary effects of this type have been found in many different investigations suggests that certain general laws may yet be found in this complex field and that we may eventually be led to a better understanding of these events.

We have mentioned the difficulty of discriminating between telepathy and clairvoyance. Our brief discussion of precognition will indicate just why the experimental task of differentiation is so enormously complicated. Suppose that our procedure was something like this. The experimenter opens a new pack of playing-cards in a dark room, puts them through a mechanical shuffler, and finally selects the target cards. The receiver in another dark room guesses these cards. Yet it cannot be said that clairvoyance has taken place, because someone will have to check the guesses against the order of the actual cards, and will thus have to perceive these cards in the normal way. The person who carried out the guessing correctly might have obtained his knowledge through clairvoyance, but he might also have been in contact with the person who carried out the checking by means of telepathy of a precognitive type. Thus, this experiment would not be adequate for establishing clairvoyance as opposed to telepathy. One possible way out of the dilemma has already been mentioned; it is the mechanical scrambler and recording device by Tyrrell.

Similar difficulties arise in trying to prove the existence of telepathy. Suppose the experimenter thinks of the names of various Zener cards without having any actual physical cards in front of him, while the receiver writes down his guesses in a different room. If now the experimenter writes down the names of the symbols he had thought of in their proper order, and a comparison with the receiver's guesses reveals evidence of E.S.P., we can still not say that we have proved the existence of telepathy because of the possibility of precognitive clairvoyance on the part of the receiver of the future physical record made by the experimenter. The way out of this difficulty is by means of a code known only to the experimenter, and never written down by him, by means of which he translates numbers drawn at random from an urn into symbols which he then tries to transmit to the receiver. The numbers are written down but not the code which translates them into the symbols, so that while pre-intuitive clairvoyance might enable the receiver to know the numbers drawn, this would still not be sufficient to enable him to translate these into the symbols he is actually asked to guess.

Experiments on both these lines have shown that both clairvoyance and telepathy must be presumed to exist. It has also been found that while many people who possess the one type of ability also tend to possess the other, this is by no means necessary, and in certain cases individuals may obtain high scores by telepathy, but not by clairvoyance and *vice versa*. The great majority of experiments, however, do not attempt to differentiate between these two abilities and must simply be taken as evidence of some all round parapsychological or extra-sensory perception capacity on the part of successful individuals.

A few words may be said in conclusion about psycho-kinesis, the last of the many parapsychological phenomena experimentally investigated. Rhine's method was simply one of letting dice roll down an inclined plane and getting his subjects to will the dice to go down in such a way as to give either a high (6, 5) or a low (1, 2) score. Routine methods of rolling the dice were developed so as to make them independent of the subject, and it has been found that strongly extra-chance scores could be obtained in this way. Certain experimental difficulties are obvious from the first; thus, dice tend to fall in such a way that the 6 or the 5 is exposed more frequently than any other number because the slight reduction in weight of those faces having a large number of spots hollowed out from the cube makes these sides come up more frequently. However, by getting his subjects to call whole series in an attempt to get *either* high or low scores, Rhine has successfully overcome this difficulty. We should be cautious in accepting these results until they have been duplicated successfully elsewhere, and altogether the amount of work done on this phenomenon is tiny compared with that carried out in the field of telepathy and clairvoyance. The evidence certainly is impressive, but not in my view conclusive, and it will need a few more years before any definite conclusions will be possible on this very important question.

Ideally, at the end of a chapter such as this, there should appear a few paragraphs dealing with theories to explain the observed phenomena. While many such theories have been suggested, there is little point in going into them in detail because they cannot be regarded as throwing very much light on our subject. Before theories can be very fruitful in science a large number of facts require to be known. Little is known in the field of extra-sensory perception, except that something seems to be active there which cannot be accounted for in terms of our ordinary rules and theories. In view of the difficulty of isolating the phenomenon and of finding good subjects, experimentation has not essentially gone very far beyond this. Certain rather interesting secondary facts are known, but much more progress will need to be made in their specific delineation before the search for a reasonable theory will become practicable. This is a disappointing conclusion, and it undoubtedly accounts for some of the hostility which orthodox science has shown towards this phenomenon. Isolated facts are not easily woven into the fabric of science, and as yet there is not in parapsychology a consistent system of facts linked together by hypotheses and theories. Some slight beginnings there are, as in the work linking personality and parapsychology, but, as we have seen there, these links are very weak and hardly to be trusted.

One of the reasons for this state of affairs, of course, is to be found in the relative youth and immaturity of parapsychology; another is the difficulty of obtaining the necessary finance for carrying out concentrated, co-ordinated, long-term work of this kind. A third reason perhaps can be found in the hostility which, until recently, research in parapsychology has aroused, and which is even now far from being completely overcome. In time, no doubt, all these difficulties will vanish and we will have the beginnings of a rational theory of parapsychology. Until then, we should perhaps not be too critical and remember that we have no proper theory of most psychological phenomena either, a fact which does not prevent us from recognizing that psychological phenomena do occur and are worthy of scientific investigation.

4

THE INTERPRETATION OF DREAMS

MANKIND has always been interested in dreams, and many attempts have been made to interpret the meaning of them. The reasons for this interest are not difficult to find. Dreams are odd and striking phenomena, similar to waking thought in some ways, but quite dissimilar in others. The objects which enter into the dream are usually everyday kinds of objects, like horses and trains and people; similarly, the place where the dream occurs is usually a familiar one, like the dreamer's house or a field or a night club. Yet what happens in the dream is often quite unlike the happenings of everyday life. People may change into each other or into animals; the dreamer may be wafted through the centuries or across the oceans in no time at all, and the most frightful and wonderful events may happen to him – more frightful and wonderful than any described in *The Thousand and One Nights*. In addition, dreams often have a very strong emotional content. This is obvious enough in the case of the nightmare, but even in the case of more ordinary dreams, strong emotions, both pleasant and more usually unpleasant, may be called forth. The presence of such emotions increases interest in dreams and makes people feel that they must be of some importance.

Factual information is scant and not very illuminating. When large numbers of dreams of people in our culture are examined, we can make a rough statistical analysis of the settings in which the dreams occur, the characters appearing in them, the actions through which they go, and the emotions which they betray. Most dreams have some fairly definite setting. In only about 5 per cent is the dreamer unaware of the setting. In another 15 per cent the dreamer is in a conveyance such as an automobile, a train, an aeroplane, a boat, an underground, or a tram. Roughly 10 per cent of dreams are set in recreational surroundings: amusement parks, at dances and parties, on the beach, watching sports events, and so on. More frequent than any of these settings, however, is the house or rooms in a house; these account for some 35 per cent. Apparently the living-room is the most popular, followed in turn by bedroom, kitchen, stairway, basement, bathroom, dining-room, and hall. Another 10 per cent of dreams are set in rural and out-of-doors surroundings. Men's dreams tend to occur more frequently in out-of-door surroundings, women's more frequently indoors. In another 10 per cent of dreams the dreamer is walking along a street or road. The remaining dreams are difficult to classify with respect to their settings.

Psychoanalysts often try to interpret certain aspects of the dream by taking into account the setting. The fact that the dream occurs in a conveyance, for instance, is interpreted in terms of the fact that the dreamer is going somewhere, is on the move; movement represents ideas such as ambition, fleeing from something, progress and achievement, breaking family ties, and so forth. Trains, automobiles, and other vehicles are instruments of power, and are thus interpreted as symbols for the vital energy of one's instinctual impulses, particularly those of sex. Recreational settings are usually sensual in character, being concerned with pleasure and fun, and imply an orientation towards pleasure rather than work. A symbolic interpretation of this kind may be even more highly specialized; thus a basement is supposed to be a place where *base* deeds are committed, or it may represent *base* unconscious impulses. We shall be concerned with the validity of such interpretations later on; here let us merely note the fact that interpretations of this type are made by some people.

In addition to a setting, the dream must also have a cast. In about 15 per cent of all dreams no one appears but the dreamer. In the remaining 85 per cent, on the average another two characters appear. Most of these additional characters are members of the dreamer's family, friends, and acquaintances. About 40 per cent of the characters in our dreams are strangers; they are supposed to represent the unknown, the ambiguous, and the uncertain; sometimes they are interpreted as alien parts of our own personality which we may be reluctant to acknowledge as belonging to us. Prominent people are seldom found in dreams; this may be because our dreams are concerned with matters that are emotionally relevant to us.

What does the dreamer do in his dream? In some 35 per cent of the cases he is engaged in some kind of movement, such as walking, driving, running, falling, or climbing. Mostly these changes in location occur in his home environment. In another 25 per cent of dreams passive activities such as standing, watching, looking, and talking are indulged in. There appears to be an absence of strenuous or routine activities in dreams – there is little in the way of working, buying or selling, typing, sewing, washing the dishes, and so forth. When energy is being expended in the dream it is in the service of pleasure, not in the routine duties of life. Women, generally speaking, have far fewer active dreams than men.

All kinds of emotions are attached to the actions and persons making up the dream, as well as to the settings. Quite generally unpleasant dreams are more numerous than pleasant ones, and apparently as one gets older the proportion of unpleasant dreams increases. The unpleasant emotions of fear, anger, and sadness are reported twice as frequently as the pleasant emotions of joy and happiness. Emotion in dreams is often taken to be an important aid in interpreting the dream, as we shall see later. In this it differs very much from colour; about one dream in three is coloured, but the attempt to find any kind of interpretation whatsoever for the difference between coloured and black-and-white dreams has proved very disappointing.

This, then, is the kind of stuff dreams are made of. What kind of interpretation can we make of them, assuming that they carry some form of meaning, however distorted, and are not merely the random after-effects of sensory stimulation encountered during the day or the immediate accompaniment of sensory stimulation present at the time the dream is taking place? Both these theories have been held, and may account for some dreams at least. We have seen a beautiful car during the day, and it may appear in our dreams. The alarm clock may strike, and instead of waking up we may have a dream of a church clock calling the devout to prayer.

A rather more adequate theory, and certainly a more poetic one, is held by savage tribes who believe that when a person is asleep his soul flies away and experiences in actual fact those things which to the sleeper appear as a dream. Such a view of course leads to complications. Thus a certain tribal chief, on hearing that one of his subjects had dreamed of having intercourse with one of the chief's daughters, demanded of him the full bride's money, on the theory that the sleeper's soul had in fact obtained the satisfaction which could in law be obtained only on paying the chief the price of his daughter. The reader may like to consider the ethical implications of this theory and ponder over possible experimental methods of disproving it; we shall, instead, summarily dismiss it, as we did the previous theory.

For the great majority of dreams such explanations as we have considered are clearly insufficient, and we encounter next two great groups of theories which attempt to interpret and explain dreams.

According to the first of these theories, dreams are prophetic in nature; they warn us of dangers to be encountered in the future, they tell us what will happen if we do this or that; they are looked upon as guide-posts which we may heed or neglect as we wish. This is probably the most common view of dreams which has been held by mankind. The prototype of the prophetic dream is of course Pharaoh's of the seven fat cattle and the seven lean cattle which Joseph interpreted. Here we have all the elements of the prophetic dream – the strong emotion indicating the importance of the dream, the symbolic way in which the information is wrapped up, and the special skill of the interpreter who can unravel the secret of the dream and can lay bare its innermost meaning.

If we take this hypothesis at all seriously, then a study of the art of dream interpretation clearly becomes of the greatest possible importance. We need only consider the possibilities opened up by dreaming in advance of the winner of next year's Derby, to indicate why people have always been fascinated by this aspect of dream study and why books on dream interpretation have so frequently been best sellers. The pattern was set by an Italian scholar called Artemidorus, who lived in the second century of the Christian era. His book was called *Oneirocritics*, which means *The Art of Interpreting Dreams*, and apart from being translated into many languages it has been imitated and copied by a very large number of writers. Essentially, books of this nature are based on the view that the dream is a kind of secret language which requires a sort of dictionary before it can be understood. This dictionary is provided by the writer of the dream book in the form of an alphabetical list of things which might appear in the dream, each of which is followed by an explanation of its meaning. Thus, if the dreamer dreams about going on a journey, he looks up 'Journey' in his dream book and finds that it means death. This may of course be rather disturbing to him, but he may console himself by the consideration that it need not necessarily be his own death which is being foretold in this fashion.

Few people would take this kind of dream interpretation very seriously; it is obviously analogous to astrology, tea-cup reading, and palmistry, in its unverified claims and its generally unlikely theoretical basis. Nevertheless, some scientists have taken the possibility of precognition seriously, as we have seen in a previous chapter, and one or two have devoted special attention to precognitive powers as shown in dreams. One of the best known of these is J. W. Dunne, whose book *An Experiment with Time* was widely read in the twenties and thirties of this century.

Let us consider the kind of dream which he considered as evidence. He reports the occurrence of an unusually vivid and rather unpleasant dream in which he seemed to be standing on high ground. This hill or mountain was of a curious white formation with little fissures here and there from which jets of vapour were spouting upwards. Dunne recognized the place as an island of which he had dreamed before; an island which was in imminent peril from a volcano. He remembered reading about Krakatoa, when the sea, making its way into the heart of the volcano through a submarine crevice, blew the whole mountain to pieces. 'Good Lord!' he gasped, 'the whole thing is going to blow up.' He was seized with the frantic desire to save the 4,000 unsuspecting inhabitants, and made considerable efforts to do so by getting the authorities to take some of them off in ships. Throughout the dream this number 4,000 seemed to have some special significance.

So much for the dream. A few days later Dunne received a copy of the *Daily Telegraph* (he was encamped at that time near the ruins of Lindley, which was then in the Orange Free State, and quite cut off from all contact with the world). In the paper he read about the explosion of the volcano Mont Pelée, which destroyed the once-prosperous town of Saint-Pierre, the commercial capital of the French island of Martinique in the West Indies. Forty thousand people were said to have lost their lives, and ships were busy for some time removing survivors.

It will be noted that the number of lives lost was 40,000, whereas Dunne had dreamed of 4,000, but, as he explains, when he read the paper he read in his haste that the number of killed had been 4,000, and in telling the story subsequently he always spoke of that printed figure as having been 4,000. He did not realize that it had really been 40,000 until he copied the paragraph fifteen years later. His explanation of the whole event is that his dream had been caused precognitively by the reading of the newspaper report, and that consequently the error in the dream respecting the number of dead was caused by the error in reading the report made subsequent to the dream. Dunne does not consider the possibility that, on the contrary, his misreading may have been caused by the memory of the number 4,000 in the dream, although even then we would have to admit a certain coincidence in his dreaming of a volcano exploding just before the actual event. Altogether, we can hardly consider this report as very convincing.

Another dream is probably a little more interesting. He dreamed one night that he was walking down a sort of pathway between two fields, and separated from them by high iron railings. His attention was suddenly attracted to a horse in the field on his left, which had apparently gone mad and was tearing about in the most frantic fashion. Anxiously he inspected the railings to see if there was any opening through which the animal could escape. Finding none, he continued on his way, only to find, to his dismay, that the animal had somehow managed to get out after all and was pursuing him full tilt down the pathway. He ran like a hare in an attempt to reach a flight of wooden steps rising up from the path. Next day Dunne went fishing with his brother, when the latter called his attention to the antics of a horse. There were two fields with a fence, and a pathway running between them. The horse was there, behaving just as it had done in the dream. The wooden steps at the end of the pathway were there too. There were certain slight differences in the scene, but by and large they were of no great consequence. Dunne began to tell his brother about the dream, but broke off because he was becoming worried that the horse might get out, as it had done in the dream. Failing to see any gap or even a gate in the railings, he said: 'At any rate this horse cannot get out', and recommenced fishing; but suddenly his brother called out to him, and he saw that the beast had, just as in the dream, got out of the field in some inexplicable fashion, and was thundering down the path towards the wooden steps. It swerved past these and plunged into the river, coming straight towards Dunne and his brother. The end of the story was rather tame, however, for on emerging from the water, the animal merely looked at the pair of frightened humans, snorted, and galloped off down the road. Again, there certainly is a somewhat surprising coincidence, but it is by no means impossible that Dunne had previously seen the horse, the two fields, the pathway, and the wooden steps. The various elements in the dream consequently might simply be memories of things seen but not leaving any conscious impression. Nor can the dissimilarities of the two stories be excluded, such as that in the one case Dunne was alone and in the other that he was accompanied by his brother; or that in the one case the horse was running after Dunne down the pathway, whereas in the actual event the horse was running by himself.

These are probably the most impressive of Dunne's dreams, and there would be no point in quoting any others. He was sufficiently encouraged by this evidence to perform a series of experiments in which he wrote down in detail all his dreams and then looked for events on the following days which could be matched with these dreams. He also got other people to do the same, and he claims that a large number of predictive dreams could be observed in this fashion. When looked at dispassionately and with the knowledge that those quoted in his book are presumably the most convincing among the many thousands which Dunne could find, the sceptical reader will see no good reason to renounce his scepticism.

As a method of proof, Dunne's attempt breaks down because there is no way of estimating the influence of chance factors, the admixture of previous acquaintance, and other similar complicating features. He himself agrees that what he has to tell is not proof in the ordinary sense and recommends the reader to try the method for himself. This, he claims, will lead to complete conviction. Even if this claim were true, and I have recorded dreams for several months without finding one which was in the slightest degree predictive of anything whatsoever, it would of course prove nothing at all. Emotional certainty that a particular belief is true still does not constitute proof, though it may be shared by a large number of people. Dunne takes this notion of proof altogether too lightly to make his work worthy of more serious consideration than that of his many predecessors.

Only one well-controlled study has been reported in the literature. This investigation was carried out in March 1932.

A few days after the kidnapping of the Lindbergh baby, but before the body had been found, the investigators put in the papers throughout the country a request for dreams concerning the kidnapping, and obtained over 1,300 replies. The dreams were then compared with the facts as established several weeks later – namely, that the baby's *naked* and *mutilated* body was discovered in a *shallow grave* in some *woods* near a *road*, and that death had been instantaneous. Only in some 5 per cent of the dreams sent in did the baby appear to be dead, and in only seven dreams were the actual location of the body, its nakedness, or the manner of its burial reasonably accurately portrayed. Only four of the seven dreams included the three items: death, burial in a grave, and location among trees. The following dream was judged to be the most accurate of the seven:

I thought I was standing or walking in a very muddy place among trees. One spot looked as though it might be a round shallow grave. Just then I heard a voice saying 'The baby has been murdered and buried there'. I was so frightened that I immediately awoke.

When it is remembered that this is the most accurate dream out of 1,300 and that it contained only a few of the facts later established, we will hardly be impressed by the precognitive abilities of the people who sent in their dreams. It could of course be argued that only a few people have this ability and that these people did not send in reports, but this would still leave us with the task of discovering those people who could supply us with the evidence. In summary, while the notion of precognitive ability is an intriguing one, it does not seem to find very much support from the study of dreams. What is indeed more needed than anything is a method, such as that discovered by Rhine, Soal, and others, in the case of clairvoyance and telepathy, which will enable us to obtain a reliable estimate of the chance factors entering into our experiment. In the absence of such an estimate, it can always be argued that coincidence is the basis of the reported findings, and that chance coincidences should not be regarded as evidence for something of such very high *a priori* unlikelihood as dreaming the future even before it has happened. It would be unscientific to deny in principle the possibility that such evidence may ultimately be found, but it must be concluded that up to now the evidence in favour of such a view does not even begin to reach a reasonable level.

We must turn to the second and quite different type of dream interpretation which is current, in order to see whether this has any more evidence in its favour. As much of this is tied up with the theory of Freud, a brief discussion of this at least is essential, although most people will already be familiar with some of its aspects. However, as in so many cases, what Freud is popularly believed to have said is not always the same as what he actually did say, and it may serve a useful function to set out the theory briefly and succinctly.

According to the Freudian theory and that of many others whose writings have preceded his by hundreds or even thousands of years, dreams do not reveal anything about the future. Instead, they tell us something about our present unresolved and unconscious complexes and may lead us back to the early years of our lives, when, according to psychoanalytic theory, the ground was being prepared for these later defects. There are three main hypotheses in this general theory which will be discussed in some detail. The first hypothesis is that the dream is not a meaningless jumble of images and ideas, accidentally thrown together, but rather that the dream as a whole, and every element in it, are *meaningful*. The second point that Freud makes is that dreams are always in some sense a *wish fulfilment*; in other words, they have a purpose, and this purpose is the satisfaction of some desire or drive, usually of an unconscious character.

Thirdly, Freud believes that these desires and wishes, having been repressed from consciousness because they are unacceptable to the socialized mind of the dreamer, are not allowed to emerge even into the dream without disguise. A *censor* or *super-ego* watches over them and ensures that they can only emerge into the dream in a disguise so heavy that they are unrecognizable.

Let us look at these three propositions in turn. The idea that the dream is meaningful is, as we have seen, a very ancient one. For Freud it follows directly from the deterministic standpoint: i.e. from the view that all mental and physical events have causes and could be predicted if these causes were fully known. This is a philosophical notion with which few scientists would wish to quarrel. It should be noted, however, that it is possible to believe that all natural events, including dreams, are caused by some agency or other without necessarily believing that dreams are meaningful in the Freudian sense. The great neuro-surgeon Penfield has shown that when needles are pushed into certain parts of the brain and an electric current sent through the needle, whole memory sequences of a specified kind run through the mind of the patient. The same memory sequence can be evoked again and again by simply re-applying the current. It might be possible that random stimulation of a physical nature of different parts of the cortex produces random combinations of past memories which are overlaid during the waking state by our sensory impressions, but which during sleep come to the fore in the form of dreams. This is not presented as a serious theory; it is merely intended to illustrate that dreams could be deterministically explained without having to accept their being in any sense meaningful. This point has often caused confusion because scientists, being generally in favour of determinism, have accepted the Freudian explanation of the meaningfulness of dreams by virtue of it being a deterministic explanation. When it is realized that many other deterministic explanations may be possible, we may be more willing to look at the evidence in favour of this particular interpretation to see whether in fact it is borne out.

Freud's argument of the meaningfulness of dreams is directly connected with his general theory that all our acts are meaningfully determined; a theory which embraces mispronunciations, gestures, lapses, emotions, and so forth. An example may be found in the story told by Jean Jacques Rousseau. Apparently he had acquired the habit of making a détour as he approached a certain boulevard. On questioning himself with regard to the origin of this 'mechanical habit', he came to the following conclusion: 'This is what my reflection discovered, for none of it had until then been present in my mind'; it was a matter of avoiding a little beggar whose chatter he disliked. 'We have no mechanical impulse,' Rousseau continues, 'the cause of which may not be found in our hearts if we but knew how to seek it there.' This is indeed the essence of the Freudian doctrine of meaning, a doctrine which was widely accepted and discussed hundreds of years before Freud was born, but of which he was an extremely effective popularizer.

Let us now turn to the second part of Freud's doctrine, namely the view that the dream is always a wish fulfilment. This is linked up with his general theory of personality. Roughly speaking, Freud recognized three main parts of personality: one, which he calls the *id*, is a kind of reservoir of unconscious drives and impulses, largely of a sexual nature; this reservoir, as it were, provides the dynamic energy for most of our activities. Opposed to it we have the so-called *super-ego*, which is partly conscious and partly unconscious and which is the repository of social morality. Intervening between the two, and trying to resolve their opposition, is the *ego*: i.e. the conscious part of our personality. In religious language we might liken the *id* to the concept of original sin and that of the *super-ego* to the concept of conscience. Classical scholars will have no need to be reminded of the striking anticipation of the Freudian doctrine which is contained in Plato's *Phaedrus*. This is what Socrates tells us in his story:

'As I said at the beginning of this tale, I divided each soul into three – two horses and a charioteer; and one of the horses was good and the other bad; the division may remain, but I have not yet explained in what the goodness or badness of either consists, and to that I will now proceed. The right-hand horse is upright and cleanly made; he has a lofty neck and an aquiline nose; his colour is white and his eyes dark; he is a lover of honour and modesty and temperance, and the associate of right opinion; he needs no touch of the whip, but is guided by word and admonition only. The other is a crooked lumbering animal, put together anyhow; he has a short thick neck; he is flat-faced and of a dark colour, with grey and blood-shot eyes; the mate of insolence and pride, shag-eared and deaf, hardly yielding to whip and spur. Now when the charioteer beholds the vision of love, and has his whole soul warmed through sense, and is full of the prickings and ticklings of desire, the obedient steed, then as always under the government of shame, refrains from leaping on the beloved; but the other, heedless of the pricks and of the blows of the whip, plunges and runs away, giving all manner of trouble to his companion and the charioteer, whom he forces to approach the beloved and to remember the joys of love.'

As one commentator reflects, 'One could hardly hope to find a more beautiful description of the three main components of man's personality – his primitive, vital impulses, his conscious or idealized self and his reason'. This part of Freud's theory too is then by no means novel and original, but has been part of educated thought for over 2,000 years.

The link-up between Freud's theory of personality and his theory of dream interpretation is a very simple one: the forces of the *id* are constantly trying to gain control of the *ego* and to force themselves into consciousness. During the individual's waking life, the *super-ego* firmly represses them and keeps them unconscious; during sleep, however, the *super-ego* is less watchful, and consequently some of the desires start up in the *id* and are allowed to escape in the form of dreams. However, the *super-ego* may nod, but it is not quite asleep, and consequently these wish-fulfilling thoughts require to be heavily disguised. This disguise is stage-managed by what Freud calls the dreamwork. Accordingly, it is necessary to distinguish between the manifest dream, i.e. the dream as experienced and perhaps written down, and the latent dream, i.e. the thoughts, wishes, and desires expressed in the dream with their disguises removed. The task of the analyst and interpreter on this view is to explain the manifest dream in terms of the latent dream.

How is this to be done? Freud uses two methods. The first

of these we will welcome as an old friend; it is simply the method of symbolic interpretation which we have already encountered in the case of Artemidorus. The other method, of much greater general interest and importance, is the method of association.

First let us consider the use Freud makes of the theory of symbolism. Very much like the old dream books, Freud provides whole lists of symbols standing for certain things and certain actions. However, where the old dream books had rather a catholic interest and spread their net widely, Freud concentrates almost exclusively on sex and sexual relations. The male sex organ is represented in the dream by a bewildering variety of symbols. Anything that is long and pointed – a stick, a cigar, a chimney, a steeple, the stem of a flower – is so interpreted because of the obvious physical resemblance. A pistol, a knife, forceps, a gun – these may stand for the penis because they eject and penetrate; similarly a plough may become a sex symbol because it penetrates the earth. Riding a horse, climbing stairs, and many, many other common-sense activities stand for intercourse. Hollow objects and containers are feminine symbols: houses, boxes, saucepans, vases – all these represent the vagina.

Members of the family are frequently said to be symbolically represented in the dream; thus the father and mother may in the dream appear as king and queen. There would be little point in giving long lists of objects and acts and their symbolic interpretation in Freudian terms (we shall encounter some of these in the course of our discussion of some dreams later on). We may also postpone a critical discussion of this Freudian theory and the elaboration of a more reasonable alternative theory until we have looked at the method of free association.

The technique of free association is essentially based on the nineteenth-century doctrines of the associationist philosophers. They believed that ideas became linked through similarity or through contiguity and that mental life could be understood entirely in terms of such associations. If ideas are linked in a causal manner, as is suggested by this theory, then we should be able to find links between manifest and latent phenomena by starting out with the former and, through a chain of associations, penetrate to the latter. In other words, what is suggested is this: starting out with certain unacceptable ideas which seek expression, we emerge finally with unintelligible ideas contained in the manifest dream. These, having been produced by the original latent ideas, are linked to them by a chain of associations, and we shall be able to re-discover the original ideas by going back over this chain of ideas. In order to do this, Freud starts out by taking a single idea from the manifest dream and asking the subject to fix that idea in his mind and say aloud anything that comes into his mind associated with that original idea. The hope is that in due course a chain of associations will lead to the latent causal idea. An example of the process of reassociation taken from M. F. Frink may illustrate the method. The original point of departure in this case is not a dream but a lapse of memory; however, from Freud's point of view both types of mental facts are determined on similar lines and are equally useful for illustrating the method.

One of Frink's friends asked him the name of a shop which sold a certain article. Frink remembered the shop but found that he had forgotten its name. Some days later, on passing the shop, which he knew very well, he saw that the name which he had not been able to remember was *Pond*. This is a type of event which, according to Freud, is motivated and has a meaning, and Frink decided to discover this meaning by means of free association. Starting out with the word *Pond*, he thought of a certain Doctor *Pond* who was a pitcher in a baseball team. From there his thoughts went on to the *Indian pond* where he used to go fishing as a child, and he saw himself throwing into the water a big *stone* which served as an anchor to his boat. Then he thought of a man called *Fisher*, who also played as *pitcher* in a baseball team. Continuing his associations, he thought of *Pond's* Extract; this product contains witch-hazel, and this reminded him that in his childhood he used to rub his arm with witch-hazel when he was *pitcher* in a baseball team. This reminded him of a rather fat boy, a member of the same team, who had once fallen head foremost into a muddy puddle and had come out in so begrimed a state that he looked just like a *pig*. This brought up the memory of another young man nicknamed *Piggy*, and Frink then recalled that he himself had been nicknamed *pig*.

His associations were interrupted for a few moments and he started again with the word *pond*. This produced the word *ponder*; then *think*; then the expression '*sicklied o'er with the pale cast of thought*'. This led him to *Hamlet*; to a certain village which he had thought of as a *hamlet*, and to a farmer in that village who had told him that one of his neighbours had in sheer malice killed two pigs and had thrown them into the farmer's well. At that point a memory of his seventh year arose suddenly which gave Frink the explanation of his failure to remember. He used to play with his brother on the edge of a pond, and a dog, of which he was very fond, used to swim in the pond. The boys used to throw stones to the dog, which the animal tried to catch. At one time the young Frink, wishing to frighten the dog, threw her a large stone, taking bad aim. The stone struck the dog squarely on the nose and she drowned. This was a terrible grief to the little boy and for months he was quite inconsolable. The memory of the accident sometimes made him cry out during the night. The psychoanalytic explanation, then, is that the word *pond* was not forgotten by chance, but that it had been thrust out of consciousness because of its painful connexion with the drowning of the dog.

Our main interest here centres on the associations produced by Frink. From the beginning these seem to be grouped around a focal point which is not seen at the outset, but which suddenly appears at the end. Take the first association – that relating to *Doctor Pond*. Frink himself is a doctor, the accident took place beside a *pond*, and the *pitcher* in baseball is a man who throws a ball. The next association is that of the *Indian pond*; this pond is situated in the same town as that in which the dog drowned, and Frink appears in it as throwing a big stone. The third association introduces a certain *Fisher* (fisherman) and again the idea of throwing. The associations leading off from the reference to *Hamlet* still contain the idea of throwing and of falling into the water, but this is not all. There is the appearance of the young man nicknamed *Piggy* and the killing of the two pigs. This may appear obscure until it is realized that the dog's name was *Gip*, which is the word *pig* in reverse.

This is a typical example of interpretation by means of free association, and the reader will probably agree that the method has a certain interest. The story tries to prove the existence of a causal relationship between the forgetting of the word *Pond* and Frink's childhood experience, but this, of course, it does not succeed in doing. The only thing it does prove, namely that terms similar in meaning tend to be associated in one's mind, hardly requires so intricate and elaborate a proof. Nevertheless, the idea of using the method of association in exploring the contents of the mind is a highly original and brilliant one, and much credit must go to the man who first introduced it into psychology. This man, contrary to popular belief, was not Freud, however, but Sir Francis Galton. Galton's name is probably best known through his initiation of the Eugenics movement, but his claims to fame extend in many different directions. He was one of the most versatile and brilliant of the nineteenth-century scientists, and his discoveries in many fields have considerably influenced our lives. He has many claims to be called the founder of modern psychology, a title usually bestowed on a plodding, methodical German called Wundt, whose contributions were of an administrative rather than of a creative nature.

Galton was one of the last universal geniuses, and he investigated and made major contributions to a great variety of subjects. One of his biographers gives the following list: 'Travel, the weather, stereoscopic maps, high-pitched whistles, blood transfusions, composite photography, finger prints, number forms and word association, correlation, twins, the sterility of heiresses, and various contrivances and inventions'. The importance of some of this work may be gathered from what the great scientist and statistician Pearson has to say about Galton's contribution to one of these fields, namely that of correlation. Talking about some empirical investigation of Galton's, Pearson has this to say:

The need for novel statistical methods which its problems demanded, led him to the correlational calculus, the *fons et origo* of that far reaching ramification, the modern mathematical theory of statistics. ... From that conception arose a new view of the universe both organic and inorganic which provides all science with a *novum organum* far wider reaching in its effects than that of Bacon, and it is as characteristic of the last quarter of the nineteenth century as the fluxional calculus was of that of the seventeenth.

Galton tried out on himself an elaborate system of word association tests and reached conclusions very similar to those later popularized by Freud and Jung. The results, he said,

gave me an interesting and unexpected view of the number of the operations of the mind and of the obscure depth in which they took place, of which I had been little conscious before. The general impression they have left upon me is that which many of us have experienced when the basement of our house happens to be under thorough sanitary repairs and we realize for the first time the complex system of drains and gas and water pipes, flues, bell wires, and so forth, upon which our comfort depends, but which are usually hidden out of sight, and with whose existence, as long as they acted well, we had never troubled ourselves.

Making use, then, of these methods of symbolic interpretations and of association, both discovered long before his time, Freud proceeded to analyse the nature of the dream. He discusses his discoveries in terms of so-called mechanisms which are active in the dream. The first of these mechanisms he calls that of *dramatization*. This simply denotes the fact, already familiar to most people, that the major part in dreams is played by visual images, and that conceptual thought appears to be resolved into some form of plastic representation. Freud likens this to the pictorial manner in which cartoons portray conceptual problems. The cartoonist is faced with the same difficulty as the dreamer. He cannot express concepts in words, but has to give them some form of dramatic and pictorial representation. He cannot say in so many words that Kaiser Wilhelm the Second of Germany was unwise in dismissing the experienced Chancellor Bismarck and in taking the conduct of affairs into his own hands, but he can dramatize this in pictorial terms along the lines of the famous *Punch* cartoon entitled 'Dropping the Pilot', in which the maniacal Emperor is seen on the bridge of the ship, while the sad-faced pilot (Bismarck) is seen descending the gangway.

In addition to visual images, verbal ones also may appear, and here the material meaning of words may often be associated with a rather uncommon meaning. Long before Freud, the Marquis Hervey de Saint-Denis, one of the most acute students of the dream, had observed that the use of verbal images by the dream-thought may sometimes have the appearance of the pun. As an example he quotes an occasion where the word 'Rosalie' aroused in the dreamer the image of a bedspread, upon which roses were embroidered. As a pun, this connexion between the name 'Rosalie' and the words *Rose-à-lit* (rose in bed) is not a good one, but it is quite typical of the way the dramatization process makes use of verbal images.

Closely related to the mechanism of dramatization is that of symbolism, which we have already encountered. Here is an example which will illustrate the general mechanism of dramatization and also that of symbolism in dreams. In this dream a young woman dreamed that a man was trying to mount a very frisky small brown horse. He made three unsuccessful attempts; at the fourth he managed to take his seat in the saddle and rode off. Horse-riding, as was mentioned earlier, often represents coitus in Freud's general theory of symbolism. What happens when we look at the subject's associations? The horse reminded the dreamer that in her childhood she had been given the French word '*cheval*' as a nickname; in addition, this woman was a small and very lively brunette, like the horse in the dream. The man who was trying to mount the horse was one of the dreamer's most intimate friends. In flirting with him she had gone to such lengths that three times he had wished to take advantage of her but each time her moral sentiments had got the upper hand at the last moment. Inhibitions are not so strong in the dream, and the fourth attempt therefore ended in a wish fulfilment.

Another mechanism acting in the dreamwork is said to be that of condensation. The manifest content is only an *abbreviation* of the latent content. As Freud puts it: 'The dream is meagre, paltry, and laconic in comparison with the range and copiousness of the dream thoughts.' The images of the manifest content are said by Freud to be over-determined: i.e. each manifest element depends on several latent causes and consequently expresses several hidden thoughts. As an example, here is a dream reported by a young woman. In this dream she was walking on Fifth Avenue with a friend, and stopped in front of a milliner's shop window to look at hats; at last she went in and bought one. Frink, who analysed this dream, obtained the following series of associations: The woman had actually been walking on Fifth Avenue with her friend, but had not bought any hats. Her husband had been in bed that day, and although his illness was not serious, she had been very uneasy and could not get rid of the notion that he might die. During the walk the young woman had talked of a man whom she had known before her marriage and with whom she had been in love. Asked why she had not married him, she explained that his financial and social position had been too far above her own. When asked to associate on the buying of the hat, she mentioned that she had much admired the hats in the milliner's shop window and would very much have liked to buy one, but could not do so because of her husband's poverty.

Clearly, says Frink, the dream was satisfying her wish by allowing her to buy a hat. However, that is not all; she suddenly remembered that in her dream the hat which she bought had been a black hat: a *mourning* hat. Frink's interpretation of this fact is as follows. The day before the dream, the woman was afraid her husband would die; in dreaming that she was buying a mourning hat she was fulfilling a death fantasy. In real life she was prevented from buying a hat by her husband's poverty; in the dream she was able to buy one. The implication is that she now has a rich husband, and we see from her associations that indeed there is a very rich man in the offing. Frink therefore concludes that the young woman is tired of her husband, that her fear of seeing her husband die is a defence reaction against her real wish for his death, and that she would like to marry the man with whom she was in love and who has enough money to satisfy all her wishes. When Frink acquainted his patient with his interpretation of her dream, she admitted that it was justified and told him several facts which confirmed it, the most important of these being that after her marriage she had learnt that the man with whom she had been in love had also been in love with her; this had revived her feelings, and she had regretted her hasty marriage. If we accept this interpretation, we see how the buying of the hat is over-determined by the threefold wish: to see the death of her husband, to marry the man she loved, and to have money.

The last dream mechanism which we will discuss is that of displacement. It is a process whereby the emotional content is detached from its proper object and attached instead to an unimportant or subsidiary one; the essential feature of the latent content of the dream accordingly may sometimes be hardly represented at all in the manifest content, at least to outward appearances; it has been displaced under some apparently innocuous object. Here is an example of such a displacement in which a girl suffering from an obsessional neurosis dreamed that she was in the presence of someone whose identity was very vague but to whom she was under some kind of obligation. As a token of her gratitude, she made him a present of her comb. The relevant details of the girl's history are as follows. She was a Jewess whose hand had been sought in marriage a year earlier by a Protestant, whose feelings she returned fully. However, the difference of religion had prevented the engagement taking place, as the girl believed that the arrival of children in such a mixed marriage would cause discord and unhappiness because of the problem of the religion in which they should be brought up; accordingly she had refused her suitor. The night before the dream, the girl had had a violent quarrel with her mother and had thought it better for all concerned if she were to leave home. She had gone to sleep thinking of ways and means whereby she could support herself without being dependent on her family. When asked to associate on the word 'comb', she answered that sometimes when someone was about to use a brush or comb which did not belong to him, she had heard it said, 'Don't do that; you will mix the breed'. This association suggests the interpretation of the dream; the person whose identity remains vague is the ex-suitor; by offering him her comb, the girl shows her wish to 'mix the breed', i.e. to marry him and to bear his children. The dream thus expresses an extremely important intention. However, the mechanism of displacement has intervened so that the idea of marrying the young Protestant is not recognizable in the manifest content and is replaced by an apparently irrelevant substitute, the gift of the comb.

We have now studied a few dreams as examples of the Freudian method, and we must try to come to some form of judgement on the adequacy of the Freudian hypothesis. It should perhaps be explained that the dreams chosen as illustrations are very much clearer, more definite, and more in line with Freudian theory than the great majority of dreams found in the text-books of Freud himself and his followers. They have all been quoted more than once by psycho-analysts in support of their theories. In order to examine Freud's hypothesis fairly, we have taken examples which should support it as strongly as any; if they do not bear out his theory, the verdict must indeed be a negative one.

Now, it will be remembered that the central piece of Freud's whole theory, the one bit that is original and not derivative, is the notion that symbols and other dream mechanisms are used to hide something so obnoxious, so contrary to the morality of the patient, that he cannot bear to consider it undisguised, even in his dream. This notion seems so contrary to the most obvious facts that it is difficult to see how it can ever have been seriously entertained. Let us list some of these objections. In the first place, the notion which is expressed symbolically in one dream may be quite blatantly and directly expressed in another. We have a highly symbolic and involved dream which is interpreted as meaning that we want to kill a relative or have intercourse with someone, only to find that in another dream these ideas are expressed perfectly clearly in the sense that we do actually kill our relative or have intercourse with this girl. What is the point of putting on the masquerade on one occasion, only to discard it on another? As Jocasta said to Oedipus 'Many young men dream of sleeping with their mothers'; if they do, why should they at times go to the trouble of dreaming that they are shooting off a revolver at a cow?

A second objection is that the symbols which are supposed to hide the dream-thought very frequently do nothing of the kind. Many people who have no knowledge of psychoanalysis are able to interpret the sexual symbols which occur in dreams without any difficulty at all. After all, let us face the fact that there are many slang expressions in use referring to sexual activities and sexual anatomy, and that these slang terms are only too often identical with Freudian symbols. There seems to be little disguise in a person's dreaming about a cock, symbolizing the penis, when the very same person would not even know the term penis and always refers to his sex organ as his 'cock'. Freud seems to have been singularly remote from the realities of everyday life.

A last point of criticism has been raised by Calvin S. Hall, whose theory we shall be considering in a minute. He asks why there are so many symbols for the same referent. In his search of the literature he found 102 different dream-symbols for the penis, ninety-five for the vagina, and fifty-five for sexual intercourse. Why, he asks, is it necessary to hide these reprehensible referents behind such a vast array of masks?

Let us see to what extent Freud's theory is in fact supported by the three dreams we have quoted. First of all let us take the young lady nicknamed 'Cheval', who at the last moment frustrated three determined efforts at seduction by her boy friend, only to have the success of the enterprise presented to her in a dream in symbolic form. According to the Freudian theory, we would have to believe that the notion of actually having intercourse with her boy friend was so shocking to this young lady, and so much outraged her moral instincts and training, that she could not even contemplate the idea in her sleep, thus having to disguise it in symbols. This, surely, is a very unconvincing argument; to imagine that a young girl, who would several times running indulge in such heated love-making that she was on the point of losing her virginity, could not bear to contemplate the possibility of having intercourse, and had to repress it into her unconscious, could surely not be seriously maintained, even by a psychoanalyst following obediently in the steps of the master!

Much the same must be said with respect to the young lady who dreamt that she bought a mourning hat. Here again it is extremely unlikely that the ideas finding expression in symbolic form in the dream – I would like to have money to buy clothes with; I would like to have married the man I was in love with; I wish I could get rid of my husband – were so abhorrent to the dreamer that she refused to entertain them consciously or permit them open expression even in her sleep. In fact, the account given by the analyst makes it clear that these ideas were quite consciously in her mind; why, then, did they require a symbolic disguise?

The 'comb' dream of the girl who did not want to 'mix the breed' is an equally obvious contradiction to the Freud hypothesis. The notion which finds disguised expression in the dream – I would like to marry my fiancé and get away from my family – was quite acceptable to the dreamer, and indeed was a constant source of conscious preoccupation in her mind. There is no possibility here of arguing that the latent dream-thoughts emerging from the *id* were so beastly, sordid, and unacceptable that they had to put on a masquerade before being allowed to emerge even in a dream.

We thus find that the three dreams which have been selected by psychoanalysts from many thousands as providing the most clear-cut support for psychoanalytic notions are, in fact, a clear disproof of the major point of the Freudian theory. We may, therefore, with some confidence, reject Freud's hypothesis regarding the origin of the mummery which takes place in dreams. It is unlikely enough on *a priori* grounds, it is self-contradictory and it is not borne out by psychoanalysis of specially selected dreams even.

Is it possible to substitute a more plausible theory for the one that we have just rejected? An interesting move in this direction has recently been made by C. S. Hall, a well-known American psychologist. His argument is as follows. The same objective fact – say sexual intercourse – may have widely different meanings to different people. One conception might be that of a generative or reproductive activity; another one might be that of an aggressive physical attack. It is these different conceptions of one and the same objective fact which are expressed in the special choice of symbolism of the dream. Dreaming of the ploughing of a field or the planting of seeds is a symbolic representation of the sex act as being generative or reproductive. Dreaming of shooting a person with a gun, stabbing someone with a dagger, or running down with an automobile, symbolizes the view of the sex act as an aggressive attack. According to this theory, symbols in dreams are not used to hide the meaning of the dream, but quite on the contrary, are used to reveal not only the act of the person with whom the dreamer is concerned, but also his conceptions of these actions or persons.

If a person dreams of his mother, and if his mother in the dream is symbolized by a cow or a queen, Freud would interpret this to mean that the dreamer is disguising his mother in this fashion because he cannot bear to reveal, even to himself, the wishes and ideas expressed in the dream and connected with the mother figure. In terms of Hall's theory, the interpretation would be that the dreamer not only wishes to represent his mother, but also wants to indicate that he regards her as a nurturent kind of person (cow), or a regal and remote kind of person (queen). The use of symbols, then, is an expressive device, not a means of disguise, and it is noteworthy that in waking life, symbols are used for precisely the same reason: a lion stands for courage, a snake for evil, and an owl for wisdom. Symbols such as these convey in terse and concise language abstruse and complex conceptions.

Certain symbols, on this theory, are chosen more frequently than others because they represent in a single object a variety of conceptions. The moon, for instance, is such a condensed and over-determined symbol of woman; the monthly phases of the moon resemble the menstrual cycle; the filling out of the moon from new to full symbolizes the rounding out of the woman during pregnancy. The moon is inferior to the sun; the moon is changeable like a fickle woman, while the sun is constant. The moon controls the ebb and flow of the tides, again linking it to the family rhythm. The moon, shedding her weak light, embodies the idea of feminine frailty. Hall concludes: 'Rhythm, change, fruitfulness, weakness, submissiveness, all of the conventional conceptions of woman, are compressed into a single visible object.'

To indicate the way in which Hall uses this theory to aid in the interpretation of dreams, we may quote an example from his book:

I was at a gas station where I worked, and my friend Bob was there also working. It seemed to me that he was new and inexperienced at the job because I was watching him check the oil on a car. He pulled out the oil dip-stick and looked at it. At this point I went up to him, rather angrily, and said 'Bob, in order to check the oil you have to wipe off the oil on the dip-stick first and then put the dip-stick back in, pull it out, and then get a reading'. He thanked me for my help and the dream ended.

When the dreamer was asked to say what came into his mind in connexion with the dream, the dreamer said it reminded him of sexual intercourse and that Bob was not doing it properly. Apparently Bob went around with prostitutes, which the dreamer felt was wrong, and he wished that Bob would stop doing this. The action of inserting the dip-stick into the oil hole was a direct representation of intercourse, and revealed a pretty mechanical conception of sexual gratification. It will be obvious again how inappropriate the Freudian theory would be to this dream.

Hall's conception of dream symbolism seems to apply quite well to many of the dreams he quotes. It does not seem to apply particularly well to many other dreams; the reader may judge for himself whether it applies to the three dreams previously quoted. The truth appears to be that any writer on dream interpretation seems to find it possible to quote a few dreams in support of his views, but that these theories cannot usually be applied to dreams quoted by people having a different theoretical outlook. This suggests that all theories of dream interpretation may have a certain limited amount of truth in them, but that they do not possess universal significance, and apply only to a relatively small part of the field. This conclusion is strengthened when it is further realized that quite probably the person whose dreams are being analysed begins to learn the hypothetical symbolic language of the analyst and obediently makes use of it in his dreams. This may account for the fact that Freudian analysts always report that their patients dream in Freudian symbols, whereas analysts who follow the teaching of Jung report that their patients always dream in Jungian symbols, which are entirely different from the Freudian!

There is one further difficulty in accepting the symbolic interpretations presented by so many dream interpreters. How, it may be asked, do we know that a motor-car stands for the sexual drive; might it not simply stand for a motor-car? In other words, how can the poor dreamer ever dream about anything whatsoever, such as a house, a screw, a syringe, a railway engine, a gun, the moon, a horse, walking, riding, climbing stairs, or indeed anything under the sun, if these things are immediately taken to symbolize something else? What would happen if you took a very commonplace, everyday event such as a train journey and regarded it as an account of a dream? The reader will see in the following paragraph how such a very simple and straightforward description is absolutely riddled with Freudian symbols of one kind or another. Relevant words and phrases have been italicized to make identification easier.

To begin with, we *pack our trunks, carry them downstairs*, and call a taxi. We *put our trunks inside*, then *enter ourselves*. The *taxi surges forward*, but the traffic soon brings us to a halt and the driver *rhythmically moves his hand up and down* to indicate that he is stopping. Finally we *drive into the station*. There is still time left and we decide to write a postcard. We *sharpen a pencil*, but the *point drops off* and we test our fountain pen by *splashing some drops of ink on to the blotting-paper*. We push the postcard *through the slot of the pillar-box* and then *pass the barrier* and *enter the train*. The *powerful engine* blows off steam and finally *starts*. Very soon, however, the train *enters a dark tunnel*. The *rhythmic* sounds of the wheels going over the intersections send us to sleep, but we rouse ourselves and *go to the dining-car*, where the waiter *pours coffee into a cup from a long-nosed coffee-pot*. The train is going very fast now and *we bob up and down in our seats*. The *semaphore arms on the signal masts rise* as we approach *and fall* again as we pass. We look out of the window and see *cows* in the pasture, *horses chasing each other*, and farmers *ploughing the ground* and *sowing seeds*. The *sun* is setting now and the *moon* is rising. Finally the train *pulls into the station* and we have arrived.

It will be clear to the reader that there is practically nothing that we can do or say on our journey which is not a flagrant sex symbol. If, therefore, we wanted to dream of a railway journey, the thing would just be impossible. All we can ever dream about, if we follow the Freudian theory, is sex, sex, and sex again. The reader may try the experiment of describing a football match or a walk in the country or a day at the office, without the use of phrases which would, according to Freud, have a sexual connotation. He would soon find that there is practically no object in common use, and no activity frequently indulged in, which cannot be made to symbolize some aspect of the sexual process.

The critical reader may feel at this point that while the discussion may have been quite interesting at times, it has not produced a single fact which could be regarded as having scientific validity. Everything is surmise, conjecture, and interpretation; judgements are made in terms of what seems reasonable and fitting. This is not the method of science. You do not argue about Ohm's Law or the Law of Gravitation or the circulation of the blood. You state a definite hypothesis, make certain deductions from this hypothesis, and then proceed to carry out experiments to prove or disprove your theory. That is the scientific method, and that is precisely what is missing in all the work we have been summarizing so far.

The blame for this state of affairs must be squarely laid at the door of the analysts, whose efforts have always been directed towards persuasion and propaganda, rather than towards impartial investigation and proof. The reader may recall our discussion of the necessity of having control groups in psychological investigations. No control group has ever been used in experimental studies of dream interpretation by psychoanalysts, yet the necessity for such a control would be obvious on reflection. According to Freud's theory, the manifest dream leads back to the latent dreams in terms of symbolization and in terms of free association. This is used as an argument in favour of the view that the alleged latent dream has caused the manifest dream, but the control experiment is missing. What would happen if we took a dream reported by person A and got person B to associate to the various elements of that dream? Having performed this experiment a number of times, I have come to the conclusion that the associations very soon lead us back to precisely the same complexes which we would have reached if we had started out with one of person B's own dreams. In other words, the starting point is quite irrelevant; as all roads lead to Rome, so a person's thoughts and associations tend to lead towards his personal troubles, desires, and wishes of the present moment. I am not suggesting that this is an established fact; I am merely suggesting that here is an alternative theory which will equally easily account for the observed facts, but which has never been tested by psychoanalysts. Many other alternative theories could be formulated and would have to be tested before anything decisive could be said about the value of the Freudian hypothesis. In the absence of such work, our verdict must be that, interesting as some of these speculations are, such evidence as there is leads one to agree with the many judges who have said that what is new in the Freudian theory is not true, and what is true in it is not new. It is possible that future experiments may lend greater credence to psychoanalytic postulates in this field, but for the moment we can only judge on the evidence so far presented.

Actually it would not be quite correct to say that no experimental work on dreams had been done. There are a number of promising leads, but, as might have been expected, these have come from the ranks of academic psychologists and not from psychoanalysts themselves. Of particular interest is the work of Luria, a Russian psychologist who attacked the problem of dream interpretation as part of a wider problem, namely the experimental investigation of complexes. His technique consisted in implanting complexes under hypnosis and observing the various reactions, including dreams, of the subjects after they had recovered from the hypnotic trance. The implanted complexes were of course unconscious in the sense that the subject knew nothing about them on being interrogated, and had no notion of anything that had transpired during the hypnotic trance. An example may make clearer just what the procedure is. It is taken from a study of my own, carried out to check some of the findings reported by Luria. The subject, a thirty-two-year-old woman, is hypnotized and the following situation is powerfully impressed upon her as having actually happened. She is walking across Hampstead Heath late at night when suddenly she hears footsteps behind her; she turns and sees a man running after her; she tries to escape but is caught, flung to the ground, and raped. On waking from the hypnosis, she is rather perturbed, trembles a little, but cannot explain the cause of her uneasiness; she has completely forgotten the event suggested to her under hypnosis. She is then asked to lie down and rest; after a few minutes she falls into a natural sleep, but is immediately woken up and asked to recall anything she might have been dreaming of. She recounts that in her dream she was in some desolate spot which she cannot locate and that suddenly a big Negro, brandishing a knife, was attacking her; he managed to prick her thigh with it. The symbolic re-interpretation of the hypnotic trance in the dream is clear enough and tends to substantiate the fact that dreams express in dramatized and symbolic form certain thoughts which in the waking state would probably be conceptualized in a more direct form. This method of investigation has considerable promise, but unfortunately very little has been done with it. One well-designed experiment would be worth more than all the thousands of anecdotal contributions published in the psychoanalytic journals, but unfortunately the trend has been towards more and more uncontrolled, unconvincing, and unrepeatable single-case studies, rather than towards a properly controlled scientific and experimental kind of investigation.

Realizing, then, that nothing certain is known, can we at least propound a general theory which summarizes what we have said and is not contradicted by any of the known facts? Such a theory might run as follows: The mind tends to be constantly active. In the waking state most of the material for this activity is provided by perceptions of events in the outer world; only occasionally, as in problem-solving and day-dreaming, are there long stretches of internal activity withdrawn from external stimulation. During sleep such external stimulation is more or less completely absent, and consequently mental activity ceases to be governed by external stimulation and becomes purely internal.

In general this mental activity is very much concerned with the same problems that occupy waking thought. Our wishes, hopes, fears, our problems and their solutions, our relationships with other people – these are the things we think about in our waking life, and these are the things we dream about when we are asleep. The main difference is that mental activity in sleep appears to be at a lower level of complexity and to find expression in a more archaic mode of presentation. The generalizing and conceptualizing parts of the mind seem to be dormant, and their function is taken over by a more primitive method of pictorial representation. It is this *primitivization* of the thought processes which leads to the emergence of symbolism, which thus serves very much the function Hall has given it in his theory.

This symbolizing activity is, of course, determined to a large extent by previous learning. To an Eskimo it would be impossible to dream of ploughing as a symbol of intercourse because Eskimos are not acquainted with the plough. To the patient who is being analysed by a follower of Freud, it would not occur to dream in Jungian symbols because he has not become acquainted with them. In general, symbols are relative to the education and experience of the dreamer, although certain symbols, such as the moon, are very widely used because they are familiar to almost all human beings.

Would it be true, then, to say that dreams are useful in the treatment of mental disorders? If we are correct in believing that dreams are simply a 'continuation of thinking by other means' (to paraphrase a famous saying), then they should be able to tell us something about the problems, wishes, and fears of the dreamer. However, it is probable that we would get as much information, and more easily, by asking him directly. The possibility remains that in a small number of cases such revelation is impossible because the patient is truly unconscious of his complexes and thoughts. If it could be demonstrated that under such conditions dreams do, in fact, reveal this unconscious material, then we would have to answer our question in the affirmative. Until evidence of a more rigorous kind than is available now is produced in favour of this hypothesis, we can only say that no confident answer can be given. If and when the proper experiments are performed, due care being given to the use of control groups and other essential safeguards, then we shall be able to end this chapter on a more positive note. At the moment the only fit verdict seems to be the Scottish one of 'not proven'.

PART TWO

PERSONALITY AND SOCIAL LIFE

5

CAN PERSONALITY BE MEASURED?

THIS question, so often asked of the psychologist, is almost completely meaningless. The answer depends on what we mean by personality, what we mean by measurement, and, indeed, one might even maintain that it depends on the meaning of the term 'can'. Do we understand this to imply that it is possible *at the moment* to carry out such measurement, or do we mean that while it is impossible at the moment to do this, in principle it can and will be done? Before going into any details, therefore, we must first of all have a brief look at what is meant by 'personality' and what meaning the term 'measurement' has in this connexion.

It is not an easy task to define personality. Allport, who has written the classic introduction to this field, discusses some fifty definitions without doing more than scratching the surface. It would certainly not help us very much in our quest to know that, to the philosopher Kant, 'personality exhibits palpably before our bodily eyes the sublimity of our nature'; that Stern defined personality as 'a multiform dynamic unity'; or Windelband as 'individuality which has become objective to itself'. We may admire without understanding, but on the whole we will probably agree with a famous sociologist; according to him, 'This word *persona* has rolled along with wonderful bounds, striking right and left, suggesting new thoughts, stirring up clouds of controversy, and occupying to the present day a prominent place in all discussions on theology and philosophy, though few only of those who use it know how it came to be there.'

Fortunately, although we may have difficulty in defining it, we can at least tell how the word 'personality' came to be there. *Persona* originally referred to the theatrical mask used first in Greek drama and later on adopted about the year 100 B.C. by Roman actors. It is said that this importation was due to the fact that a popular Roman actor wanted to hide an unfortunate squint behind these masks. In the writings of Cicero the word was then used to denote how a person appears to others, but not as he really is, and also a conglomeration of personal qualities. Very roughly, this combination of meanings, referring both to the inner psychological qualities of a person, and also to the impression he gives to other people, has persisted and is contained in our modern psychological usage of the term 'personality'.

As such, however, it is far too all-embracing to be particularly useful. It seems to be almost co-extensive with behaviour, and therefore with psychology as a whole, which is usually defined as a study of behaviour. Can we nail it down a little more precisely? We can do so, but only by ceasing to regard it as a strict scientific term which can have a precise meaning, such as atom, reflex, planet, acid, or molecule, and treating it instead as a term descriptive of a field of study. In this way we shall be able to get a much better notion of what the exact place of personality is in modern psychology.

We may start out by, first of all, looking at the place of psychology as a whole among the sciences. We will find that it derives its unique importance from the fact that it acts as a kind of bridge between two very large and important groups of disciplines. On the one hand, it is closely related to the biological sciences, like physiology, neurology, anatomy, biochemistry, zoology, genetics, and so forth; many of its theories are built on the findings of these sciences, and any advance in them is immediately reflected in psychological research and theorizing.

On the other hand, psychology is intimately related to the social studies, like sociology, economics, history, anthropology, social philosophy, psychiatry, and so on. These are sometimes called the social sciences, but it seems to me that at their present stage of development the term science is a little misleading as applied to fields characterized more by speculation and blind empiricism than by experimentally derived laws of general applicability. However that may be, clearly these various fields of study depend very much on the existence of a well-developed body of knowledge relating to the behaviour of individuals. A properly developed science of psychology is indispensable to their development, and the

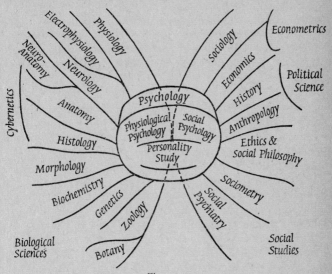

Figure 3

need for such a science is clearly evidenced by the fact that in its absence many of them have been forced to develop their own *ad hoc* and frequently absurd systems of what one can only call *quasi* psychology. The concepts of 'economic man' and 'rational man' are two of the attempts made by economists and sociologists to lay some kind of psychological foundation for their studies.

The picture, in fact, is very much like that shown in Figure 3, which clearly demonstrates the bridge-like position of psychology. However, this notion of psychology as a uni-

G

fied subject standing between the biological sciences and the social studies is not quite accurate. Psychology itself, as will be seen in the diagram, is divided into two; on the one hand, physiological psychology, which has its main affinities with the biological sciences, and on the other hand, social psychology, which has its main affinities with the social studies. The gap between these two groups of studies is a very deep one. Physiological psychologists publish their papers in one set of journals; social psychologists publish theirs in another. There is little reference from one group of journals to the other, and few readers are equally familiar with both sets. Consequently, the gulf between the biological sciences and the social studies runs right through the centre of psychology.

Within the discipline of psychology, then, clearly a concept is needed to bring these two sides together. This central role falls to the concept of personality, which thus acquires its unique importance in psychology by bringing together two sets of workers otherwise isolated from each other. It does this, not so much by emphasizing a special field of study, but rather by imparting a certain point of view to groups of studies which otherwise might have remained quite unrelated. An example may illustrate the difference which a change in point of view of this kind may make.

Physiologists for many years have been interested in defective dark vision. They have shown that there are physiological causes for it, some connected with the structure of the retina; others with dietary deficiencies. During the First World War several governments showed a considerable interest in the diagnosis and the distribution of night blindness because, obviously, soldiers suffering from this disability could not be used for certain purposes and might, if not diagnosed in time, become a danger both to themselves and to their comrades. Consequently, physiologists and physiological psychologists were asked to make estimates of the number of cases to be expected to fall into this category of the night blind. In fact, these estimates turned out to be absurd under-estimates of the true number of people who actually had visual defects in the dark, and the question arose as to the cause of this very considerable discrepancy.

The answer became clear when it was found that many of the people who were suffering from dark blindness also seemed to be somewhat emotionally unstable individuals. Detailed investigations disclosed that in many people who were, in fact, night blind, there appeared to be no physiological causes of any kind which might be responsible for their condition. In these cases particularly, the emotional instability and presence of neurotic symptoms were very marked, and several experimental studies have since disclosed that there is quite a close relationship between the difficulty of seeing in the dark and the possession of certain neurotic personality traits. Thus, what caused the original estimates to be so much in error was the fact that physiologists and their psychological colleagues treated the particular part of the central nervous system which subserves dark vision in isolation. They dealt with the various parts of the eye, the retina, the optic nerve, and so forth, in complete disregard of the individual person of whom these various structures formed a part. This, of course, is in the best tradition of physiology, which tries to isolate certain structures and study these under conditions, as far as possible, removed from any disturbances by other parts of the central nervous system.

This type of segmental analysis is certainly valuable and important, and nothing that is said here should be construed as being in any way critical of work of this type. However, it must be realized that in the intact animal, or in the living human being, such interaction between different structures is not the exception, but the rule. Consequently, the study of segmental processes in complete isolation does not tell us very much about the behaviour of the complete organism. The physiological study has to be supplemented, and it is here that the concept of personality comes in. At the moment that physiological or any other processes are studied from the point of view of their interaction with other parts of the individual they become part of the study of personality. Thus, personality study is not differentiated from physiological psychology by the phenomena it studies, but rather by the conditions under which these phenomena are studied, and by the setting in which experiments are carried out and information sought. Both the physiological psychologist and the psychologist interested in personality study may do work on dark vision. Where, however, the physiological psychologist studies dark vision as far as possible under conditions which exclude the influence of personality factors, or what we may call 'central processes', to the personality oriented psychologist the phenomena of dark vision are of interest precisely to the extent to which they are influenced by these 'central processes'.

The reason for this will be obvious. If we are interested in such 'central processes' as liability to fear, or anxiety, we soon come up against the difficulty that there is no direct way of measuring them in the present state of our knowledge. We are reduced to finding certain measurable phenomena which show a relationship with the central processes in which our real interest lies. To discover, therefore, that night blindness, when found in people not suffering from physiological defects, is closely related to liability to fear and anxiety is of considerable importance because it enables us to use a measurement of defective dark vision as a measure, albeit an indirect and perhaps a not very satisfactory one, of the central processes which really engage our interest.

Much the same might be said of conditioning. Most people nowadays are familiar with Pavlov's famous experiment, in which he showed that by pairing the sound of a bell and the giving of food to a dog, the latter could be 'conditioned' to react by salivation to the bell alone, i.e. when no food was given. This mechanism of conditioning, which has frequently been studied by physiological psychologists, is of interest to workers in the field of personality because it can be shown that individual differences in the speed with which such conditioned reflexes are formed have very important correlates in the behavioural field, and can thus be used as explanatory concepts to account for differences in 'personality'. A later chapter will develop this line of argument in detail.

So much for the relationship between personality and physiological psychology. What about its relationship with social psychology? Here the connexion is perhaps more obvious. Social psychology, strictly speaking, deals with the behaviour of people in groups. It attempts to formulate laws which will enable us to predict what people will do under certain conditions when two or more are co-operating or acting in competition, or interacting with each other in some other way. Such laws of interaction must inevitably introduce in some way certain variables related to the individual persons entering into the relationship. Thus, social psychology is depending very much for fundamental information on the student of personality.

As an example, we might perhaps mention here the formation of social attitudes and voting behaviour in an election. These clearly are social phenomena, and certain general laws can be discovered regarding them. Yet it would be impossible to give anything like a full account of the events the social psychologist is interested in without paying considerable attention to personality factors in the people concerned. Again an attempt will be made in a later chapter to spell these very brief comments out in greater detail, and to show how, through the intermediary concepts of personality study, the laws of conditioning can be used to account for many of the phenomena of attitude formation, voting behaviour, and so forth.

This discussion of the place of personality in psychology generally may have done something to indicate roughly the field of study with which we shall be concerned. No attempt will be made now to give a clear-cut definition because it is doubtful if any such definition will be universally acceptable, or would, indeed, add very much to the reader's understanding of the topic we shall be dealing with. The contents of this chapter should give a rough idea, at least, of the kinds of topic psychologists who are interested in personality do, in fact, study, and the kind of methods they use in their study.

If personality is a field of study characterized by a particular point of view, then obviously we cannot 'measure' personality, just as little as we can measure the universe. All we can do is to measure certain aspects of personality or of the universe. Our question, therefore, becomes modified immediately. Unfortunately, the problem of measurement is a very complex and somewhat technical one, and it would be out of place to discuss it here in any detail. A few remarks must suffice to indicate the general line of the argument. Measurement has been defined as the assignment of numerical values to objects or events according to rules. This is a very broad definition, but it is difficult to see how it could easily be narrowed down without excluding processes universally regarded as constituting measurement, and without introducing artificial breaks where, in actual fact, none seem to exist. If this definition be accepted, and it has been widely accepted among scientists in general, then we can see at once that many of those who argue that measurement of personality variables is impossible do, in fact, themselves use measurement in their daily work.

Thus, the psychoanalyst who apparently argues against the possibility of measurement being applicable to the complexities of the human being does not hesitate to say that Mr Buxtehude has an unresolved Oedipus complex, while Miss Schwangerschaft has not, but by thus assigning a numerical value of one to the gentleman, and a numerical value of zero to the lady, he has, in fact, carried out an elementary form of measurement. At least, he has *attempted* to carry out an elementary form of measurement; we would still have to inquire into the reliability and validity of this measurement, as well as into its meaningfulness. Quite likely we would find that this measurement, so called, would have very little relation to actual fact. But that, of course, is a different problem; whether the attempt was successful or not, it has in fact been made, and consequently our psychoanalyst cannot argue that measurement is impossible in this field unless he wants to condemn his own practice at the same time.

Much the same is true of a great deal that is done by psychiatrists, sociologists, and others who are temperamentally opposed to measurement. What, in fact, they do is not to substitute something else for measurement, but to use elementary, inappropriate, and illogical forms of measurement where complex, appropriate, and relevant methods are available. Like Monsieur Jourdain, in Molière's famous play, who discovered with considerable surprise that he had been talking prose all his life, many people in these fields may be surprised to find that they have been carrying out measurement most of their lives.

It cannot, therefore, be reasonably maintained that measurement is impossible or inappropriate to the variables which the student of personality is interested in. What I think most people who make statements of this kind are really trying to say is that complex forms of statistical manipulation are not appropriate to the measurements which are, in fact, made, and that only the roughest and simplest kind of treatment is acceptable. This, however, is not a really tenable argument; in fact, quite the opposite appears to be true. Where measurement is very accurate, complex mathematics are seldom needed because the relationships and functions involved are quite clear and obvious. When there is a considerable amount of error in the measurement, however, then it becomes very necessary indeed to use complex statistical methods to get estimates of the amount of error involved, and to tease out the complex relationships existing between data. This sorting-out process is a difficult one requiring considerable technical competence, and certainly no one not possessing this competence is likely to make a worth-while contribution to this issue.

Having now agreed, in broad outline, on what we mean by 'measurement' and what we mean by 'personality', let us have a look at the methods used by psychologists and psychiatrists in their endeavours to pin down the very elusive qualities associated with individual human beings.

First and foremost, we find there a method which has been used since the beginning of time, although only in recent years has it become formalized and subjected to experimental study. This is the method of rating, i.e. the attribution of traits, abilities, attitudes, and so forth to other people on the basis of our observation of their behaviour. All of us at some time or other have decided that Mr Meetglad is sociable, Mrs Puddlebasin talkative, Mr Greaseproof humorous, and Miss Groansharp critical. When we make a statement of this sort, what we are doing in fact is to attribute a trait of a certain kind to these persons. We do this without realizing that we are carrying out a very primitive type of analysis, followed by a very primitive kind of measurement. The analysis leads us to posit the existence of a given trait; the measurement makes it possible for us to assign each person to one of two categories, i.e. those having or not having that particular trait. We may, in fact, go further than that and have not two but several categories. Thus, we may say that some people have a very good sense of humour; others have a good sense of humour; some are average; some have a poor sense of humour; and some a very poor sense of humour indeed. Thus, we would assign people to one of five categories and thereby get a rather more refined type of measurement. But in essence this refinement is irrelevant and we may, for the purpose of this discussion, disregard it.

What about the validity of measurements of this kind? Unfortunately, the evidence is fairly strongly opposed to our paying very much attention to ratings made along these lines, particularly when they are made by persons who have not been trained specifically to be aware of the many difficulties and complexities involved.

In the first place, when we rate a person as having a good sense of humour, what precisely do we mean by this? We might mean:

(1) A person who laughs readily, i.e. one who is a merry sort of person, happy, good-natured, and so forth.

On the other hand we might mean:

    (2) A person who has a ready wit and tells amusing stories and makes other people laugh.

Or again, we might mean:

    (3) A person who laughs about the same sort of things that we laugh about and who therefore agrees with us in his tastes.

Again, we might mean:

    (4) A person who is capable of laughing at himself, i.e. a person who is not pompous, conceited, or blown up with his own importance.

These are only some of the ways in which the concept 'having a good sense of humour' was defined by competent and highly intelligent people who were asked to say what they meant by certain terms. It is clear that simply to know that person A thinks that person B has a good or a poor sense of humour does not tell us very much unless we know precisely what person A means by having a 'good sense of humour'. He may be able to tell us, of course, but even when he does so, it will often be found that he is mixing up two or three, or even all four of the different possibilities discussed above, so that he may rate one person as having a good sense of humour for one reason and another person for another reason. All this would not matter if the various traits associated with these various definitions were closely related, in that a person who laughed readily was also the one with a tendency to tell witty stories, to laugh at himself, or to agree with the rater in the things he found funny. However, an experimental study has shown that in actual fact there is no great tendency for these different traits to hang together; indeed, a person who has a tendency to tell witty stories frequently does not laugh at all readily at such stories told by somebody else, and he often finds it very difficult to laugh at himself. Thus, what appears to be a very simple rating procedure in fact turns out to be a highly complex process which is very difficult, if not impossible, to interpret in any meaningful sense.

Even if there is some agreement on just what the trait being rated is supposed to mean, it may nevertheless be impossible ito base any meaningful rating on ordinary observation. Thus, in one study a large group of neurotic patients was seen by two or more psychiatrists each. In view of the importance which the trait of suggestibility is often thought to have in producing neurotic symptoms, and in view of the considerable amount of discussion which it has received in the psychiatric literature, one might have thought that there should be fairly general agreement between psychiatrists as to whether a given person was or was not suggestible. Yet in actual fact it was shown that there was no agreement at all between them; a patient may be called highly suggestible by one, non-suggestible by a second, and average by a third. Clearly, whether or not a patient was rated as 'suggestible' depended not on any qualities within himself but rather on which particular psychiatrist happened to carry out the rating procedure.

This is an example of a fundamental difficulty which is inherent in all ratings. What the rater says about the ratee may be taken as evidence about some quality inherent in the ratee, but it may also be taken as evidence of some quality inherent in the rater. Two examples may show what I have in mind. If the same set of schoolboy essays is rated by two schoolmasters on a 100-point scale, one may on the average give a mark of 80, the other a mark of 40. We would not regard this as showing anything about the quality of the essays, but would rather say that one schoolmaster was more severe in his marks than the other. In other words, we would use his rating to come to a conclusion, not about the things rated, but about him, the rater. Or let us consider another situation in which a person is asked to rate on a scale of excellence both Shakespeare's *Hamlet* and the latest Hollywood masterpiece. We would not regard his verdict as telling us very much about Shakespeare and his excellence, but we would regard it as telling us something about the person who made the rating.

This difficulty is quite inescapable, of course. We are throughout dealing with a process of interaction between two people, and what we have to do is to analyse this interaction rather than accept any part of it as being objectively true. There is ample evidence to show that this statement is, in fact, correct. Just one such study will be quoted because of its importance. The hypothesis on which this study was based may be phrased as follows. An individual judging others with respect to a given trait will be determined in his judgement not only by objective reality, but also by his own possession of this trait. His judgements will be influenced in two different ways, according to whether he is conscious of the fact that he himself possesses the trait in question, or whether he is unconscious of this fact. If he is unconscious of possessing the trait himself; if, in other words, he lacks insight, then he will tend to attribute a *greater* amount of that trait to other people, while, when he has insight into his possession of that trait, he will tend to attribute a *lesser* amount of it to other people.

The experiment was run along rather simple lines. A group of people was chosen, each of whom knew the others quite well, and they were all asked to rate themselves and each other on a number of traits. As an example, let us take the trait of stinginess. First of all, those people were selected who were considered stingy by the majority; they, in other words, might be considered to possess this trait to an above-average degree. They were then divided into two groups, i.e. those who had insight and rated themselves as being stingy, and those who lacked insight and rated themselves as not stingy.

As a next step, the ratings made by these two groups of judges of all the other people in the group were compared with the average ratings made by the whole group. The hypothesis predicted that those judges who were stingy and had insight would be rather lenient, and not attribute stinginess to other people, while those judges who were stingy and did not have insight would be rather strict, and attribute stinginess to other people to a greater extent than objectively justified. This, indeed, is precisely what happened, and we can see, therefore, that to understand the meaning of a rating given by one person of another, we must have some knowledge, not only of the meaning attributed to the terms used by the rater, but also to his own possession of the trait in question and to his insight or lack of insight. This, of course, enormously complicates the whole problem of ratings.

Unfortunately, these are not the only difficulties that arise; there are many more. One of the most ubiquitous is the so-called 'halo' effect, a term used to denote a tendency common among human judges to like or dislike the ratee as a whole, and thus attribute all the desirable and admirable traits to him if we like him, or to attribute all the undesirable and not so admirable traits to him if we dislike him. Thus, again, the relationship of the rater to the ratee influences the ratings given, and makes it more subjective and less valid than we would like it to be. It is very difficult to get around this halo effect unless, perhaps, it could be done by always having two judges for each one of our ratees, one who liked and one who disliked him intensely. However, this is a difficult thing to arrange in practice, and the end result might be that everyone would receive an average rating because the two judges would completely cancel out.

A last point which should be mentioned is that there seem to be very considerable differences in rating ability among human beings. Some people apparently have an almost uncanny ability to come up with the right answer, while others are almost constantly wrong in their ratings and their predictions based on these ratings. Thus, it was found during the war that in the War Office Selection Boards, where a number of judges made predictions as to the 'officer quality' and future career of young officer candidates, some people had a batting average of correct predictions very much in excess of that of their colleagues, while others were quite unusually incompetent. This finding has recently been sub-

jected to experimental tests in the United States along
several different lines. In one experiment the ratee was asked
to fill in a personality questionnaire of the kind to be discussed presently. Having done this, he was asked to go into
another room, where he had to stand on a platform, smoke
a cigarette, walk up and down, write on a blackboard 'Mary
had a little lamb', and recite a poem. He did this in front of
a fairly large group of people – the 'raters' in this experiment – who observed him carefully and were then required
to fill in the personality questionnaire in the way in which
they thought he himself had filled it in. It thus became possible to compare the actual answers given by the ratee with
those which the raters thought, from their brief acquaintance, he would have made.

It was found again that some people were very much better than others, and this ability to carry out a task of this
kind was apparently a fairly general one, because when the
experiment was repeated several times with different people
taking the part of the ratee, it was the same raters, again and
again, who succeeded in estimating correctly the answers
that had been given to the questions in the personality
inventory.

In a rather more thorough investigation a slightly different method was used. Short interviews with several ratees
were recorded on a sound film and were then played to
groups of judges who had to answer questions about the personality of the interviewees. The answers to these questions,
which dealt partly with verbal behaviour, partly with behaviour in various life situations, were known from an ex-
haustive study of each subject's life-history, test performance, and so forth. In this way, the judgements of the ratees
could be compared with actual fact. Again it was found that
considerable differences existed in the ability of the raters to
judge the personalities of the subjects, and that psychological ability appeared to be a prominent characteristic of a
given judge, regardless of which of the several subjects he
was rating.

Important as this psychological ability undoubtedly is,

very little is, in fact, known about it. As you might have expected, intelligence and emotional stability tend to be positively correlated with it, but the relationship is not close enough to make selection on this basis very fruitful. One might think that special training in psychology and psychiatry would be of help, but in actual fact this does not appear to be so. Students of the natural sciences are usually superior to other groups in making judgements of this kind. Psychiatrists have been found to be reasonably accurate in predicting verbal behaviour, but not in predicting behaviour in actual life situations. This, in a way, is perhaps what one might have suspected. Practically the only relationship between the psychiatrist and his patient is one involving words and verbal behaviour; unfortunately, what a person says and what a person does are not necessarily the same thing, and one cannot extrapolate from the one to the other.

Perhaps the superiority of students of the natural sciences over psychiatrists and clinical psychologists is not to be wondered at either. Physicists, chemists, engineers, and so on, are trained to deal with facts and not to indulge in speculation and complex theorizing unsupported by evidence. Psychoanalysts and other clinical workers, who have not undergone this type of training, all too easily take their highly speculative theories seriously, forgetting the very small factual basis supporting them, and make unwarranted and complex generalizations and predictions which are not in accord with reality. It is not known whether this is the correct explanation of the findings, but it certainly is a possible one, and it is to be hoped that experimental evidence will soon be forthcoming to prove or disprove it. There is, in fact, a good deal of evidence to show that experts in the more esoteric fields of clinical psychology tend to be less accurate in their predictions than beginners, and the reason for this appears to lie mainly in precisely this tendency for over-elaboration on insufficient evidence on the part of the expert.

With such very marked differences apparent between different judges, it seems reasonable to expect that while good judges might produce worth-while results, poor judges could not be relied on to give ratings of any reasonable degree of usefulness. Unfortunately, good judges are rare and difficult to find, and the procedure for detecting them is so complex and cumbersome at the moment, that it has never in fact been used, except for experimental purposes and in the laboratory. It might be hoped that in the selection and training of psychiatrists, psychoanalysts, and clinical psychologists, room would be found for the application of experimental procedures of this type, if only to demonstrate to the majority the fallibility of human judgements on such complex questions and problems. However, to date all that can be said is that for the great majority of people the method of rating is a very unreliable and insecure way of arriving at accurate measures of personality variables, and that clearly other methods, if available, would be preferable.

In discussing these other methods, as we shall do presently, we must bear in mind one great difficulty which makes this branch of psychology particularly frustrating and unsatisfactory. This difficulty relates to the almost complete absence of any reliable criteria against which we can evaluate our methods and tests. In psychology, a test is considered valid when it can be shown, in fact, to measure what it attempts to measure. For instance, let us suppose that we have been given the task of preparing a battery of tests for the improved selection of sagger-makers' bottom knockers. While, technically, this may not be an easy task, in principle it is capable of a relatively straightforward solution, because we have a criterion against which to measure the adequacy of any test which might be suggested. We could give our test, or battery of tests, to 1,000 sagger-makers' bottom knockers, record their scores, and then correlate these scores with the actual number of bottoms knocked per day, or per week, or per year, by each one of our subjects. Once these records had been made available by the sagger-makers, the relative capacity of their bottom knockers could be established, and the relationship of this ability to the test scores would be known. We could then retain those tests which showed a high relationship with bottom-knocking ability, and eliminate those of low or moderate predictive ability.

There would, of course, be all sorts of practical difficulties. Thus, London bottoms and Glasgow bottoms might not be of exactly the same size, or again, the instruments used might not be identical. Apprenticeship schools might differ, and there might be an overall agreement among bottom knockers not to produce more than a certain number of specimens each day. While practical difficulties of this kind certainly make the life of the industrial psychologist more adventurous and troublesome than it would otherwise be, they are not insuperable, and ways and means can usually be found to take into account troublesome factors of this kind.

The difficulty in the personality field is that for those variables in which we are really interested there is no outside criterion of any kind. If there was some certain way of knowing who had and who did not have a good sense of humour, then we could easily correlate any judgements used against the true facts and find out in this way who was and who was not a good judge. In a similar way we could construct tests of 'sense of humour', retaining those which correlated highly with our criterion, and throwing out those which did not. However, if we did have such a perfect criterion, then, of course, we would have no need of either ratings or tests; the fact that both ratings and tests are still used indicates more clearly than anything that no objective and valid criterion is in practice available.

The extraordinary difficulty of finding a good criterion may be illustrated by certain experiences gained during the war, when the problem of pilot selection became a crucial one. There are, quite obviously, considerable differences between people in their ability to learn to fly and to pilot a plane. It would be a very inefficient and expensive method to train everybody who applied, and to count those as failures who smashed up a plane, which might have cost half a million pounds. Consequently, a number of objective tests, of the kind to be described presently, were constructed because it was thought that the abilities measured by these tests would be relevant to the art of flying a plane. However, no relationship whatever was observed between scores on these tests and actual flying ability. This seemed unreasonable, because much previous work had shown that such a relationship did, in fact, exist, and consequently the criterion of flying ability became suspect. This criterion, which on its face appeared quite a reasonable one, consisted in the rating of an experienced instructor, who carefully observed the pupil going through a series of predetermined manœuvres; each manœuvre was rated separately as to the excellence of its execution, and the instructor then gave an over-all estimation of the number of points gained in these various manœuvres and his over-all impression of the candidate in flight.

In order to check up on the reliability of this criterion a number of candidates were asked to go through the set of manœuvres, watched this time by several independent instructors who made their judgements without consulting with each other. When their ratings were compared, it was found that there was hardly any agreement between them at all. They all marked down a candidate who broke off the under-carriage of his plane in an attempt to land, up-ended the plane, and finally managed to break its back. However, this candidate constituted the solitary case on which there was universal agreement. For the rest, the subjective opinions of the judges were so divergent that, quite clearly, no reasonable criterion could be expected from unreliable ratings of this type. It took a very long time indeed before it became possible to objectivize the procedure.

The main alternative method to that of rating has traditionally been the questionnaire or personality inventory. In this, the subject in whom we are interested is asked to answer a number of questions about himself; from his answers to these questions we try to arrive at some conclusions about his personality. This method obviously has a number of drawbacks and difficulties to which we shall turn presently. These, however, have not prevented it from working

H

very efficiently in certain situations, and of all the methods of collecting data of relevance to personality study in psychology, the questionnaire has probably been the most widely used.

It originated very much as did intelligence tests, in response to a practical emergency. During the First World War the American army was getting worried over the large number of recruits who were boarded out because of neurotic disorders of one kind or another. To the army this was a serious matter. It meant, for one thing, that large numbers of medical personnel, nurses, orderlies, and so on, had to be employed to look after these neurotics, special hospitals had to be set up, psychiatrists had to be employed to determine the degree of incapacity, and last, but not least, a considerable financial sacrifice was involved in boarding out the men under this category. It has been calculated that it cost the United States Government 75,000 dollars in all for just one neurotic to be 'separated' from the army, as this somewhat painful process is called in the United States. When 75,000 dollars are multiplied by hundreds of thousands of cases, it will be clear that it would be of tremendous help to the authorities to be able to diagnose the potential neurotic before he ever joined the army. Such early diagnoses would be exceedingly helpful, not only to the army, but probably even more to the potential neurotic. It would prevent him from going forward to an almost certain nervous breakdown, and he would probably be far more useful to the country doing a civilian job involving little stress and not precipitating all the neurotic symptoms with which we have become so familiar in the last fifty years, than as an emotional victim of army life and hazards. From the ethical point of view, this argument has sometimes been attacked because it means that the burden shouldered by different individuals is not the same, but whatever the ethical implications may be, few armies would, for practical reasons alone, refuse to employ a selection procedure which would 'screen out the neurotic', if such screening were possible.

The person to whom the difficult task of creating such a

sieve was entrusted was Woodworth, one of the most eminent of American psychologists. Realizing that laboratory experiments would not be feasible under army selection conditions, Woodworth drew up a questionnaire which recruits had to answer. This questionnaire consisted of very simple questions which had to be answered by underlining 'Yes', 'No', or, where the answer was difficult, by underlining a '?'. The questions themselves were obtained by going through several text-books on psychiatry and noting all the symptoms associated with neurosis, such as having many headaches, having nightmares, worrying about one's health, often feeling miserable, lacking self-confidence, having feelings of inferiority, or worrying too long over humiliating experiences. Woodworth put together over 200 questions of this kind in his final inventory, but it was never actually employed for selection, as the war had come to an end by then. The reader who is interested in the kinds of question asked may read through a very much briefer questionnaire used in Great Britain, which is printed below. It consists of forty questions, and the score is simply the number of 'Yes's' underlined by the subject. The average score of groups of normal subjects is about 10, that of neurotics about 20. (The reader should not take it too much to heart if, on going through the questionnaire, he finds that he gives 20 or more 'Yes' answers. This does not mean that he is a neurotic. Inventories of this kind can give useful leads to the experienced psychologist and they may single out people for further investigation; in themselves they should never in any circumstances be used to arrive at a conclusion about a person's mental health.)

MAUDSLEY MEDICAL QUESTIONNAIRE

Read through these questions and underline the correct answer, either 'Yes' or 'No'. Do not omit any item. It is important that you should be quite frank.

(1) Do you have dizzy turns?   Yes   No
(2) Do you get palpitations or thumping in your
      heart?   Yes   No

(3) Did you ever have a nervous breakdown?   Yes   No

(4) Have you ever been off work through sickness a good deal?   Yes   No

(5) Did you often use to get 'stage fright' in your life?   Yes   No

(6) Do you find it difficult to get into conversation with strangers?   Yes   No

(7) Have you ever been troubled by a stammer or stutter?   Yes   No

(8) Have you ever been made unconscious for two hours or more by an accident or blow?   Yes   No

(9) Do you worry too long over humiliating experiences?   Yes   No

(10) Do you consider yourself rather a nervous person?   Yes   No

(11) Are your feelings easily hurt?   Yes   No

(12) Do you usually keep in the background on social occasions?   Yes   No

(13) Are you subject to attacks of shaking or trembling?   Yes   No

(14) Are you an irritable person?   Yes   No

(15) Do ideas run through your head so that you cannot sleep?   Yes   No

(16) Do you worry over possible misfortunes?   Yes   No

(17) Are you rather shy?   Yes   No

(18) Do you sometimes feel happy, sometimes depressed, without any apparent reason?   Yes   No

(19) Do you daydream a lot?   Yes   No

(20) Do you seem to have less life about you than others?   Yes   No

(21) Do you sometimes get a pain over your heart?   Yes   No

(22) Do you have nightmares?   Yes   No

(23) Do you worry about your health?   Yes   No

(24) Have you sometimes walked in your sleep?   Yes   No

(25) Do you sweat a great deal without exercise?   Yes   No

(26) Do you find it difficult to make friends?   Yes   No

(27) Does your mind often wander badly, so that you lose track of what you are doing?   Yes   No

(28) Are you touchy on various subjects?   Yes   No

(29) Do you often feel disgruntled?   Yes   No

(30) Do you often feel just miserable?   Yes   No

(31) Do you often feel self-conscious in the presence of your superiors?   Yes   No

(32) Do you suffer from sleeplessness?   Yes   No

(33) Did you ever get short of breath without having done heavy work?	Yes	No
(34) Do you ever suffer from severe headaches?	Yes	No
(35) Do you suffer from 'nerves'?	Yes	No
(36) Are you troubled by aches and pains?	Yes	No
(37) Do you get nervous in places such as lifts, trains, or tunnels?	Yes	No
(38) Do you suffer from attacks of diarrhoea?	Yes	No
(39) Do you lack self-confidence?	Yes	No
(40) Are you troubled with feelings of inferiority?	Yes	No

In view of the great ease with which questionnaires can be drawn up and the large number of people who can be tested simultaneously without difficulty, questionnaires became very popular indeed in the years between the wars. They provided so much grist for the statistical mill of the psychologist's calculating machines that few people managed to ask critical questions about the meaningfulness of data so acquired. Gradually, however, doubts began to grow, even in the most enthusiastic. Many people had experiences of a kind to make them somewhat suspicious of the truthfulness of the answers given by subjects. Thus, one might see some unfortunate individual sitting down with his questionnaire, his hands trembling and sweating with excitement, his face getting pale and flushed alternately, and his tongue licking his lips, his whole body in a tremor of nervousness; on going over to reassure him, one would find that after the question, 'Are you generally a nervous sort of person?' he had boldly put the answer 'No'!

Doubts of this kind came to a head in the 1930s because some very odd results indeed came out of the statistical mill. To explain the consternation caused, we must go back a little to the 1920s again. While following Woodworth, most questionnaires had dealt with the diagnosis of neurotic disorders and emotional instability, the translation of Jung's book on *Psychological Types* made people interested in the investigation of extraversion and introversion, and many questionnaires were drawn up for this purpose. The procedure followed was pretty much the same as that used by

Woodworth. Jung's book would be gone through with a fine-tooth comb and statements about the behaviour of the typical extravert or introvert could then be transformed into questions to be answered 'Yes' or 'No'. In this way, long and detailed questionnaires and inventories were drawn up for the measurement of a temperamental trait which, according to Jung's hypothesis, was completely different and unrelated to neuroticism.

For about ten years psychologists went along their way happily measuring neuroticism and introversion with these different instruments, when suddenly someone hit upon the bright idea of comparing the scores made by the same group of people on different types of questionnaires. Now, if all the neuroticism inventories measured neuroticism, presumably the same people, i.e. the emotionally unstable ones, should have high scores on all the questionnaires, while another group of people, i.e. the emotionally stable ones, should have low scores on all the questionnaires. Similarly, with respect to the introversion questionnaires, all the people who were introverted should have high scores on all the questionnaires, while the extraverted ones should have low scores on all the questionnaires. And as neuroticism and introversion were supposed to be quite unrelated to each other, the fact that a person had a high or a low score on neuroticism should not in any way determine his score on an introversion questionnaire.

The many investigations conducted to test these hypotheses all arrived at the same conclusion. The relation between one neuroticism inventory and another was not at all close; the relationship between one introversion measured and another was not at all close; worst of all, the relationship between a measure of introversion and a measure of neuroticism was just about as close as that between two measures of introversion or two measures of neuroticism! In other words, we are dealing with haphazardly grouped items, or questions, which do not succeed in measuring any known or hypothesized form of behaviour, and which, because of their arbitrary selection, cannot even be used to test any kind of worth-while hypothesis. Questionnaires of this type, therefore, are useless, misleading, and must be regarded as quite fatal to the development of the scientific study of personality. It is small wonder, then, that questionnaires fell very low indeed in the estimation of psychologists and that it needed a complete revolution in their construction before they were readmitted to the armamentarium of the student of personality.

The reassessment began by noting that one very fundamental assumption had been made by questionnaire constructors which had little basis in fact. The assumption was that a person in answering a question would be giving an objectively true answer. Now, there are many reasons why this is not only unlikely, but impossible. Let us take such a question as 'Do you have frequent headaches?' Let us assume that the person who is filling in the questionnaire is willing to give a truthful answer. What shall he say? Does one headache a week qualify as being frequent, or should it be more than two a week, or perhaps one every day? How severe ought a headache to be in order to qualify? Perhaps the question means 'more frequently than the average'; but what is the average? How many headaches do people have in the course of a year? It is clear that the answer is subject not only to the actual number of headaches which a person has and their severity, but also to his estimate of what the questioner had in mind, his estimate of what the average number of headaches is in the community, and various other factors as well. How can we then attribute any direct meaning to the 'Yes' or the 'No' which is the only answer permitted to the subject? If we regard this reply as a truthful account of his own experience, we must come to the conclusion that it is quite impossible to interpret in any reasonable manner. If the reader will go through the forty questions in our questionnaire, he will find that nearly all of them are of a similar kind and subject to a similar criticism. How easily do one's feelings have to be hurt in order to answer 'Yes' to question 11? How difficult does it have to be for one to get into a conversation with strangers before one answers 'Yes' to question 6? How shy does one have to be to say 'Yes' to question 17, and how worried about one's health to say 'Yes' to question 23? It will be obvious that the whole basis of the questionnaire, as it used to be conceived, is at fault.

Another difficulty which arises is that a person may not know the truth about himself and may therefore not be able to give a correct answer. As we have seen before, a stingy person may be quite unconscious of his stinginess and completely lack insight. Under those conditions we can hardly expect him to give us an answer which will be very revealing or diagnostic of the true state of affairs. Few people, for instance, who have a poor sense of humour are conscious of this fact. In a well-known experiment the question was put, 'Do you have a better sense of humour than average?' Ninety-eight per cent of those who answered the question claimed to have a better than average sense of humour!

A third point, which has always created difficulties in accepting questionnaire responses at face value, lies in the fact that these are so easy to fake. Most people want to be seen in the best light; consequently, they tend to 'put their best foot forward', or in other words to deny those traits and those behaviour patterns which are socially regarded as being unreliable, immature, unstable, and so forth. Why should we expect a person to indict himself in a questionnaire; what right have we to expect him to tell the truth about himself if that truth is uncomplimentary and would show him up as a rather poor sort of fish? We have no guarantee at all, then, that a person would even attempt to tell the truth, even assuming that he did know the truth and that he could make any sense out of our questions.

In recent years the whole basis of interpretation of questionnaires has shifted, and a serious attempt has been made to get over these difficulties. In the first place, psychologists have more or less abandoned the idea that the answer a person gives should be intrepreted as a truthful self-revelation. We are now concerned, not at all with the interpretation of answers, but merely with the objective fact that a person puts a mark in one part of the paper rather than in another. Thus, it is a fact that a person underlines the 'Yes' or the 'No' after the question 'Are you touchy on various subjects?'; it is a subjective interpretation of this objective fact to assume that he has answered it in a truthful manner and that in fact he is touchy on various subjects. To what use, it may be asked, is the objective fact of a given endorsement if we cannot interpret it? The answer is a very simple one indeed. Let us take two groups of people between whom we want to differentiate. For the purpose of illustration, let us take a group of normals and a group of neurotics. We might, of course, have taken a group of introverts and a group of extraverts, or a group of epileptics and a group of patients with brain damage. The procedure is quite general, and can be applied whenever two criterion groups can be distinguished.

Let us now apply our questionnaire to a group of 1,000 normals and 1,000 neurotics, and let us note merely the objective fact of how many in each group underlined the 'Yes' and how many underlined the 'No' alternative printed after each question. Let us take the question, 'Do you suffer from sleeplessness?' It has been found that 32 per cent of neurotics answer this in the affirmative, whereas only 13 per cent of normals answer it in the affirmative. Now, this is an objective fact. We are not here concerned with the *reasons* why a greater number of neurotics endorse this question. It might be that neurotics are truly more given to sleeplessness than are normal people. It could be that neurotics are more given to complaining, although, objectively, normal people suffer more from sleeplessness. It could be that both normals and neurotics suffer equally from sleeplessness, but that this presents a much greater stress to the emotionally unstable neurotic. Whatever may be the true reason, the fact remains that neurotics and normals are differentiated objectively in their behaviour, and that consequently, when dealing with people whom we want to classify into either of these groups, the endorsement of the 'Yes' answer to this question makes it more likely that they belong in the neurotic group than that they belong in the normal group. Knowing the percentage endorsements of known members of the two groups, we can calculate exactly the probability of a given person belonging to either of the two groups from knowing his answer to this particular question.

Figure 4 shows the existing differences in endorsements of normal and neurotic groups of 1,000 each on sixteen items in the Maudsley Medical Questionnaire. In making a judgement one would, of course, not rely on the answers to single questions alone, but probabilities can be combined, and by the time we have combined probabilities on forty questions

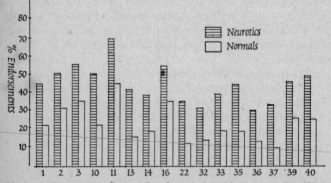

Figure 4: Percentage of normal and neurotic subjects answering 'Yes' to selected questions from the neuroticism inventory given on page 195.

we can come to a fairly reasonable estimate as to whether a person belongs in the neurotic group, in the normal group, or whether his status is indeterminate, being somewhere in between the two. We would, of course, want to make certain of the validity of the argument by following up groups with high and low scores, but, by and large, we may feel reasonably content that in changing our basis of interpretation we have left behind the morass of unwarranted interpretation and are now on fairly firm ground.

We also have a method now which enables us to eliminate poor items and retain good items. Any item which does not succeed in differentiating between normal and neurotic groups would, on these grounds, be a poor item, however prominent it might be in the psychiatric text-books, while any item which did give a good differentiation between a normal and a neurotic group may be a good item, although it may not even be mentioned in the text-books. Our approach is a purely empirical one, and this enables us to call to our aid complex statistical and mathematical analyses. Thus, brief and simple questionnaires like the one presented on an earlier page can be constructed on an empirical basis and are, in fact, more valid and more reliable than the very much longer ones current in the 1920s.

But how can we get over the difficulty of faking? How is it possible to prevent our subjects from answering all the questions in the positive 'healthy', non-neurotic direction? The answer is that, while it is not possible to do this, it is possible to detect tendencies of this kind and either to make allowances for them, or to disregard the result of the questionnaire. The method used, that of the so-called 'lie-scale', is essentially a very simple one. A person who wants to give a particularly good impression of himself does so by answering 'No' to all questions which would put him in a somewhat less good light than that in which he wants to be seen. Consequently, all we have to do to catch him is to make up a scale of items which, while they put people in a rather poor light, are nevertheless of such a nature that anybody would have to admit to the answer 'Yes' if he was at all honest. As an example we might take a question like the following: 'Have you ever told a white lie?' Certainly, to have to admit to having told lies is to put oneself in a poor light, yet very few people could truthfully answer 'No'. If a person does answer 'No' to this question, and to a large number of others of a similar kind, then we can be fairly certain that his questionnaire answers also are not to be trusted. It is, of course, conceivable that a person might, quite truthfully, answer 'No' to all the questions on the lie scale, but in that case he would be a saint, and questionnaires are not constructed to deal with saints.

Another method which has very much improved the

accuracy of questionnaire measurement has been that of detailed internal statistical analysis. This analysis involves the calculus of implication, which is discussed in more detail in the chapter on 'Personality and Politics'. Briefly, what this means is simply that the psychologist analyses the relationships between answers to different questions. Logically, questions such as 'Are your feelings easily hurt?' and 'Do ideas run through your head so that you cannot sleep?' are quite independent; it would be possible to answer 'Yes' to one and 'No' to another. In actual fact, people who answer 'Yes' to one tend to answer 'Yes' to the other, and *vice versa*. In other words, there is a *factual implication*, so that from knowing a person's answer to the one we can predict his answer to the other. It is possible to give a numerical statement of the degree of implication, and the statistical psychologist has worked out methods to analyse the network of implications running through all the questions in a questionnaire. The methods used are too technical to discuss in detail here, but they have helped enormously in making questionnaires more reliable, in cutting out dead wood, and generally in improving measurement along these lines.

Modern questionnaires, then, are usually quite different in their method of construction and interpretation from those earlier ones which encountered such severe criticism. A great deal of work has usually gone into their construction as compared with the *a priori*, happy-go-lucky methods which were responsible for the original neuroticism and introversion inventories. Detailed experimental studies with different diagnostic groups are usually carried out, and a complex system of statistical analysis along the lines of the calculus of implication has to be gone through. The resulting instruments have considerable usefulness from the practical point of view, and may aid the psychologist in his attempts to measure personality.

In certain ways there undoubtedly are similarities between ratings and questionnaires. Thus, the psychiatrist who wants to rate a person's degree of emotional instability, or neuroticism, will ask him a series of questions in an interview, which is essentially very similar to the questions contained in the questionnaire. Indeed, experiments have shown that there is considerable agreement between the questionnaire replies given by large samples of people, and the ratings of the same people made by a highly skilled psychiatrist who interviewed them. If the outcome is so similar, why, it may be asked, do we feel more confidence in the questionnaire than in the rating procedure?

There are several reasons for this. In the first place, a great deal of work has gone into the exact choice and wording of questions in the questionnaire. The forty items in the Maudsley Medical Questionnaire are the remains of almost 1,000 which were tried out, most of which were discarded when it was experimentally found that they did not discriminate as well as those which were retained. The psychiatrist who interviews a patient does not usually perform the considerable amount of work which would be involved in the careful selection of questions on an objective basis. Consequently, his choice is almost inevitably inferior to that leading to the construction of a questionnaire.

In the second place, data, once they have been gathered, have to be interpreted and compared. This is best done by statistical procedures relating the scores obtained by a given person to replies given by large control groups whose responses are known. The psychiatrist seldom asks exactly the same questions of any two people, and he never keeps exact statistics to tell him what the means and averages of different groups are. Consequently, he does implicitly and vaguely in his head what the psychologist does explicitly and with the use of calculating machines.

In the third place, the psychologist using an inventory or questionnaire is careful to collect large groups of normal people, which will give him a base-line in terms of which to make his interpretation. The psychiatrist hardly ever sees normal people in the course of his work and therefore lacks this kind of objective basis.

An actual experiment may show the quite remarkable

differences in judgement which these various sources of errors may produce among psychiatrists. These figures relate to the medical examination in the United States of all literate recruits to the United States Army, prior to their induction. This work was carried out during August 1945 in some fifty stations all over the country. Fourteen per cent of these candidates were rejected for psychiatric reasons, and it is very instructive to analyse the reasons given for rejection in the various induction stations. There is ample evidence to show that candidates going to these various stations did not differ very much from each other, so that differences in diagnosis cannot be due to the candidates themselves, but must be due to the examining psychiatrists.

First of all, then, let us consider the percentage of psychiatric rejections in these various induction stations. As mentioned above, the overall percentage is 14. In some induction stations only ·5 per cent, i.e. only one person in 200, was rejected for psychiatric reasons. At another induction station the percentage was 50·6, i.e. every other candidate was rejected for psychiatric reasons. To put it slightly differently, for every one inductee rejected for psychiatric reasons in one centre, there were over 100 rejected in another!

When we look at the reasons why people were rejected we find again considerable variation from one centre to another. Of all those rejected for psychiatric reasons, 40 per cent on the average were diagnosed as 'psychoneurotic'. However, this average concealed a very large amount of variability. Thus, in one centre 2·7 per cent were diagnosed as psychoneurotic; in another, 90·2 per cent. Differences in other psychiatric categories were equally large, or larger, and it must be quite clear that ratings of this type are subject to all the sources of error mentioned in the preceding paragraph.

In contrast, questionnaires given at various centres to similar groups of candidates did not disclose any such variability because it was now possible to objectify the selection method, to set definite standards, and thus to gain all the advantages of an objective as opposed to a subjective approach. This is only one example of many which could be given, but it does illustrate that, although in principle there may not be very much difference between the procedure of interviewing and rating, on the one hand, and the procedure of administering questionnaires, on the other, yet there are very great advantages attached to the latter procedure which should not be ignored.

We must now turn to a third method of investigation which is very much more important and scientifically fruitful than those considered hitherto, and which will become more and more the standard method of personality investigation. Here, what we are using is not what one person says about another, or what a person says about himself, but rather we make an actual measurement of the observed behaviour of a person in a situation or a test so constructed as to call forth the type of behaviour in which we are interested. It will be easiest to explain this type of measurement by including in the discussion a consideration of a theoretical point mentioned at the beginning of this chapter, but not discussed in full. We noted at the beginning that the man in the street discusses personality variables in terms of such concepts as 'traits', and we have followed his example so far without going in any detail into the very important question of whether there is any evidence for the existence of such traits, and what precisely we understand by this whole notion. Let us remedy this omission and begin by considering a given trait, say that of persistence.

What do we mean when we say that a given person is persistent? We mean, surely, that he tends to carry on an activity in the face of boredom, or pain, or exhaustion, long after other people less persistent than himself might have stopped. Implied in the notion of this trait of persistence is the assumption that persistence will be shown by a given person, not only in one particular situation, but in a wide range of situations. We would not call a person persistent if he only continued one particular type of activity against fatigue and boredom, but let himself be put off continuing other activities. Thus, the notion of generality is quite essential to our concept of a trait; a trait is something which is shown in a large number of different situations.

The difficulty caused by this requirement is dimly noted in ordinary language too. Thus, we have a concept of 'cowardice' as a trait, but quite obviously this does not work too well. The V.C. may faint in the dentist's chair; in other words, he may be a coward in one situation and a hero in another. The schoolboy may be physically brave, but may not dare to show that rare quality of moral courage. It becomes a factual question to find out whether a given hypothetical trait is, in fact, general in the sense of being displayed in a wide variety of situations, or whether, in fact, all we are dealing with is a specific response to a specific situation.

How would this apply to the problem of the measurement of persistence? What we would do here would involve a whole series of steps which may be taken as exemplifying the method employed by the modern psychologist in measuring a particular trait of personality. In the first place, we would make a theoretical statement of the nature of the trait under investigation somewhat along the lines indicated in the preceding paragraph, where we defined persistence as the tendency to carry on an activity, in spite of fatigue, pain, or boredom. The second step would then be the construction of a large number of tests or situations making possible for the subject the demonstration of different degrees of the trait in question. Here are a few such tests, quoted more or less at random from the very large literature that has grown up around the concept of persistence. Most of these have been used in connexion with schoolchildren, but many of them, have been adapted for use with adults also, and the results have been just as favourable.

Here, then, is our first test. The subject is given a large jig-saw puzzle which he is told to fit together. He is told that this is a test of intelligence, or some other kind of ability, and that he has as much time as he wants in order to do the test. Before handing the jigsaw puzzle to the subject, however, the experimenter has removed some of the pieces and has substituted others for them in such a way that it is quite impossible to complete the test successfully. (This, of course, is done in such a way that the candidate has no idea of what has happened and cannot, in fact, guess at any stage that his task is objectively impossible.)

The subject begins to put the test together, gradually gets tired as he fails to advance beyond a certain point, and finally is discouraged and gives up completely, saying 'This is too difficult for me', or 'I don't think I'll be able to do this'. In extreme cases, subjects have even been known to throw the test out of the window, hurl it at the experimenter, or burst out crying and leave the room in tears. However they may terminate the experiment, the time from the beginning to the end is taken as their score, because this is the period during which they have continued with the task.

Now let us look at the next test. The subject here is asked to pull a dynamometer as hard as he can. (This is an instrument measuring the strength of a patient's pull against a steel spring, the result in pounds being registered on a large dial.) Having found the strongest pull of which the subject is capable, the experimenter then instructs him to pull the dynamometer at exactly half that strength for as long as he can. The length of time during which he is capable of doing this is then taken as another measure of his persistence (not of his strength – this variable is controlled by making the tasks relative to the initial pull).

A third test may be given consisting of one of those Chinese puzzles in which eight carved pieces of wood have to be put together in the form of a cross. The subject is shown the completed cross, which is then taken to pieces, and the test proper begins. While, theoretically, the candidate may succeed in doing this, the task is so difficult that, in practice, no one has managed it before giving up. Again the length of time taken before giving up is a measure of the candidate's persistence.

A fourth test might involve an item in an intelligence test which was well above the candidate's ability to solve. All items in the test are timed separately, and the time which the candidate is willing to spend on an item too difficult for him to solve is a measure of his persistence.

Hundreds of other similar tests can be used, and have been used, but the reader will be able to see the general underlying principle without an unnecessary duplication of instances. Instead, we will go on to the third stage of the measurement of persistence. If our hypothesis that persistence is a general trait is correct, and if these are all measures of persistence, then it must follow that the person who is persistent in any one of these tests should be persistent in the others, and that a person who lacks persistence in one of these tests should also lack persistence in the others. Consequently, what we must do is to administer a whole series of thirty or so tests to a group of subjects, give each subject a score on each of the tests, and then investigate statistically the degree to which success in one test predicts success in all the others, and failure in one test failure in all the others.

There is ample evidence to show that agreement between different tests exists to a quite considerable extent. It might have been thought, *a priori*, that the intellectual child might be persistent with a difficult intelligence test item, say, but lack persistence in the dynamometer pull, while, conversely, the athletic child might be persistent in connexion with the dynamometer, but lack persistence on more intellectual tasks. Up to a point, this is true; there is a tendency for intellectual tasks to hang together, or for physical tasks to hang together more closely than they do from one group to the other, but the difference is slight and the over-all agreement considerable. Consequently, it appears that we can justifiably talk about a trait of persistence as being manifested in all these tests. Having shown this, we can then conclude that the best measure of persistence is a person's average performance on a well-selected battery of tests of this kind. By well-selected in this connexion we mean that the tests should cover as many different areas of ability and interest as possible; that they should be adequate for the age groups for which they are designed; that they should not take too long to administer;

and that they should not require too much complex apparatus.

Having designed our battery of tests for the measurement of persistence, we must next demonstrate that these tests actually do measure persistence rather than something else. It might be, for instance, that these are all measures of intelligence, and that the intelligent child tends to do better than the stupid one. This may not seem likely on *a priori* grounds, but psychologists are justly suspicious of *a priori* grounds and prefer some empirical evidence before coming to a conclusion. One possible way of answering a question of this kind is to administer intelligence tests to the same children who have been given the persistence tests; it is possible then to show statistically that whatever it is that the persistence tests have in common, it is not intelligence. Another method of showing the validity of our test battery in a positive rather than in a negative way is to find some reasonable outside criterion and correlate the test results with it. It will be clear from our discussion of outside criteria that we cannot be very hopeful of finding a very good criterion, or one giving high correlations with our tests, but we would nevertheless be rather suspicious of our results if we found that in correlating them, say, with teachers' estimates of persistence there was no correlation at all. Equally, we would be rather suspicious if estimates of a child's persistence given by his classmates did not correlate at all with his performance on the test. In actual fact, reasonably high correlations are found, so that there seems to be little doubt that the test battery measures more reliably and more validly what schoolteachers and classmates indicate by their ratings.

A third method which is also often used would be to make certain deductions from the hypothesis that what we are measuring is persistence, and then go on to test the truth of these deductions. Thus, it seems reasonable to suppose that, given equal intelligence, a persistent person would do better at school or university than a person lacking in persistence. Experimentally, this would lead us to apply our battery of persistence tests to a group of schoolchildren, or students, and pick out a set of highly persistent, as well as a set of non-persistent, subjects. We would then administer intelligence tests to these groups and equate the persistent and non-persistent ones in intelligence by eliminating from the more intelligent group one or two of the most intelligent, until the groups were equal in I.Q. Our prediction now would be that the more persistent group, although no more intelligent than the non-persistent group, should do better in their school work, or obtain better degrees at university, than the non-persistent group. There is ample evidence to show that this is in fact so, and that persistence contributes noticeably to success. We may thus rest at this point in the secure conviction that we have succeeded in measuring, with a given amount of reliability and validity, the trait of persistence, and that we have also succeeded in adducing evidence to show that this trait is not a mere artefact of the imagination.

I have given as an example a trait where the outcome of the set of experiments performed by many authors has been very positive indeed. As the next example, I will give a trait where the outcome has been very much more complex, and where the notion of a unitary trait has, in fact, not been borne out by the evidence. This is the trait of suggestibility, and the investigations carried out here have an important lesson to teach. First of all, let us start by noting roughly what is meant by suggestibility. It is a state or trait causing a person to perform certain acts without having any motivation of his own to do so, or even in spite of having a certain degree of motivation to the contrary. Psychologists have, for many years, been constructing tests of suggestibility as so conceived, and a few of these may be mentioned:

(1) *Chevreul Pendulum Test.* The experimenter draws a chalk line across the table. In his hand he holds a little pendulum made of a small piece of metal, suspended from a thread, which he holds in his hand. He tells the subject that the magnetic lines of the earth go along the chalk line he has drawn on the table, and that they act on the pendulum, making it swing to and fro. As he says so he slowly causes the pendulum to swing along the line on the table. He then

hands it on to the subject, telling him that he should try to hold it quite still and steady over the centre part of the line on the table, but that, in fact, he will be unable to do so. The magnetic lines of the earth will cause the pendulum to sway to and fro, to and fro, to and fro. In actual fact, many subjects accept this suggestion and, quite unwittingly and unconsciously, move their arm in such a way that the pendulum begins to swing along the line suggested.

(2) *Body Sway Test.* In this, the subject is told to stand quite still and relaxed with his eyes closed, his heels together, and his arms by his side. He is told specifically that he should go on standing like that while a record is being played to him. This record endlessly repeats the suggestion: 'You are falling; you are falling forward; you are falling forward; you are falling; you are falling forward now. ...' The actual amount of sway produced by the suggestion is measured by running a thread from the collar of the subject over a series of wheels on to a kymograph marker, which produces a graphic record of the forward and backward sway of the subject on a piece of paper, which is being pulled along by a motor over the surface of a metal drum. Again, some subjects accept the suggestion and sway to a considerable extent; some even fall outright and they have to be caught by the experimenter, who is standing in front of them.

(3) *Arm Levitation Test.* In this test the subject stands with his eyes closed and his right arm raised sideways to shoulder level. He is told to keep it there while a series of suggestions is played over to him on the gramophone to the effect that his arm is getting lighter, that it is rising, and so forth. Again, a record is made of the number of inches that the arm moves in an upward or downward direction.

(4) *Odour Suggestion Test.* In this test the subject is told that he is going to be subjected to a test of his smell sensitivity. He is seated in one corner of the room, while the experimenter goes to the other corner of the room, picks up a bottle containing attar of roses. The bottle is uncorked and the experimenter slowly carries it across to the subject, telling him to say 'Now' the moment he gets the faintest sniff

of the perfume. When the subject says 'Now', the experimenter ostentatiously takes up a measuring tape and measures the exact distance between the bottle and the tip of the subject's nose. This is then entered into a big red book, and the experiment repeated with oil of cloves and camphorated oil. The fourth time, however, the bottle the experimenter picks up contains nothing but distilled water. He again carries it across to the subject, the implied suggestion of the whole procedure being that the bottle again contains some kind of perfume. Many subjects accept this suggestion and call out 'Now' when the experimenter reaches the same point where they previously recognized the smell.

(5) *Progressive Weights Test.* In this test the subject sits at a table, and around him, arranged in the form of a semicircle, are fifteen boxes numbered 1–15, but otherwise identical to all appearances. They differ, however, in weight, the first box weighing 20 grams, the second 40 grams, the third 60 grams, the next 80 grams, and all the remainder weighing 100 grams. The subject is instructed to pick up the first box, then the second box; his task is to say whether the second is heavier than the first. He replies in the affirmative and is then instructed to pick up box 2 and box number 3. Again, the second box is the heavier, and so he continues, always finding the second box heavier until he goes on to boxes 5 and 6, which, of course, are both objectively equal. Many subjects accept the suggestion implied in the procedure that the second box is always heavier than the first, and go on saying 'heavier' through the rest of the trial, in spite of the objective quality of the weight of the boxes.

(6) *Memory Suggestion Test.* In this test the subject is shown a picture containing a large number of details. He is asked to memorize the details of the picture for 15 seconds and then the picture is taken away and he is asked a series of questions about the contents of the picture. One of these might be, 'Was the cat lying on the chair in the right corner or the left corner of the room?' There was no cat at all in the picture, but many people accept the implication of the ques-

tion and firmly convince themselves that there was a cat on one of the two chairs.

These are only some of the many tests which have been used for the measurement of suggestibility. When a sufficient number of them are applied to groups of people and we inquire again, as we did in the case of persistence tests, whether a person who is suggestible in one test is also suggestible on the others, we find that, in this case, the answer is in the negative. The first three tests mentioned, i.e. the Chevreul Pendulum test, the Body Sway test, and the Arm Levitation test, do, indeed, correlate together quite highly. The next three tests, i.e. the Smell Suggestion test, the Progressive Weights test, and the Memory Suggestion test also correlate together, although the relationships are very much lower than in the case of the first three tests. However, when the first three tests are correlated with the last three tests, it is found that there is no relationship whatsoever. In other words, a person who is 'suggestible' as defined by his performance on the first three tests may, or may not, be 'suggestible' as defined by the last three tests; it is impossible to make any kind of prediction because there is no relationship at all between these two meanings of the term. We are dealing with two quite unrelated types of suggestibility – primary suggestibility and secondary suggestibility, as they have been called.

Not only are these two types of suggestibility not related to each other; they behave quite differently in a number of ways. Thus, primary suggestibility is not at all correlated with intelligence; intelligent people are no less suggestible than dull ones. Secondary suggestibility, however, does correlate with intelligence. Here the more intelligent ones are less suggestible and the dull ones are more suggestible. Again, primary suggestibility is closely related to hypnosis; a person who is highly suggestible also tends to be easily hypnotizable. This is not true of secondary suggestibility. A person who is suggestible along the lines defined by this set of tests is neither more easily nor less hypnotizable than a person who is non-suggestible. These are only some of the differences observed between these two types of suggestibility, but there are many more, and they leave no doubt at all that we are dealing here with quite different traits.

Nor are these the only two types of suggestibility. A third variety, which does not seem to correlate with either of the other two, and which has been called tertiary suggestibility, is demonstrated in the following type of test. A social attitude inventory is given to a group of people, calling for their opinions on a variety of social issues. The filled-in questionnaires are then collected and scored. A new set of questionnaires is now constructed containing many more questions than the old one, but incorporating all the old questions also. This time, however, the students are told how each question has been answered by some prestigeful person or group, such as the President of the United States, members of the local Chamber of Commerce, or even their own Professor. These new questionnaires are now handed out after an interval of about three or four months, care having been taken to construct the hypothetical 'prestigeful' answers for each person in such a way that in half the cases they agree with his previous replies, and in half the cases they contradict his previous replies. In this way it becomes possible to measure the amount of change produced in his replies by the presentation of the answers of the prestige group or person. If he is suggestible, then we would expect him to change a number of his answers in the direction of the replies given by the prestige group. This does, indeed, happen and people differ considerably in the amount of suggestibility shown in a test like this.

Thus, we find that there are at least three types of suggestibility, and probably several more different types quite unrelated to those mentioned so far will be unearthed by future experimentation. It will now be clear why, in our rating experiment, there was so little agreement among different raters of the 'suggestibility' of the subjects whom they rated. There simply is no one trait of suggestibility which can be rated in this way, and unless we make it clear which kind of suggestibility we are concerned with, we are caught in the snares of semantic confusion. Before such semantic confusion can be cleared up, however, we must clarify the hypothesis embodied in the trait names by the sort of experimental work just described. Because it enables us to do this on an objective basis, the objective test appears to be so much superior to either the rating or the questionnaire.

The methods discussed so far illustrate only one of the many ways in which objective tests can be used for the measurement of personality traits. It will have been noticed that what is done is essentially this. We start out with a popular notion of some kind of trait; we then go on to refine this notion, express it in terms of objective tests, study its implications statistically, and finally emerge with a much more refined and accurate notion than the one we started out with. In this respect what we are doing in the field of character and temperament is essentially similar to what had been done previously in the field of ability. The methods of isolating and measuring persistence and suggestibility are precisely analogous to the methods used for isolating and measuring verbal ability, perceptual ability, memory, or intelligence. The reader familiar with my discussion of these topics in *Uses and Abuses of Psychology* will see the parallel without any difficulty.

However, objective tests enable us to do considerably more than this. In what we have said so far we have been concerned simply with an improvement in the description of behaviour. There has been no mention of any fundamental laws governing behaviour, nor of any deduction from such laws to indicate why a person showed much or little persistence, or suggestibility, or whatever trait we might be concerned with. Descriptively we have succeeded in isolating certain continua on which we can assess a given subject's position with a certain degree of accuracy. However, this clearly is not enough, although it is a useful first step. After all, an individual cannot do anything with these continua except sit on them, and we would like to be able to do a good deal more. We would like to know why a given individual finds himself in the position he occupies; we would like to know how we can change his position; and we would like to be able to deduce all this from some general kind of law. It will be the task of the next chapter to indicate how this can be done and how we can arrive at more fundamental types of measurement. The topic is too important and too complex to be squeezed into a few paragraphs at the tail-end of this chapter.

Nor will we deal with another type of measurement which is also of considerable importance. This is the field of psycho-physiology, or psychosomatic relationships, and great strides have been made in it in recent years owing to the advances in electronic apparatus which can be used for the refined measurement of slight physiological changes which are indicative of emotion. Again, the field is too complex to be compressed into a few sentences, and I have tried to deal with some aspects of it in an earlier chapter, where I discussed the lie detector apparatus, essentially based on these psycho-physiological relationships.

There does, however, remain to be dealt with in this chapter a group of tests which have blossomed during the last twenty years to a surprising extent, and which have been so widely used that no chapter on the measurement of personality could be complete without at least some mention of them. I am referring to the so-called 'projective techniques', which differ from the methods so far considered by taking a conscious pride in being subjective rather than objective, and which try to deal not with certain traits in isolation but with what is often called the 'total personality'. The typical result of an examination by means of one of the projective techniques is not a rating of a given trait or a given set of traits, but a personality description in which an attempt is made to convey a total impression of the person who has been tested and examined.

The actual term 'projection', as used in connexion with these tests, is something of a misnomer. Originally, the term was used by Freud to characterize the tendency to ascribe to the external world repressed mental processes which were not consciously recognized; as a result of this repression the content of these processes was supposed to be experienced as part of the outer world. We have already encountered an example of this process of projection in our description of the experiment on ratings in which people, unconscious of the fact that they themselves were stingy, 'projected' this stinginess on to others. As Freud would have put it, having repressed any knowledge of this reprehensible trait in themselves, they tended to project it outwards and found evidence for it in other people, contrary to objective fact.

While this was the original meaning of projection, the term was broadened considerably by later writers and now means simply a tendency on the part of an individual to express his thoughts, feelings, and emotions, whether conscious or unconscious, in structuring some relatively unstructured material. It is in this that the projective tests differ most from the objective tests considered hitherto. In an objective test there is a correct answer, a right and wrong way of doing things, or at least a numerical measure of success and failure. In the projective test all this vanishes. The subject may be shown a picture and asked to write a story about the contents; what situation is depicted in the picture; how the situation came about; how it will end; what will happen to the main characters, and so on. The hypothesis underlying this method is that in telling this story the subject will inevitably draw on his own hopes and fears, his own conscious and unconscious emotional complexes, and will reveal them in some way in the story. Clearly, reading back from the story to this hypothetical complex, feelings, and so on, is a very hazardous matter, and equally clearly, there is no right or wrong way of telling a story. This technique, called the Thematic Apperception test, has been used very widely, and there is some evidence that certain types of mental content at least are indeed recognizably expressed in stories told. Thus, in one experiment groups of students whose political sympathies were known, were shown photographs depicting clashes between police and strikers. The stories they told about these pictures were then scored according to the amount of sympathy shown with the police or the strikers respectively, and these scores were found to be highly correlated with the known political attitudes of the students. In other words, right wing students made up stories in which the strikers had committed various crimes and were unreasonably resisting the loyal and patriotic police forces. Students with opinions tending towards the left, on the other hand, made up stories in which the brutal and licentious police were beating down hard-working, honest men rebelling against intolerable injustices.

Another test which has become very widely known is the so-called Rorschach test. In this, a set of ink-blots, some coloured, some just black and white, is shown to the subject, who is given the following instructions. 'People see all sorts of things in these ink blots; now tell me what you see, what it might be for you, what it makes you think of.' Interpretation of the results is attempted by noting four things. First, where on the card does the subject see whatever he claims to see? Does he make use of the whole card, or does he just see a tiny detail somewhere in the corner? This is called analysis by location. Secondly, the examiner tries to find the so-called determinants of the ink blot which the subject has used in constructing a response, such as the form, the colour, the shading, and so forth. Thirdly, the examiner studies in detail the content of the response, i.e. what kind of thing did the subject see. Lastly, the popularity or originality of the response is taken into account; some people give only stereotyped replies, others see highly original and unusual things in the ink-blot.

Certain relationships have been worked out between these various categories and personality characteristics. Thus, a tendency to give responses based on the whole card rather than on parts of it is supposed to indicate a tendency towards making broad surveys of presented material, a tendency which, if exaggerated, indicates a person fond of expansive generalities and neglectful of obvious detail. Conversely, great attention to small details in the blot is supposed to denote habitual attention to the concrete and a more practical approach. Taken to extremes it is supposed to indicate pedantry and obsessions of thoroughness and cautiousness.

The tendency for responses to be dominated by colour is supposed to indicate habitual impulsiveness, eccentricity, capacity for intense emotional experiences, and in extreme cases violence and flightiness. Attention to form rather than to colour is supposed to indicate intellectual steadiness or introversion. Determination of responses by the shading characteristics of the blot is supposed to indicate a considerable degree of repression.

A whole mythology has grown up around the Rorschach test to such an extent that there are acknowledged 'Rorschach experts' in the United States who do not use any other methods, but simply study the responses given by patients to these ink-blots. Many psychiatrists, despairing of ever encompassing the complexities of neurotic behaviour in the interview situation, have grasped at the Rorschach as the proverbial man grasps at a straw, and pay considerable attention to its verdict. Unfortunately, the evidence regarding its validity indicates that if the various possible diagnoses were written on the different faces of a die, and the die then cast at random, the diagnosis arrived at by this somewhat chancy method would not be considerably inferior to that arrived at by the Rorschach expert in all his panoply. A single experiment must suffice to illustrate the truth of this observation.

In this experiment, a whole group of projection tests, including the Rorschach, was given to prospective pilots in the United States Air Force. These were followed up over a period of years, and finally two groups were selected, those who had unmistakably broken down with neurotic disorders of one kind or another, and those who had made a spectacularly good adjustment in spite of considerable stress. In other words, out of a very large group of people, two groups were chosen representing, respectively, those making the best and those making the worst kind of adjustment. Their projective test records were then taken out of their files and given to recognized experts in the field, the instructions being to say which records would predict good adjustment and which would predict poor adjustment. The experts were familiar with the criterion used, had had experience with the type of task on which they were engaged and, on the whole, regarded it as a reasonable experiment in which they could expect to be successful. In actual fact, not one of the experts succeeded in predicting with better than chance success the future performance of these airmen. They failed when using a single test; they failed when using all the tests together; and they failed when their predictions were combined in all possible ways. Only one single result was statistically significant, and that was significant in the wrong direction!

If this result is typical of experimental attempts to validate the Rorschach, then the reader may rightly ask why it has achieved such universal fame and is so widely used. The answer is a rather complex one, but it may perhaps be premised by a little story which will illustrate some of the mechanisms at work. Quite a few years ago I was studying French literature and history at the University of Dijon. Also attending courses there was a young Viennese girl, without whose presence at the University my French would now be much better than it is. Unfortunately, the ratio of men to women at this University was deplorably high and a good many French students were offering to teach this young lady French outside the official lecture hours. (Nobody offered to teach me French!) However, she was very interested in dancing, and I was fortunate enough to be allowed to take her to the official mid-term dance, the great social event of the town.

On the way to the dance, to my mortification I sprained an ankle and could only hobble to the place where the festivities were being held. I desperately searched my brain for a way of retaining the young lady's interest without having to go on to the dance-floor, and finally hit on what still seems to me a very ingenious idea. We were sitting down at a large table with a rather international group of students, and I casually mentioned that I was an expert graphologist and could tell anybody's character from their handwriting. (Of course, I knew nothing whatsoever about graphology, but a desperate situation calls for desperate remedies.) The response was literally overwhelming. Everybody pulled letters and other documents out of their pockets, demanding that I should tell the character of the people concerned. Many surreptitiously slipped away to write something down themselves in order that they might at long last learn something about their own character.

To cut a long story short, I managed to retain my companion's interest throughout the evening, and I probably did more good for the renown of graphology as an exact science than I have ever been able to do damage to it in my more professional writings. About 95 per cent of the 'clients' reported themselves amazed at the uncanny accuracy of my characterizations. I think any scientist who would have come in to challenge the claims of graphology at that time would have had a very hard time indeed. What happened?

When we write a personality characterization there are a number of factors which are acceptable to the person to whom it is meant to apply, although objectively there may be no connexion at all. In the first place, there are a number of traits which most people think they possess, although in reality they may not possess them at all. An example of this has already been given when it was pointed out that 98 per cent of the population consider that they have an above average sense of humour. If, therefore, we want to write a description which will be acceptable to almost anybody, we would merely have to introduce a sentence like 'You have a very good sense of humour'; 98 per cent of the population, at least, will agree with us that this correctly describes them and will marvel at the accuracy with which we have been able to diagnose their handwriting, or read their Rorschach, or analyse their Thematic Apperception test. Similarly, most people at times have feelings of insecurity; most people feel that their real worth is not always being appreciated and that they have sometimes been pipped at the post by people less able than they. Just fill your whole personality description with universally acceptable statements of this kind, and everyone will recognize his own picture in them.

That this is true has been experimentally demonstrated on several occasions. The experimenter gives his students an outline, say, of the beliefs of graphologists or of Rorschach experts; he then asks them to submit a sample of their handwriting, or actually to undergo the Rorschach test. He takes the records away with him and after a few days hands out to each member of the class a typed statement of what the Rorschach or the graphology specimen has revealed about each student's character. The students are given a few minutes to read through their characterizations and are then asked whether they consider these to be accurate descriptions of their own personalities. Usually ninety to ninety-five out of one hundred raise their hands. The experimenter then asks one of them to read out his own characterization. All the others then realize that each one of them has been given the same personality description and that what they all agreed to as being representative of themselves was, in fact, an overall set of traits applicable to practically everyone.

The second factor working in favour of the analysis is the vagueness and ambiguity of the terms used. The persons whose characters are being analysed almost inevitably pick out that meaning of a term or phrase which they consider applicable to themselves, forgetting all the other meanings which might not be so applicable. These two factors work particularly strongly in the case of neurotic and psychotic patients, where the Rorschach is most frequently applied. It is perfectly safe to say in every case that the patient is anxious or depressed; if he is not overtly so, then it can always be argued that some other symptom acts as a defence against his anxiety which thus remains unconscious. This policy of 'heads I win, tails you lose', which is so characteristic of psychoanalysis as a whole, has been triumphantly applied by the Rorschach experts, and serves to make any experimental examination of their tenets difficult.

We must therefore rule out entirely the personality description as being in any way an acceptable proof of the accuracy of the projective type of technique. We can see why graphologists, palmists, and other self-styled scientists are so successful in bamboozling the public, and why astrologers can still persuade the more gullible members of the public of their occult powers. The fact that clinical psychologists and psychiatrists have fallen for a similar type of trick does not argue too well for their critical acumen and scientific outlook.

If we rule out the personality characterization, what then are we left with? Frequently another method is used which has become known as the matching method. In this an attempt is made to rule out the many sources of error inherent in a simple assessment of personality description. What is done instead is this. Five patients, say, are given the Rorschach test; their records are then analysed and the personality descriptions resulting therefrom are handed over to another expert who is also given the case records of the same five people. His task, then, is to match the case records and the personality descriptions. If he succeeds in doing so, then it is argued there must be some truth in the personality description, because otherwise how could a correct matching be obtained?

Unfortunately, this method also is subject to so many sources of error as to be practically useless. It is very frequently possible to get from the record indices of a person's background, intelligence, and upbringing which may serve to identify him, but which are completely independent of the purpose of the test. Thus, in one experiment dealing with graphology, which I carried out myself, the subject was asked to copy the questions of a questionnaire which he also had to answer; the answers were then cut off and the handwriting specimen supplied to an expert. One subject in numbering the questions left out number 13 and put 12a instead. No wonder he was called 'superstitious' by the expert and recognized and correctly matched because of this single adjective.

I

Another person in a similar study of the Rorschach gave many anatomical responses and was correctly identified as a medical student, the only one in the sample of five.

What is required in studies of this kind is to have the matching done, not only by the expert in graphology, or the Rorschach, or the Thematic Apperception test, but also by a very intelligent person who is quite ignorant of the rule of interpretation of these various tests. I have found in a number of investigations that by relying entirely on external cues of the kind mentioned, such an independent observer was actually more successful in performing correct matchings than Rorschach and graphology experts! Without control experiments of this kind matching is not a safe method to use as evidence.

What has been said about the Rorschach applies in very much the same way to the other projective techniques which have been used at various times. As the reader may be interested in learning something about the kinds of methods which have been used, a few of them will be enumerated. An auditory version of the Thematic Apperception test is the so-called Tautophone test, or 'verbal summator'. This consists of a set of phonograph records on which a series of vowel patterns are repeated. These records are played to the subject at a low intensity and at some distance, so that an illusion is built up that the subject is actually listening to human speech. Instructions are to report what the man on the record is saying as soon as it can be understood. The subject's record is then analysed in some detail.

Another method, rather similar to the Thematic Apperception test, is that of story-telling, in which subjects are asked to tell stories about people or situations which are described to them, or even about musical pieces or odours which are used to stimulate fantasy. Alternatively, a story may be begun and the subject left to finish it.

A slightly more analytical type of test is the incomplete sentences test. The beginnings of some sentences are given to the subject, and he is then required to write in the endings. Such beginnings as the following are used:

My hero is ....
I worry over ....
I become disgusted with ....
I feel ashamed when ....
I fail ....
My father used to ....
The men around here ....

It is hoped in these cases that the continuation written in by the subject will reveal something about his attitudes, fears, and complexes.

Handwriting analysis is another one of the so-called projective techniques in which various characteristics of a person's handwriting are used to arrive at a personality description of him. Thus, for instance, anxiety is supposed to be shown by narrow distances between words; narrow distances between lines; lines beginning at the extreme left without a margin; slants and flourishes to the left; heavy pressure or irregular losses of pressure; and small slow writing with occasional abrupt losses of height. While there is some slight evidence that graphology may be worthy of further study, at the present time it can certainly not be considered to be either a reliable or a valid technique.

Drawing, painting, and play have all been used as projective techniques. Interpretations are made of the drawings or paintings the child makes, either quite spontaneously or of certain suggested subjects, such as a tree, or a house, or a man. Similarly, play may be analysed in a standard situation in which the subject is supplied with a number of dolls representing the father, the mother, the baby, and so on. When the child pushes the father doll's head into the toilet, for instance, this may be interpreted as denoting aggressive feelings towards the father!

What strikes one most about all these projective techniques, apart from the fact that little attempt is usually made to show that they are valid indicators of personality, and the further fact that negative results are quietly disregarded by the 'experts' making use of these techniques, is the fact that they seem to be based on a logical fallacy. The argument in

their favour is usually put something like this. Everything
we do, it is said, is determined by conscious or unconscious
mental processes of one kind or another. According to this
basic 'dynamic' theory, anything that we do may be used to
argue back to the causal factors which are responsible for
our action. If that be so, then the best techniques for diag-
nosing personality would clearly be those which will give the
greatest freedom of choice in structuring our environment.
It is for this reason that stories, paintings, play activities,
Rorschach interpretation, and so on, are considered so
valuable.

This argument appeals to many people because the major
premise of it is probably quite true. There is, of course, no
clearly convincing proof of this, but it is not unreasonable to
suppose that most of our major activities are, in fact, performed for some reason, or that this reason is in some sense
diagnostic of our personality. Because most of the activities
studied by the expert in projective techniques are caused by,
and diagnostic of, features of personality, it does not follow
that we are able to argue back from the finished product to
the causal mechanism. Perhaps I can best explain this by
means of a somewhat fanciful example.

It is often said that Jaguar sports cars are bought by sporting young men. In other words, buying a Jaguar sports car
is regarded as a kind of projection test in which the personality of our 'sporting young man' finds an outlet for its various
characteristic features in the speed, power, etc., of this particular car. Let us assume that this argument is correct.
What the projective technique expert now asserts is that we
can argue back from the purchase of a Jaguar sports car to
the possession of these various psychological features. This,
however, would logically be true only if we could say that
only sporting young men buy Jaguar cars. However, it is possible, and indeed probable, that many other types of people,
for many other types of reasons, also buy Jaguar sports cars,
thus completely invalidating the inversion of the original
argument. Thinking of the relatively limited number of
people in my acquaintance who have bought Jaguar sports

cars, I found the following reasons for the purchase: the first one was an American business man who would have preferred a more orthodox family car, but who said that the re-sale value of a sports car in the United States was very much higher than that of a British family car. Another business man bought it because, as a salesman, he had to get around the country very quickly and make long trips over to the Continent, where he found the speed invaluable. A third one bought it to impress his girl friend. Presumably, there are many more reasons why a person might buy a particular car, reasons which would make it extremely hazardous to argue back from the purchase to his personality.

But it is precisely this logically fallacious argument which underlies all the projective techniques. Because, it is said, a person of vehement emotion makes use of the colour of the Rorschach in his choice of interpretations, therefore a person who makes choice of colour in his interpretations must have strong emotions. Even if the first part of the argument were true, which it is not, the second part would by no means follow. There are many other reasons which might cause a person to be particularly conscious of the colour of the blot, and which might lead to quite different views of the subject's personality if they were taken into account.

In brief, then, the projective technique experts very much call to mind the famous story of Tartarin de Tarascon. Those familiar with Daudet's classic will remember that Tartarin was the greatest hunter in that lovely little town in the *Midi*. Unfortunately, as there were no animals to hunt in the neighbourhood, all that the Tarasconais could do when they sallied out on a bright sunny morning was to throw their caps into the air and shoot at them; the one who had the most holes in his cap was the winner. Tartarin, not content with the reputation he gained in this way, wanted to extend his field of operations and go lion-hunting in Africa. The more he talked about this, and the more vividly he described the exploits he would be going to accomplish, the more he became convinced that he had actually been there and was describing feats actually accomplished. For a long time his fellow townsmen fell under the same spell, but finally it was broken and he had to carry out his great plans in actual fact.

His adventures in Africa were many and various; the most important of them, perhaps, was that he did finally manage to shoot a blind, old, and mangy lion who had been used by the Arabs very much as a dog is used by beggars to hold a cap before passers-by to throw their coins into. This miserable animal was skinned and the hide sent back to Tarascon. When he finally arrived back, followed by a camel which he had somehow managed to acquire, he was rapturously greeted by the townsfolk, who had blown-up the fact of this one, mangy, moth-eaten skin into a glorious victory over hundreds of wily and dangerous kings of the desert.

In very much the same way, projective techniques experts started out by emphasizing the ways in which they would provide validation for their methods. Gradually they persuaded themselves, and those whom they could induce to listen to them, that the validation had already been accomplished. However, when finally the realization dawned that nothing of the kind had really happened and they were forced to try to hunt for some tangible and palpable evidence, they set out boldly, only to return with mangy, moth-eaten, and useless data, based on logical fallacies and completely lacking even the most elementary types of control necessary in this kind of work.

6

PERSONALITY AND CONDITIONING

THIS chapter deals with a series of experiments and theories due to a man who was perhaps the greatest psychologist in the brief history of that science. Pavlov himself, curiously enough, considered himself to be a physiologist and had an exceedingly low opinion of psychology altogether. Nevertheless, his great contribution, by general consent, has been to psychology and his physiological speculations have been received very coldly indeed by his fellow physiologists.

Most people have heard something of his work and the term 'conditioning', originally introduced and defined by him, has become fairly widely known, yet the true importance of his work is seldom realized, and even among psychologists many misconceptions are rife. A good rousing summary and elaboration of these misconceptions can be found in the writings of George Bernard Shaw, particularly his chapter on 'The Man of Science' in *Everybody's Political What's What*, and in *The Black Girl in Search of God*.

What Shaw has to say is interesting, although in fact it is almost complete nonsense. It is interesting because it shows clearly how a highly intelligent person can utterly misunderstand the aim and purpose of scientific experiments. This lack of understanding of scientific methodology and purpose will be startling to anyone with even a modest background in scientific discipline, but it is worth taking seriously because it is so widespread.

What then is Shaw's argument? To him Pavlov is 'the prince of pseudo-scientific simpletons'. All he did was 'to devote twenty-five years of his life to experiments on dogs, to find out in the data for his biological theory, whether their mouths watered, and if so, how much (counted in drops of saliva) when they had certain sensations, such as the sight or smell of food, the hearing of words or noises, the feeling of certain touches or the sight of certain persons or objects'. In this way he discovered that habits or 'conditioned reflexes' could be produced by association. 'This remarkable discovery', so Shaw makes Pavlov say, 'cost me twenty-five years of devoted research, during which I cut out the brains of innumerable dogs and observed their spittle by making holes in their cheeks for them to salivate, instead of through their tongues.' 'Why did you not ask me?' said the black girl. 'I could have told you in twenty-five seconds without hurting those poor dogs.' 'Your ignorance and presumption are unspeakable', Shaw makes Pavlov reply. 'The fact was known, of course, to every child, but it had never been proved experimentally in the laboratory, and therefore it was not scientifically known at all. It reached me as an unskilled conjecture; I handed it on as science.'*

We may discard in Shaw's argument his emotional obsession with Pavlov's alleged cruelty to his dogs and also the somewhat patronizing attitude Shaw takes to Pavlov's work, implying that if only he, Shaw, could have taken off a few weeks from his important work to set Pavlov on the right track, then everything might have been all right. Shorn of these red herrings and of the rhetorical bombast which Shaw uses to twist the argument, he is essentially saying this: Pav-

---

* That some of the facts of conditioning were known previous to Pavlov's work cannot, of course, be doubted. As an example we may perhaps quote from the play by the famous Spanish playwright, Lope de Vega, which was written about 1615 called *El Capellan de la Virgen*. This is the story, somewhat freely translated: 'Saint Ildefonso used to scold me and punish me lots of times. He would make me sit on the bare floor and eat with the cats of the monastery. These cats were such brutes that they took advantage of my penitence. They drove me mad stealing my choicest morsels. It did no good to chase them away. But I found a way of coping with the beasts in order to enjoy my meals when I was being punished. I put them all in a sack, and on a pitch black night took them out under an arch. First I would cough and then immediately beat the daylights out of the cats. They whined and shrieked like an infernal pipe organ. I would pause for awhile and repeat the operation – first a cough, and then a thrashing. I finally noticed that even without beating them, the beasts moaned and yelped like the very devil whenever I coughed. I then let them loose. Thereafter, whenever I had to eat off the floor, I would cast a look around. If an animal approached my food, all I had to do was to cough, and how that cat did run!'

lov discovered that by occurring at the same time, two events became linked in the mind of a person or a dog, and that in this way habits are created. This fact is known to everyone, but it took Pavlov twenty-five years to discover it. What fools these scientists be!

One might in a very similar way dismiss the contribution which Newton made to physics. The argument would run something like this: 'Objects when left unsupported tend to fall to the ground. This is known to everyone, but it took Newton twenty-five years to prove it.' Most people will be able to see the weakness in this argument; precisely the same weakness is contained in the argument as applied to Pavlov. Of course we all know that things fall to the ground, but few of us know the laws according to which they do so. We all know that habits are formed, but few of us know precisely how they are formed and how they can be broken. The fact that we have a vague acquaintance with certain natural phenomena can hardly be taken to mean that a scientific study of these phenomena is unnecessary. Common sense may vaguely recognize the sort of thing that is happening, but science requires more than that. It requires description and explanation. These two terms and the meaning which they have in science are so important that a brief discussion appears indicated.

Fundamentally, description and explanation cannot be considered to be entirely different processes. How do we explain why objects fall to the ground? We explain it in terms of the law of gravitation. How do we find the law of gravitation? We discover it by the detailed 'description' of things falling to the ground. Explanation is simply the reference back of the individual facts to general laws, laws which in turn are derived from the detailed observation and description of individual facts. Some of these individual facts may be known to common sense, and common sense may even be able to make some vague kind of generalization. However, this is never sufficient for the scientist. The common-sense descriptions are vague and couched in words rather than in numbers, and do not take account of many possible sources of error. Common-sense generalizations are vague, intuitive, and often contradictory. It is only necessary to compare the common-sense generalization 'objects tend to fall to the ground when left unsupported' with the actual formula giving the behaviour of falling bodies as $\frac{1}{2}gt^2$ to realize the tremendous difference between common-sense concepts and explanations and scientific laws and formulae.

The main difference between description and explanation, then, is essentially one of breadth and latitude; description is essentially of individual phenomena, explanation is in terms of laws derived from large numbers of individual phenomena and applicable to literally infinite numbers of further individual events. It is these laws which science is always reaching out for, and an advance in their direction is of the greatest possible importance in the development of the science. In arriving at such laws and generalizations it often becomes necessary also to invent or discover certain concepts which are of a peculiar abstract nature. Newton's gravitational force was such a concept; Pavlov's 'conditioning' is such another. These terms do not refer to actual observable objects or events, but to hypothetical constructs which make thinking about observable events easier and which may enter into our equations describing and 'explaining' the behaviour of objects, animals, or human beings.

This notion of explanation by reference to general laws should be contrasted with a rather different notion which is frequently encountered and which is particularly apposite to psychological phenomena. We often think we have 'explained' somebody's behaviour when we succeed in showing that it was in some ways similar to behaviour with which we were already intuitively familiar. Thus, we all know what it is to feel annoyed and to want to strike another person whom we consider to have been responsible for this annoyance. When we, therefore, find one person striking another, and when we further learn that this other person has annoyed the one whose aggressiveness we are trying to explain, then we feel that we have a complete explanation of the situation. 'He was annoyed', we say, 'and therefore he knocked down the chap who annoyed him.' Generally this is not in any sense an explanation of what happened. People often get annoyed without knocking down other people. Why, then, in this particular case, did the aggressive act happen, while in another case it did not? We might say that in the one case the annoyance caused was greater than the other, but if we are asked how we know this, we can only say that it must have been so, because in the one case violence ensued, while in the other case it did not. Reasoning along these lines is clearly unsatisfactory. All scientific explanation is circular, and consequently we could hardly complain in this case that the reasoning is circular. Our objection is to the fact that the circle is too narrow and small; at no point do we have general concepts and laws entering in which are defined *objectively and independently of the facts which they are called upon to explain.*

The law of gravitation is derived from the observation of falling bodies and is in turn used to explain the behaviour of falling bodies. So far the argument must be conceded to be circular, but in accounting for the speed with which a given brick – which I dropped from the roof-garden of the Maudsley on to the tennis-court – fell, I do not make use of any information obtained from this particular brick. I refer back to a general law discovered when Galileo dropped various objects from the Leaning Tower of Pisa, three hundred years ago. But in accounting for the aggressive behaviour of a given person in terms of the strength of his annoyance, I make use of his actual behaviour to indicate his degree of annoyance. There is no general law here, but simply a begging of the question. An actual example of how we can go from the popular man-in-the-street kind of psychological explanation, often called a 'mentalistic' explanation by Pavlov and his followers, to the more fundamental and scientific explanation which has become possible through the work of the Russian School, may be useful as an illustration.

You are at the dentist's, and the drill is biting into one of your molars, suddenly touching the nerve; you grip the arms of the chair as strongly as you can and you may notice a slight lessening in the pain experienced. This, at least, is the reaction of some people. Others may seek distraction by pinching their thighs, by digging their finger-nails into their hands, or even by doing complex problems in spherical trigonometry in their head. Again the common-sense explanation as always is readily forthcoming. Our attention, so it is said, is distracted from the pain, and consequently we feel it less sharply. The greater the distraction, the greater will be the lessening of the pain. How do we know which distraction is greater and which is less? Well, simply by noticing the degree to which the pain is lessened. This is simply another example of circular reasoning in which any general term is conspicuously missing. The lessening of the pain is attributed to the distracting stimulus, and the strength of the distracting stimulus is measured by the lessening in pain. There is no possibility of proving or disproving such a theory because no independent verification is possible. What, then, can we do to get away from this mentalistic interpretation and achieve a kind of theoretical formulation which is capable of generating broad generalizations and which can be submitted to the ordinary scientific processes of proof?

We may start with a perfectly general law discovered by Pavlov and called by him 'Negative Induction'. (Actually to be strictly accurate, the first mention of such a law is due to the German psychologist and physiologist Hering. It did not, however, play any considerable part in his theory and he did not use it to anything like the same systematic extent as did Pavlov.) By Negative Induction, Pavlov meant the experimental demonstrable fact that a positive stimulus applied in one part of the brain may cause the depression of activity in other parts of the brain. The kind of defining experiment which he uses to demonstrate this is as follows: A dog has been conditioned to respond with a flow of saliva to a metronome giving 120 beats a minute. By saying the dog has been 'conditioned' is meant just this: the dog, standing on a table in a sound-proof room, strapped in a harness which makes it impossible for him to jump off the table, can be presented with various stimuli by the experimenter, who is standing outside the room. He can observe the animal through a one-way screen, without being himself observed, and he can count, through an electrical transmission system, the number of drops of saliva secreted by the dog. When the experimenter sets the metronome going, the dog can be seen to glance towards the source of the sound, but does not salivate. The metronome, therefore, is what may be called a neutral stimulus, i.e. it does not produce the reflex which is being measured. After a few repetitions of the stimulus, the dog ceases even to look towards it and becomes quite inured to the presence of the metronome. Now a piece of food is presented to the dog, which has not been fed for several hours. Considerable salivation takes place. Food, then, is the unconditioned stimulus, i.e. the stimulus which without training brings forth the response or reflex. (The proper translation of Pavlov's terminology would be 'conditional' and 'unconditional' rather than 'conditioned' and 'unconditioned'. What we call a conditioned response is one which is conditional upon training; what we call an unconditioned response is one not conditional upon training. Similarly, an unconditioned stimulus is one which produces its effect without any intervening training period.)

Now the conditioning procedure commences. A number of training trials are given, in each of which the sound of the metronome is followed by feeding the dog a relatively slight amount of food. After ten or so training trials, the metronome is presented without any food, and now it is found to have acquired some of the properties of the unconditioned stimulus because now salivation follows the metronome alone. Further training trials increase the strength of the association until finally salivation to the metronome alone produces as many drops of saliva as does presentation of the food. The previously neutral stimulus, i.e. the metronome, by being paired with the unconditioned stimulus, the food, has itself become conditioned and produces the salivary reflex.

We are now in a position to follow Pavlov's experiment for Negative Induction. The dog having been conditioned to the metronome, another neutral stimulus (a buzzer, say) is now presented to it and reinforced by food each time it is presented. After a number of presentations, four drops of saliva are produced when the buzzer is applied. Now, for just one trial, the metronome stimulus is presented to the dog (together with food) and then the buzzer. This time no salivation whatsoever follows the buzzer. In other words, the presentation of a strong positive conditioned stimulus has inhibited the occurrence of the rather weaker conditioned response associated with the other stimulus. This, then, is an example of Negative Induction, or the inhibition of action in one part of the brain caused by action elsewhere. Let us now apply this conception to the dentist's chair. A strong stimulus (gripping the arms of the chair, pinching oneself, or thinking of some difficult problem) is applied by the victim at the same time as the drilling proceeds. By the law of Negative Induction we would expect this new stimulus to produce inhibition in the remainder of the brain and thus to lessen the pain of the dentist's drill.

The reader may object to this explanation as being purely anecdotal and presenting nothing but an analogy. Such an objection is perfectly reasonable and correct, but it does leave out one vital feature. We are now in a position to take our problem into the laboratory, to quantify the variables concerned, and to conduct an experimental test of the adequacy of our explanation. What we have stated is merely a hypothesis; we can now go on to prove the correctness of various deductions which can be made from this hypothesis.

First of all we must quantify the variables concerned. It is difficult to measure the pain caused by a dentist's drill – which in any case is constantly variable; it is also difficult to measure the strength of the grip exerted on the chair by the hypothetical subject of our illustration. Consequently, let us substitute for the dentist's drill a psychological torture instrument, the dolorimeter, which measures pain in units called dols. This consists essentially of a beam of light concentrated through a system of lenses on the forehead of the subject of the experiment. By increasing the amount of light, the experimenter also increases the amount of heat generated, and the illuminated spot on the subject's forehead will begin to feel warm, and finally warmth will give way to the sensation of pain. This pain can then be increased until the experimenter's research is completed, or until the subject decides that psychological research is not his cup of tea! The amount of heat produced on the subject's forehead by this instrument can be measured with great exactitude, as it is proportional to the current fed into the apparatus. So much, then, for the quantification of the pain stimulus.

The grip on the chair is easily replaced by asking the subject to grip a dynamometer. A description of this apparatus has already been given in a previous chapter; it simply consists of a steel spring which has been compressed by the subject; attached to this spring is a dial with a pointer indicating the amount of pressure exerted. This quantifies the inhibiting stimulus.

Lastly, we must somehow quantify and objectify the very subjective notion of pain. As long as we have to rely on our subject's saying 'Oh! Ouch!' or something similar whenever the stimulus begins to be painful, it can always be objected that perhaps he was not paying attention sufficiently, or that other subjective sources of error determined his reaction. Fortunately, there are several objective indices which indicate the exact moment when pain is experienced. One of these is the psycho-galvanic reflex, which is discussed at some length in a previous chapter. More useful still, in this connexion, is the so-called pupillary reflex. When pain is being inflicted on a person, his pupils get larger reflexly, and it has been shown that in the dolorimeter a slight increase in the size of the pupil can be demonstrated *just before* the subject reports the first sign of pain. In other words, we have here an objective indicator of the pain threshold of an individual at any time.

We are now ready for our experiment. The subject is sitting at a table, his forehead blackened with burnt cork; the dolorimeter is sending out its rays at relatively low intensity, so that the subject's sensations are of warmth rather than of pain. At the same time a film camera focused on his eyes is taking pictures of his pupils. Now the current in the dolorimeter is increased until the experimenter discovers that the pupil of the subject has increased in size. The experiment is then stopped, the film is developed, and the exact point determined when the subject's pupil first begins to show an increase in size. This is then correlated with the setting of the dolorimeter at that moment, and we thus obtain an estimation of the pain threshold of this subject, i.e. the precise amount of heat required to give rise to the sensation of pain. A number of readings are, of course, taken, in order to have a more reliable estimate, but they are precisely alike in the method of determination of the pain threshold.

The whole procedure is now repeated, with one important difference. This time the subject is required to pull the dynamometer at a certain rather low level of strength, say with a pull equivalent to ten pounds. Again a number of determinations of his pain threshold are made, the theory being that through Negative Induction the pain threshold should now be higher, i.e. the subject should be capable of experiencing a slightly higher degree of heat without showing the pupillary reflex indicative of pain. This is indeed found to be so, and the experiment is repeated with increasingly strong pulls on the dynamometer. A pull of ten pounds is followed by one of twenty, then of thirty, then of forty, and then of fifty pounds. Each time the theory predicts a further rise in the pain threshold of the subject, and each time such a rise is indeed observed. When the experiment is over we can plot the increase in pain threshold as a function of the amount of pull exerted on the dynamometer, or in Pavlov's words: 'the amount of Negative Induction as a function of the positive stimulus given'. In this way we can quantify the variables with which we are dealing, study the functional relationships between them, and demonstrate the adequacy of our theoretical formulations to deal with phenomena of this type. The advance over mentalistic explanation in terms of concepts like 'attention' and 'distraction' is obvious.

In the explanation which we have given of the phenomena of attention and distraction, the concept of Negative Induction has been used as if it did not allow for any further analysis. This, however, is not true. Pavlov has in fact carried the matter just a step further, but before we can discuss his theory of excitation and inhibition we must look at another set of experiments which led him to postulate the existence of these two profoundly important properties of the cortex. This will not only give us a better understanding of the experiments just described, but it will also lead over directly to an explanation of certain extremely important determinants of personality differences.

Let us go back, then, to the original conditioning experiments in which the dog becomes conditioned to neutral stimulus by pairing this with an unconditioned stimulus. What are the conditions under which the conditioned reflex is formed? In the first place, the animal must be in a good state of health; the dog that is not well, or is in active pain does not form conditioned reflexes easily or well, possibly because of Negative Induction. The dog must be in an alert state; a dog that is drowsy or sleepy may not even notice the neutral stimulus, and therefore will not be able to connect it up with the food. The dog should be hungry; in a state of repletion even food will not produce salivation, and consequently there is little hope of conditioning the neutral stimulus to do so. There should be an absence of strong disturbing stimuli, as otherwise Negative Induction would inhibit the formation of the conditioned reflex. The conditioned stimulus itself should be neither strong nor unusual; if it is either, it will itself produce Negative Induction, and therefore inhibit the formation of the conditioned reflex.

Lastly, the external stimulus which is to become the signal for a conditioned reflex must overlap in point of time with the action of the unconditioned stimulus. In other words, it is no good putting on the metronome, switching it off again, and giving the dog the food ten minutes later. Nor would it be any use giving the dog the food and then switching on the metronome.

Actually, there is an exception to this general rule. This exception, however, is a very important one, as it shows how a whole chain of conditioned reflexes can be established. Supposing we have conditioned our dog to salivate at the sound of a metronome; we now wish to make him salivate whenever we switch on a dim light in front of his eyes. It would be easy to achieve this by pairing the light and the food stimulus. It can also be done, however, without ever establishing any contact at all between the light and the food. The method is as follows: switch on the light, then switch it off again, allow a few seconds to elapse, and then put on the metronome. After a number of repetitions of this association between light and metronome, the light itself produces salivation. This is called the establishment of a secondary conditioned reflex, or a reflex of the second order, and it has proved possible to go further than this and to establish conditioned reflexes of still higher orders. Thus, we could now condition the dog to respond with salivation to a buzzer by pairing the buzzer with the light in the manner outlined above. Through the establishment of conditioned reflexes of the higher order, the network of connexions in the cortex can thus become exceedingly complex.

What stimulus may be used to produce a conditioned reflex? The list is almost endless. It could be any agent whatsoever in nature which acts on any adequate receptor organ. It could be any change in any such stimulus, i.e. increasing the loudness of a tone, or decreasing the brightness of a light. It could be any combination of stimuli, e.g. the sound of a buzzer *and* the switching on of a light. It could be the cessation of a stimulus, i.e. turning off a light or a buzzer. It could be a simple time interval; thus by feeding a dog every half an hour, the dog will, after a while, begin to salivate shortly before he is due to be fed. Of particular interest, however, is another type of stimulus known as the trace reflex, which is important because it again extends the range over which the conditioned reflex can work. Thus, a dog can become conditioned to the time elapsing from the application of the stimulus to the giving of the reward, i.e. the food. If we condition a dog to a buzzer applied at the same time as the dog is being fed, thus establishing a conditioned reflex to the buzzer, we can transform this into a trace reflex by gradually increasing the interval between sounding the buzzer and feeding the dog. Thus a trace reflex extends the possible action of conditioning in point of time, just as a secondary conditioned reflex extended it from the point of view of different stimuli.

One further method of increasing the range of conditioned reflex activity must be noted. Suppose that we condition a dog to salivate to a tone given off by a tuning-fork vibrating at a rate of a thousand vibrations a second; suppose we now sound another tuning-fork, vibrating at a rate of 800 vibrations a second; will the dog salivate? One might argue that he has been conditioned to a sound, and that therefore he should salivate. One might also argue that he has been conditioned to a particular sound and that as the sound now presented is a different one, he should not salivate. In actual fact, the dog will not stand on principle, but will compromise between these two extremes. He will salivate, but rather less than he would to the exact tone. Quite generally, the greater the similarity between the conditioned stimulus and the one applied to the dog, the greater will be the strength of the conditioned reflex. An actual example from Pavlov's work will make this clear. A dog had been conditioned to salivate when touched on the thigh. He also salivated on being touched elsewhere on the body, but the further away from the thigh the touch was applied, the less was the salivation elicited (Table 2 below will show this most clearly).

TABLE 2

hind paw	33 drops
thigh	53 drops
pelvis	45 drops
middle of trunk	39 drops
shoulder	23 drops
foreleg	21 drops
front paw	19 drops

This general rule is known as the law of *stimulus generalization*. In other words, by conditioning a particular stimulus S_1, we also simultaneously condition a whole group of stimuli S_2, S_3, S_4 .... S_n, in such a way that a conditioned reflex is obtained to any of them in proportion as they resemble the original stimulus. Without this law the whole process of conditioning would be of purely esoteric interest; exact identity of stimuli is difficult enough to produce in the laboratory, and would be quite impossible to achieve in everyday life. If, therefore, conditioning was dependent on identical repetition of stimuli, its range of application would be so small as to be minimal. Through stimulus generalizations, however, it becomes extended and applicable to everyday events.

All the phenomena discussed so far are treated by Pavlov under the general term of 'excitation'. By this he means essentially that when a stimulus is applied to any sense organ – a light shone into the eye, a sound striking the ear, a touch applied to the skin – nervous excitation is produced which travels through the central nervous system to the cortex and there interacts with any other kind of nervous excitation produced simultaneously. The precise neurological details of what happens are largely unknown and in any case do not concern us, as this is not a book on neurology. We may note, however, that there is ample neurological evidence that a passage of a nerve current through the chainwork of nerves does not leave this chain-work in its former state, but tends to modify it in certain ways. This modification appears to take place largely at the synapses, i.e. the points where different nerves or neurons meet, and where the nervous impulse is handed over from one set of neurons to another. These synapses are a kind of switching station, and the passage of the nervous impulse of a certain strength, and going in a certain direction, has certain lasting effects on the synapses which make the subsequent passage of a similar nerve impulse in the same direction easier. It is probable that these semi-permanent modifications occurring at the synapses are at the basis of the phenomena of learning, habit and conditioning, although it would almost certainly be wrong to say that a given habit is in any sense located in a particular synapse or set of synapses. The picture is very much more complicated than that, but for the purposes of this chapter enough has been said to give the reader an idea of what is meant by 'excitation' in the context of Pavlov's theory.

Pavlov's discovery of some of the facts of excitation is important enough, but far more important, novel, and fruitful have been his discoveries of a large group of other facts which complement those of excitation and go by the name of inhibition. The necessity of postulating such a complementary set of factors became obvious quite early in Pavlov's work and was forced on him by facts which have been reproduced since in many laboratories.

One type of inhibition we have already encountered. It is called 'external inhibition' by Pavlov, and its consideration was forced on him when he found that conditioned reflexes could very easily be disrupted, or even completely inhibited, by strong external stimuli. During the first years of his work he did not realize the necessity of having sound-proofed laboratories, and the many sights and sounds of the open rooms in which he tried to condition the dogs produced so many distracting stimuli that it was very difficult indeed to obtain worthwhile results. External inhibition of this type is so universal that the investigator has no difficulty in observing it. Quite on the contrary, his difficulty will be in getting rid of the disturbing effects introduced by it.

External inhibition is a fairly obvious kind of effect which one might have anticipated. The various types of internal inhibition, however, are rather less obvious. First to be discovered was the phenomenon which was to be known as that of 'extinction'. Let us suppose that a conditioned salivary response has been set up to a buzzer; let us now suppose that the buzzer is sounded a number of times without reinforcement, i.e. without being followed by the presentation of food. Gradually the number of drops of saliva secreted will diminish, until finally no saliva is produced at all. When this stage is reached, the response is said to have been *experimentally extinguished*, and superficially the situation now appears to be very much as it was before conditioning took place. The previously neutral stimulus is neutral again in the sense that it produces no reaction.

Why, it may be asked, do we require an added concept of inhibition? Would it not be simpler to say that the animal originally learned to respond with salivation owing to conditioned stimulus and that now, owing to lack of reinforcement, he has gradually forgotten to respond in this manner? There are two reasons why this view is not acceptable. In the first place, it requires an active process of extinction to make the animal 'forget'. Conditioned responses not actively extinguished are retained over periods of months and years, so that the passive process of forgetting cannot be appealed to in any reasonable manner.

What is more conclusive, however, is another phenomenon consequent upon extinction; namely, the phenomenon of *recovery*. Take again the dog who was conditioned to the sound of a buzzer and whose conditioned response was then extinguished to the point where no salivation whatsoever occurred to the buzzer. Test him again the next day, and the conditioned response will again be present as strongly as ever. It can again be extinguished, but after a reasonable pause, recovery will once more take place. The conditioned response, once it is firmly established, can be extinguished dozens of times, but it will always return, like the proverbial bad penny. These facts make it quite essential to conceive of inhibition as an active process which is produced by experimental extinction and which counteracts the effects of excitation. The experiment suggests one important characteristic of inhibition which follows inevitably from the facts given so far. If the observed behaviour of the animal is conceived of as the algebraic sum of so many units of excitation minus so many units of inhibition, then we may say that when extinction is completed the amount of inhibition present in the animal equals the amount of excitation. The next day, however, the animal, without any further training, makes a positive response again. This means that now there are more units of excitation present than of inhibition. In other words, *inhibition dissipates more quickly than excitation*. This very important property of inhibition we shall have ample opportunity of returning to later. For the time being we may put down the sequence of events in a typical extinction experiment in a figure which may serve as a graphical illustration of what we have described so far (Fig. 5*a–b*).

An important and useful extension of the concept of inhibition is that of disinhibition. We have already seen that excitation can be inhibited by a disruptive external stimulus. What would happen if such an inhibiting stimulus were to be applied to an organism already in an inhibited state, such as for instance a dog in whom the positive conditioned reflex had just been extinguished? According to the theory, the external inhibitory stimulus should inhibit the internal inhibition, and consequently the positive conditioned reflex should again be produced. This is indeed what is found. Extinguish the conditioned reflex in a dog, then shine a bright light into his eyes or ring a loud bell behind his head, and quite suddenly the extinguished reflex will emerge again and the dog will salivate to the conditioned (and extinguished) stimulus. The experimental demonstration of this inhibition adds one further argument to the acceptance of inhibition as an active process.

We have quite vaguely mentioned that the most likely locus for excitation lies in the modification of the structure of the central nervous system, particularly at the synapses. It is here also that we must look for the locus of inhibition. Little is known about the precise anatomical details, but it may be mentioned that in recent years it has been possible to detect, under the microscope, physical changes at the synaptic level corresponding to excitatory and inhibitory functions. It is impossible as yet to say whether what has been observed under the microscope is indeed the physiological basis, directly or indirectly, of the psychological concepts of excitation and inhibition. Much detailed work will be required before any such identification can be made with any confidence. However, even if this possibility should not stand up to closer scrutiny, the value of a theory such as Pavlov's would still be unimpaired. It serves to summarize existing

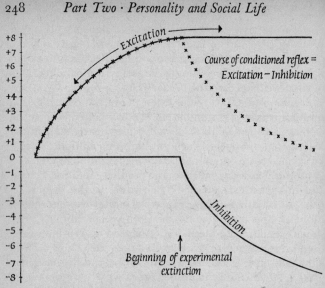

Figure 5*a*: Hypothetical course of extinction experiment in which the strength of the conditioned reflex is determined by the algebraic sum of excitation and inhibition

knowledge, it serves to direct our attention to areas of significance from the point of view of future research, and it tells us precisely what to look for in our neurological and microscopic studies. Few other theories in psychology can claim as much.

Extinction, though probably the most widely studied form of inhibition, is not the only one. Another important variety is what Pavlov has called *differential inhibition*. In this type of experimentation the animal is first conditioned to salivate to a particular stimulus, such as for instance the sight of a circle. When the animal is now shown an ellipse, we know that because of stimulus generalizations he will again salivate, although somewhat less than to the circle. If now we proceed to feed him every time he is shown the circle, but never when he is shown the ellipse, his response to the ellipse will be inhibited, so that after a while salivation will occur only after the circle is shown and never after the ellipse is shown.

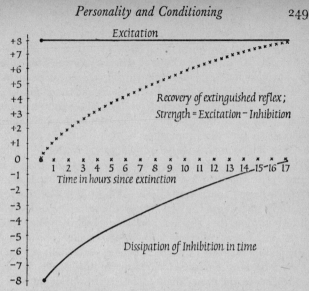

Figure 5*b*: Hypothetical course of recovery experiment in which the recovery in the strength of the conditioned reflex is determined by the dissipation of inhibition in time

This method of differential inhibition has been found important for two reasons. In the first place, by its use we can learn something about the sensory acuity of dogs. Suppose we want to know how much like a circle we can make an ellipse while still keeping the two distinct from the point of view of the observer. With human observers this presents no difficulties, as we can rely on the verbally expressed judgement of our subjects. But suppose we are interested in knowing the answer to this question in the case of dogs. In view of their limited vocabulary we cannot use the same method as with humans. What we can do, however, is to start out with a conditioning experiment contrasting a circle with a rather narrow ellipse, reinforcing the former and extinguishing the latter. When the dog, through differential inhibition, has succeeded in making this distinction, we take another ellipse, slightly rounder than the first, and extinguish the dog's responses to this. We go on in this way, substituting ellipses more and more like a circle, until finally, when we reach an ellipse, the ratio of whose height to its width is about 8 to 7, the dog's discriminatory capacity breaks down. This point, then, marks his discrimination threshold for this particular type of stimulus. We can, of course, repeat the experiment with any other type of stimulus in which we may be interested, thus exploring in considerable detail the dog's ability to make sensory discriminations.

This achievement, while important, is rather less significant from the point of view of personality study than is an observation made by Pavlov in the course of this experiment. He discovered that when the breaking point was reached, i.e. the point where the dog was unable to make the correct differentiation, the dog then had what can only be described as a kind of nervous breakdown. Its behaviour suddenly changed in a variety of ways. It became extremely agitated, started barking, refused to remain in the stand, became aggressive to the experimenter, lost previously conditioned reflexes, refused to go back into the experimental room, and even refused food, although hungry. This unusual behaviour might extend well outside the laboratory and even involve such symptoms as sexual incapacity. Quite clearly we are dealing here with a very unusual and profoundly important type of reaction. We need not concern ourselves too much with the rather semantic question of whether what Pavlov had discovered was truly an 'experimental neurosis'; the similarities certainly are striking, but we are so ignorant of what precisely is involved in human neuroses that it is at present impossible to consider Pavlov's discovery as anything more than an analogy.

His theory regarding the origin of this experimental neurosis certainly fits in with a conception of human neurosis shared by many observers. In Pavlov's view the experimental neurosis in his dogs was due to a conflict; a clash in the cortex between excitatory and inhibitory potentials elicited by the different stimuli which had acquired excitatory and inhibitory properties respectively but which at the perceptual level could no longer be distinguished from each other. Physiologically it is difficult to see precisely what such a clash between excitatory and inhibitory potentials may mean. Psychologically the theory certainly cannot be dismissed without serious consideration.

This is so particularly because in another type of situation, also involving a clash between excitatory and inhibitory potential, Pavlov was successful in also producing experimental neurosis. Certain strong and painful stimuli lead to defensive reactions on the part of the animal and inhibit the secretion of saliva and digestive activity altogether. When a stimulus of this type, say a strong electric shock, is used as a conditioning stimulus for salivation, we have a clash between the normal reflex response to strong electric shock (drying up of saliva) and the conditioning response (salivation). Under these conditions, if Pavlov's theory is right, experimental neurosis should occur again, and indeed the facts bear out the hypothesis.

In these experiments we see the first link between the laws of conditioning on the one hand and the experimental study of personality on the other. Interestingly enough, Shaw, who never seems to have got beyond the first chapter of Pavlov's book, does not even mention these discoveries, possibly because even his black girl could not have told him about them in twenty-five seconds from her abundant store of common sense.

There are one or two other varieties of inhibition, but these are rather less important and we need only mention them in passing. One of them is so-called 'Conditioned Inhibition'. It may be remembered that in elaborating a secondary conditioned reflex, the new conditioned stimulus is linked with the reflex through a conditioned stimulus previously elaborated, and that this is linked up by presenting the animal with a new stimulus, turning it off again and letting several seconds elapse before the previously conditioned stimulus is applied. This lapse of several seconds between the new and the old conditioned stimulus is absolutely essential for the elaboration of higher order conditioned reflexes. If the new stimulus is applied in conjunction with the old conditioned stimulus, i.e. with no, or only a very short, time interval between them, then the new conditioned stimulus acquires inhibitory properties and is called by Pavlov a 'conditioned inhibitor'. These inhibitory properties can be demonstrated by applying it simultaneously with some previously established conditioned stimulus. It will have the effect of inhibiting the flow of saliva well below that which would normally be forthcoming.

Another type of inhibition Pavlov has called the 'inhibition of delay'. We have already mentioned the existence of trace reflexes in which the conditioned response does not occur for a minute or two. Clearly, during this intervening period, inhibition is present and suppresses the active emergence of the reflex. That this view is the correct one can be shown by the simple device of applying a disinhibiting stimulus shortly after the conditioned stimulus has been given. The animal will immediately respond with salivation instead of waiting until the expiration of the time interval to which the trace reflex had become conditioned.

One last type of inhibition must be mentioned. This is 'inhibition with reinforcement'. As Pavlov puts it 'the cortical cells under the influence of the conditioned stimulus, always tend to pass, though sometimes very slowly, into a state of inhibition'. Pavlov was led to this belief by observing that in certain circumstances it was not necessary to extinguish the conditioned reflex along the lines described above. By simply repeating the original conditioning procedure, i.e. the presentation of the conditioned stimulus followed by the presentation of the food, a few hundred times, the animal would finally cease to show any kind of conditioned response. This was a rather mysterious effect for which Pavlov does not present a very convincing explanation. There seems to be no doubt that inhibition with reinforcement does occur, and there seems to be no doubt either as to the fact that the conditioned stimulus does acquire inhibitory properties. This can be shown in the same way as before, by pairing it with another newly elaborated conditioned stimulus and showing that it actively depresses the rate of salivation by this newly elaborated stimulus.

Having now outlined very briefly some of the facts on which Pavlov's theory of excitation and inhibition is based, we may note one further theory of his which again links it very closely with the theory of personality. While interested in the general laws of cortical behaviour, Pavlov could not help noticing very marked individual differences in the behaviour of the dogs with whom he was working. To take one example, some dogs were easy to condition but rather difficult to extinguish; others formed conditioned reflexes only with difficulty but were very quick to extinguish. These two types of dogs also differed considerably in their general behaviour, and in terms of his theory, Pavlov considered these differences due to innate properties of the central nervous systems of these dogs. His explanation ran along the following lines. In the average dog there is a certain balance between the development of excitatory and inhibitory potential. In some dogs the ratio of excitation over inhibition is relatively high, and this disturbance of the balance leads to their being easily conditioned and difficult to extinguish. Conversely, in some dogs the ratio of excitation over inhibition is unusually low; this leads to difficulties in conditioning and to easy extinction (these consequences of a disturbance in the excitation to inhibition ratio follow quite naturally from Pavlov's conception of all excitation as responsible for production of conditioned reflexes and of inhibition as being responsible for their extinction).

In the last few years of his life, Pavlov became interested in mental abnormality and spent a good deal of time in psychiatric hospitals observing symptoms of mental patients. He was struck with the apparent similarity of some of these symptoms to the behaviour difficulties of his dogs and tried to account for them in terms of his concepts of excitation and inhibition. In doing so he followed Janet, a famous French psychiatrist, by dividing neurotic patients into two great groups; on the one hand there are the hysterics, people characterized by a histrionic personality, a certain lack of moral scruple, an overt interest in sexual matters, and considerable liking for the society of other people. Symptoms appearing in the more extreme forms of hysteria are paralyses, perceptual dysfunctions such as blindness or deafness, and amnesias in which certain episodes or whole parts of the individual's life might be forgotten (many of these symptoms, the reader may recall, were observed in Mesmer's patients, and indeed nothing can demonstrate the lack of a physiological basis of these hysterical symptoms more clearly than the fact that they can be alleviated and often completely removed under hypnosis).

The other great group of disorders has been labelled in many different ways at different times; perhaps the term 'dysthymic' describes them best. People in this group are shy and unsociable in their behaviour, have strong emotions, are given to anxiety and depression, and may even develop obsessional and compulsive habits. Whereas the hysteric's symptoms find an expression which is easily observable in the outer world, those of the dysthymic are readily available only to his own introspection. Everybody can observe the paralysed limb or the functional blindness of the hysteric, but the guilt-ridden anxiety and deep depression felt by the dysthymic may often escape notice. Not all neurotics fall into one of these two groups. Indeed, the majority would probably be found in a mixed group containing symptoms characteristic of both hysterics and dysthymics. However, it is possible in a rough-and-ready manner to arrange patients in a continuum all the way from almost pure hysteria through various mixtures to the other pole of almost pure dysthymia.

Pavlov was struck very much by the fact that the symptoms of the hysterics were always of an inhibitory nature. Paralysis involved an inhibition of the motor-effector system. Anaesthesias and other perceptual dysfunctions involved an inhibition of the affector-perceptual mechanism. Amnesias involve the inhibition of part of the cortical systems subserving memory. Conversely, the symptoms of a dysthymic seemed to him to show evidence of an excess of excitatory potential and a failure to develop sufficient inhibitory potential. This hypothesis, then, based upon these observations and conjectures, runs as follows: hysterical symptoms are developed by individuals in whom the excitation-inhibition balance is tilted in the direction of excessive inhibition. Dysthymic symptoms develop in individuals in whom the excitation–inhibition balance is tilted in the direction of excessive excitation.

Pavlov never followed this work up by actually putting his theory to experimental test, but this has been done since and the results support his view. It follows from his theory that hysterics should be difficult to condition in view of the excess of inhibitory over excitatory potential, whereas dysthymics should be very easy to condition in view of their excess of over-excitative inhibitory potential. Several attempts have been made to test this deduction and results have always tended to support Pavlov's view.

The reader may be interested to know how conditioning experiments are performed in human beings. While it is possible to use the salivary reflex, this is a little messy, and other reflexes have usually been preferred. One of these is the eye-blink reflex. Here the unconditioned stimulus is a puff of air to the eyeball; the reflex associated with this stimulus is a rapid closure of the eyelids. If now the conditioned stimulus, which might be a tone delivered through a pair of earphones, is made to precede the puff of air by about half a second a number of times, then the eye-blink will become conditioned to the tone, and occur even although no puff of air is delivered to the eyeball. Another method frequently used involves the psycho-galvanic reflex, i.e. the sudden drop in the resistance of the skin to an electric current which follows any sudden stimulus and which we have described in an earlier chapter. In the experiment the subject may be shown a series of words on a screen. Every time one particular word is shown to him an electric shock is administered. Very soon the psycho-galvanic reflex which always accompanies the shock becomes associated with the word itself, which thus becomes a conditioned stimulus. Many other methods have been used, but these are probably the most popular.

The relation between ease of conditionability and neurotic symptomatology is certainly interesting, but it does not seem to find any easy application to normal personalities. The bridge is provided, however, by a well-known psychiatrist – C. G. Jung. As is well known, Jung postulated the existence of a continuum from extraversion to introversion on which all human beings could be placed. From his account, the extravert emerges as a person who values the outer world both in its material and in its immaterial aspects (possessions, riches, power, prestige); he is sociable, makes friends easily, and trusts other people. He shows outward physical activities, while the introvert's activity is mainly in the mental, intellectual sphere. He is changeable, likes new things, new people, new impressions. His emotions are easily aroused, but never very deeply. He is relatively insensitive, impersonal, experimental, materialistic, and tough-minded.

It may help the reader if this somewhat abstract description of the extravert and the introvert is rounded off with a number of examples. These are taken quite at random from real life and from fiction; the only thing they all have in common is that all are good examples of strongly introverted or extraverted people. In looking through the list the reader must remember that both extraverts and introverts can be bright or dull, stable or unstable, normal or mad. In saying that two people are extraverted there is no implication that they are alike with respect to all the various personality traits which psychologists have discovered. They are alike only with respect to those traits which form the syndrome or constellation of traits which constitutes extraversion–introversion. If the reader will thus read quickly through the two lists given below, trying to abstract what is common to all the people in each list, he may obtain an intuitive understanding of the nature of extraversion and introversion.

Let us start out, then, with a baker's dozen of introverts, followed by a similar number of extraverts. Here are the introverts: Hamlet, Sherlock Holmes, Robespierre, Savonarola, Spinoza, Cassius, John Stuart Mill, the March Hare,

Sir Stafford Cripps, Faust, Cato the Elder, Don Quixote, and Kant.

Next the team of extraverts: Mr Pickwick, Bulldog Drummond, Boswell, Mr Punch, Caliban, Dumas, Donald Duck, Churchill, Pepys, Cicero, Falstaff, and Toad of Toad Hall.

It would be wrong to credit Jung with the discovery of this personality dimension. The very terms extraversion and introversion can be found as far back as the sixteenth century, and in more modern times the English psychologist Jordan and the Austrian psychiatrist Gross both anticipated Jung in putting forward theories very similar to his. He did, however, popularize this particular typology and he made one important contribution to it. He pointed out that *hysterical disorders tend to develop in extraverted persons, whereas introverts are more liable to symptoms of the dysthymic type*. This link-up of extraversion and hysteria on the one hand and introversion and dysthymia on the other has received ample experimental support. We can, therefore, extend Pavlov's hypothesis and say that where the excitation–inhibition balance is tilted in the direction of an excess of excitation we are likely to find introverted individuals, whereas when the balance is tilted in the opposite direction we are liable to find extraverted individuals. According to this theory, then, we would expect extraverts to be difficult to condition and introverts to be easy to condition. This deduction also has received experimental support.

In extending Pavlov's theory, however, we have lost the connecting link between excitation and inhibition on the one hand and personality on the other. While his hunch that hysteria and excessive cortical inhibition were related was merely based on reasoning by analogy, at least it did provide a link between these concepts. There appears to be no direct link between inhibition and extraversion or between excitation and introversion. To provide such a link will be the last task of this chapter. In order to do so, however, we must go on a slight theoretical detour.

In Pavlov's theory of conditioning what is required for learning is mere contiguity. Pair the conditioned stimulus with the unconditioned stimulus and the mere occurrence together of these two stimuli will have the desired effect of associating the conditioned stimulus with the reflex or response. Yet this seems to run counter to a very basic principle of human learning, the so-called *law of effect*, according to which learning takes place only when a reward or a punishment is provided. The typical experiment which illustrates the law of effect is the so-called Skinner Box, named after the well-known American psychologist who first constructed it. Essentially it is a sound-proof box with a glass lid, completely empty on the inside except for a small movable lever near the bottom and a trough positioned near the lever. The hungry rat is placed into this box; in the course of its exploration it accidentally depresses the lever, which is wired to a food magazine in such a way that a food pellet is delivered into the trough. The rat quickly eats the pellet and soon learns to press the lever in order to get further pellets of food. The difference between the Skinner experiment and the Pavlovian one is this: in Skinner's experiment the learnt response, i.e. the lever pressing, is instrumental in providing the reward. In other words, the rat is rewarded for making this particular response. In the Pavlovian experiment the learnt response, i.e. salivation, is not in any way instrumental in producing the food; the animal would have obtained just as much food if it had never learned to salivate to the conditioned stimulus. Hence Skinner's type of experimentation is often referred to as 'instrumental conditioning', whereas the Pavlovian variety is often referred to as 'classical conditioning'. One other difference will be noticed: 'instrumental conditioning' deals with conditioned responses involving muscles and bones, whereas the responses involved in 'classical conditioning' make use of glandular secretions and other activities associated with the autonomic rather than with the central nervous system. In a slightly different terminology, instrumental conditioning involves voluntary activities and classical conditioning involves largely involuntary activities.

Thus there is much to be said in favour of the view which

asserts that these two types of learning are differentiated in many important ways and that the laws according to which they operate are not by any means identical. There is no point in going into this matter in any considerable detail now, but we must notice how these two different types of learning complement each other and contribute to the acquisition of different kinds of skill by the human infant as he grows up.

Roughly speaking, there are two different kinds of activities which the young child has to learn. The acquisition of the first kind of activity is relatively easily accounted for in terms of the law of effect. The young baby has to learn for instance to suck at the mother's breast. He solves this problem very much as the rat solves the problem of the Skinner's Box. Random movements of the head and mouth, perhaps guided to some extent by the mother, produce milk and a reduction in hunger, just as pressing the bar produced a pellet of food in the case of the rat. A few repetitions enable the infant to learn this series of events and to make use of this instrumental conditioning for the satisfaction of his bodily wants. This may serve as a prototype for the very many different kinds of activities in which what the individual learns benefits him directly and immediately. The law of effect ensures the success of this type of instrumental conditioning.

However, there are many activities which would be pleasurable and rewarding in themselves, but which society cannot permit. In the young child indiscriminate urination and emptying of the bowels may serve as an example. In older children and adults, we might use as an example the uncontrolled release of aggressive and sexual urges. The difficulty of controlling what is often called one's 'animal nature' is proverbial; the miracle is that it can be done at all. Instrumental conditioning and the law of effect do not help us here; quite on the contrary, they would suggest that the highly pleasant and stimulating consequences of satisfying one's aggressive and sexual urges immediately and without regard for the consequences should be learnt very firmly indeed. How then is it possible for the process of socialization to work? The answer is quite briefly that Pavlovian conditioning is required as an additional variable. Unpleasant autonomic responses such as pain and fear become conditioned in the process of training to anti-social activities, and the individual, by not indulging in these anti-social activities, secures the immediate reward of a reduction in these painful autonomic responses. This may be a difficult idea to digest at first, and an example may make the conception more readily intelligible.

Let us take the little brown bear. Like the human infant, he also has to learn two types of activities: those which are immediately beneficial to himself, and those on which society has to insist as a condition of survival. As an example of the first type of activity let us take the provision of food. The mother bear has to teach him that blueberries are good to eat. She has little difficulty in doing this; she simply picks him up by the scruff of his neck, carries him to the nearest blueberry bush, and dumps him into it. In the course of his somewhat uncoordinated efforts to get out of the bush, he accidentally squashes a few of the berries with his paws and then reflexly licks his paws. The reward provided by the taste of the blueberry juice ensures that through the agency of instrumental conditioning he will from now on assiduously hunt for blueberries.

But the mother bear has another much more difficult job. The father bear, being somewhat cannibalistically inclined, would like nothing better than to make a meal of his son. The only way in which the mother can protect him is by teaching him to climb up the nearest tree whenever she gives him the signal that father is coming. She also has to teach him to stay on the tree until she gives a signal that all is clear. Now she can hardly explain these things to the little bear, and she encounters the additional difficulty that he finds life on the ground much more amusing than going up a tree and staying there, very bored and very much against his will.

However, being, like most animals, a good psychologist, she sets about her task very much according to the dictates of Pavlovian conditioning. Picking up the little brown bear by the scruff of his neck, she takes him to the nearest tree, honks very loudly, and then gives him a painful bite on his undercarriage. The little brown bear, surprised and hurt, seeks to escape from his suddenly aggressive mother and shins up the tree. After a while he tries to come down again, but the mother rears up and gives him another painful nip to send him upwards again. Finally, she gives two honks to indicate that the trial is over and that the little bear may come down again. The whole procedure is repeated a number of times, until finally the little bear has learnt his lesson and the vigilance of the mother can protect him from the baser instincts of his father. In fact, so well has he learnt his lesson that when the mother bear finally decides that he is old enough to fend for himself, she simply sends him up the tree by giving the warning signal and then goes away and leaves him for good. He is so well conditioned not to come down without her permission that he will stay on the tree for hours, even days, until hunger pains finally drive him down.

What has happened? By pairing the warning signal (the conditioned stimulus) with the painful bite on his backside (the unconditioned stimulus), the mother has set up a conditioned reflex in which the warning signal produces a powerful fear reaction on the part of the little bear; a fear reaction which can be relieved only by the action to which he has become conditioned, namely that of shinning up the tree. Thus the conditioned autonomic response becomes, as it were, an intermediary in the law of effect; the reward which the young bear gets for obeying the social laws of his clan is a reduction in anxiety rather than any external reward. Much the same happens when he is on top of the tree and wants to come down before having received the all-clear. As he begins to go down the tree, the stimuli he encounters have become conditioned in his past experience to the powerful and painful bite received from his mother; consequently, the conditioned response, i.e. fear or anxiety, become stronger and stronger until finally he climbs upwards again in order to relieve his anxiety.

This account of the behaviour of the little brown bear may appear a little fanciful, but there is good experimental evidence in favour of the major theoretical points made here. Admittedly, the experiments were carried out on rats rather than on bears (even American departments are seldom well enough equipped to be able to support a few hundred bears in order to allow graduate students to complete their Ph.D. theses). Nevertheless, the general outline of what has been said is probably accurate enough to stand critical scrutiny.

You thus arrive at the point where we consider conditioning the essential substratum of the socialization process. Where the religious person talks about conscience as restraining the evil-doer, the psychologist would point to the conditioning process as the agent responsible for the presence of the conscience in the mind of the evil-doer. In a similar way, where Freud attributes unselfish and ethical actions to a *super-ego* derived from parental teaching and example, the psychologist would consider Pavlovian conditioning as the method by means of which this goal is reached. There is, in principle, no issue between the religious, the Freudian, and the Pavlovian approaches. The main difference is that neither the Freudian nor the religious approach provides an experimentally testable hypothesis to tell us the precise method by means of which the final result of socialization is brought about. Perhaps Shaw's black girl could have elaborated a testable theory in twenty-five seconds, but her rather aggressive behaviour, denoting a strongly hysterical and extraverted personality, makes one doubt whether she had much of a notion of the meaning of the socialization process.

We are now in a position to link up, as we promised to do, the conditioning process on the one hand and extraversion–introversion on the other. We start out with the known fact that there are marked individual differences in the excitation–inhibition balance, differences which manifest themselves in different degrees of conditionability. Given that some individuals are easier to condition than others, and assuming for the moment that all individuals are subjected to a similar process of socialization, it would follow from our general theory that those who are most difficult to condition should be relatively under-socialized, while those who are relatively easy to condition would be, comparatively speaking, over-socialized. Over-socialization and introversion should therefore, in terms of our theory, go together, as should under-socialization and extraversion. Is this really so? The experimental evidence is not as extensive as one might wish, but as far as it goes it definitely supports this view. Let us look again at our neurotic extraverts and introverts, the hysterical and dysthymic groups respectively, because in them we see to an exaggerated extent certain qualities characteristic of extraverts and introverts altogether. Close to the hysterics, but even more extremely extraverted according to their test performances, are the so-called psychopaths: these are people characterized by an almost complete absence of social responsibility. Many of them are pathological liars who tell lies almost by preference and regardless of the certainty of being found out. Others commit thefts without regard for the inevitable consequences; others again go absent without leave or contravene other rules and regulations pointlessly and in spite of the certainty of being found out and punished. Psychopaths generally seem almost completely lacking in this conscience or super-ego, which is so essential in making civilized life possible. Typically enough they also as a group are the most difficult of all to condition and the most strongly extraverted in terms of experimental tests.

Hysterics also tend to share the lack of a strong 'inner light', as it were, which serves them as a guide to action. They are easily swayed by momentary passions, by bad companions, or by the standards of any small group of which they happen to be members; while less extreme than psychopaths, they also may rightly be considered under-socialized.

Dysthymic groups show precisely opposite characteristics. Where hysterics and psychopaths try to 'get away with it' on every conceivable occasion, and even often under conditions where detection is inevitable, the typical dysthymic not only does not indulge in anti-social activities, but tends to worry excessively over the very slightest infringement of the social code which most people would dismiss with a shrug of the shoulders. Where the psychopath might seduce his girl-friend without a qualm, or commit bigamy in order to gain his immediate ends, the typical dysthymic would worry endlessly over ethical issues involved in a single innocent kiss. Even relatively mild peccadilloes may lead him to quite excessive methods of atonement, such as compulsive hand-washing a hundred times a day to cleanse himself of some relatively unimportant misdoing. Small wonder, then, that what characterizes the extravert most is to prefer action to thought, whereas to the typical introvert, thought is preferable to action. The stress of the socialization process is largely on the inhibition of action; the abandoning of aggressive or sexual activities of one kind or another. Consequently, the introvert – the over-socialized person, who has learnt his lesson too well – tends to generalize this rule to all activity and prefers to seek salvation in his own thinking. Conversely, the typical extravert, not having heeded the lesson of the socialization process, prefers the immediate satisfaction of his impulses through action.

This, then, is the general picture emerging from Pavlovian theory and modern research. There are many i's to dot and t's to cross before we can feel certain about the exact relationships described here in broad detail, but it does not seem likely that the main outline of the picture will require any major revision. In any case, the substance of the chapter will serve to show how personality measurement can be geared to fundamental psychological theories which may be far away from the more obvious type of personality test described in the last chapter. It is in the further advance of such more fundamental measurement that the greatest promise for an increase in our knowledge of personality would seem to lie.

7

POLITICS AND PERSONALITY

THERE are two contradictory points of view widely held
among many people nowadays, and frequently even held by
the same people at different times. Some believe that a person's political opinions are the results of objective experiences, of thought, and of definite decision; they are consciously arrived at after a thorough weighing of the evidence
and are modifiable by logical argument and factual proof.
The opposite view is that political opinions are the reflec-
tions of personality, determined largely by irrational motives
of one kind or another, not amenable to logical argument or
factual disproof, and altogether an expression of personality
rather than a reaction to external reality. Many people feel
that the former of these two views adequately characterizes
the voting behaviour of themselves and their friends; the
second type of motivation may be recognized more easily in
those voting for the opposite camp.

Among those who usually, or at least at certain times,
hold the view that personality factors are at least partly responsible for political views and social attitudes, there is
again a good deal of agreement on what are the basic traits
which are responsible for a person's choice of political party.
Their political opponents, so they declare, are driven to their
opinions by their lack of intelligence, their emotional instability, and their chronic selfishness, which makes them
put class before country; conversely, those who think like
themselves are characterized by high intelligence, emotional
stability of an outstanding quality, and an imperturbable
integrity which makes them scorn prizes held out by rival
politicians.

Unlikely as such beliefs might appear, they have given
rise to a considerable amount of experimental work in the
social sciences, particularly in the United States. Quite a
large number of researches have been conducted on the

hypothesis that Socialists, who form a relatively small minority group in America, are lacking in emotional stability. The results, by and large, have failed to disclose any such differences between Socialists and members of the Democratic and Republican parties respectively. Other studies, involving the measurement of intelligence, have shown a slight degree of superiority of the more radical as opposed to the more conservative; this superiority, however, seems to have been restricted to University students in the 1930's and does not seem to apply to less highly selected samples at different times during this century. Altogether, it may be said that attempts, until quite recently, to link up personality and political beliefs have been restricted to the contrast between conservative and radical opinions and have nearly always resulted in failure. It is interesting to inquire into the reasons for this failure and to show how, by more determined application of the scientific method, success can be achieved in this field also.

We may begin by taking account of two contradictory types of statement which are frequently made and which, being partial in their application, impede rather than further the scientific study of social and psychological issues. The first point of view to be mentioned here is one frequently held by the more old-fashioned social scientists in this country, by many politicians, and, implicitly at least, by many groups of people who have only a tangential relation to social science, such as historians, economists, and sociologists. This point of view might best be expressed in the following form. Empirical investigations in the social sciences have a much lower and much less important status than have philosophical arguments, scholarly reviews of opinions held by well-known writers (preferably dead), and argumentations about possible causes of historical events. Factual studies are looked upon with distaste because they force a reconsideration of cherished values and beliefs, and because they do not usually fall in line with patterns of thought formed many years ago.

This vague distaste for empirical work, which is quite

common in this country, has recently found a somewhat more virulent expression in the United States. The 83rd Congress established in 1953 a special committee to investigate Tax Exempt Foundations, under the chairmanship of Mr Rees. This committee collected evidence on the support given by the Foundations to Social Science Research, and made a special point of the criticism of empirical investigations. The views expressed are so illogical and unclear that it is difficult to know precisely what is implied. The type of insinuation made is exemplified by statements like the following: 'It may not have occurred to (foundation) trustees that the power to produce data in volume might stimulate others to use it in an undisciplined fashion without first checking it against principles discovered through the deductive process.' If this statement means anything – a point which is, of course, debatable – it means that facts should not be discovered if they disagree with principles discovered through the deductive process, i.e. if they disagree with the *a priori* opinions of a person, or group of persons, in charge of an inquiry, or conducting a Congressional Committee investigation. This type of argument is, of course, quite common in Russia (and in Hitlerite Germany), where either no factual investigations in the social sciences are carried out at all, or where the investigator is told beforehand in no uncertain terms what kind of results are expected from him. It is, however, a little disturbing to find such views expressed in what is, effectively, an agency of the Congress of a democratic nation.

It is easy to see why such distrust of factual empirical research in the Social Sciences should arise among politicians and others who have an axe to grind. Their success and their very existence are predicated upon their ability to persuade a large enough number of the population that the particular beliefs they hold, and the panaceas they advocate, are in some way advantageous to the community as a whole. They are opposed by other politicians asserting precisely the opposite, and, with the usual swing of the pendulum, both sides in due course have their intoxicating draught of power given to

them by the electorate. They are well used to this particular
type of game and, by and large, have no ill feelings towards
their opponents.

The matter immediately becomes charged with emotion,
however, when the social scientist appears and says, 'Here
we have two opposite sets of hypotheses; let us not waste
time in *talking* about which is nearer the truth, but let us
and carry out an *experiment* to see which hypothesis is, in
fact, nearer the truth.' Such a proposal is almost invariably
considered by the politician as a threat to his particular
position in society. He has no means himself of carrying out
an investigation of this kind and, quite usually, he will even
be incapable of understanding the results if they are presented to him. He knows how to deal with a fellow politician
and with arguments he has heard a thousand times before,
but the party line will give him little support against the up-
start social scientist who takes these theories seriously and
actually wants to find out whether they work or not!

While it is thus easy to see why politicians should be
somewhat chary of employing the empirical approach, it is
difficult to see why the man in the street should have any
objections against it. As the President of the Social Science
Research Council has put it: 'To approach a problem empirically is to say: "Let's have a look at the record." To
apply the empirical method is to try to get at the facts.
Where feasible, counting and measuring and testing are
undertaken. There is nothing necessarily technical about
empirical methods and there is no simple distinctive empirical method as such. Congressional investigating committees normally follow an empirical approach. To imply
something immoral about using an empirical method of inquiry is like implying that it is evil to use syntax.' The alternative to an empirical study is speculation, aimless debate,
and unsupported theorizing. As John Locke, the famous
British philosopher, often called the father of empiricism,
said to a friend who mentioned to him some rationalistic
speculations by a Continental philosopher, 'You and I have
had enough of this kind of fiddling'.

In spite of the Rees Committee, then, we may conclude that the social sciences, if they are to be anything at all except idle speculation and arid, dry-as-dust scholasticism, must have an empirical foundation; in other words, they must be securely founded on ascertained facts. But is this enough? Many social scientists seem to feel that the answer here is 'Yes', and it is this second belief which I think requires even more careful analysis and refutation than the first. It is less obviously nonsensical but, none the less, it is probably equally fatal to the development of a true science of personality and social life. The reason for this belief is a very simple one. Science is defined as *systematic* knowledge, not just as knowledge, and while the empirical content is certainly an absolutely essential part of it, the system, or organization, of this empirical content is at least equally important. What the scientist is looking for is not a large number of disconnected facts; it is rules or laws which bind together large groups of facts and make it possible, once a law is known, to deduce these facts from it. Results have been published in many different countries of thousands of different Gallup Polls on all sorts of issues. These results provide a considerable amount of empirical content, but they do not make Gallup Polling into a science. Only if it were possible to find some general rule or law running through all these results, and making it possible to deduce the individual results from the general law, would all this work make a genuine contribution to science.

A simple example may illustrate this point. Hundreds of thousands of stars have been discovered in the sky. All of these are approximately circular in appearance, and there is little doubt, therefore, that they are, in fact, spherical, or very nearly so. Let us suppose that a new star has been discovered. If we were asked to give an opinion as to its shape, what would our answer be? Presumably, very few people would fail to predict that this newly discovered star would also be spherical, and the most common reason given for this prediction would be that in the past all stars have been observed to be spherical, and that the new one, presumably, would not be an exception. This kind of argument does not lack empirical content (after all, a large number of stars have actually been observed in the past), but nevertheless it is not a scientific argument. The scientist, when asked his opinion, would make the same prediction as the man-in-the-street, but he would make it on quite different grounds. He would argue that, according to Newtonian laws of physics, any large body made up of physical substances would, in the course of time, assume a spherical shape. He would be able to make this prediction even if no other stars had ever been seen before, by a simple deduction from certain known laws. It is the existence of such laws and the possibility of going deductively from the law to the individual fact, and inductively from a set of facts to a given law, that characterizes science as opposed to the mere collection of isolated and unrelated data.

Empirical work is at the foundation of science, but empirical research is not enough. It must be guided by and lead to theories of general significance and laws of deductive power. Only under these conditions can we talk about a field of study as being a science. As T. H. Huxley once put this point in his pithy way, 'Those who refuse to go beyond fact rarely get as far as fact; and anyone who has studied the history of science knows that almost every great step therein has been made by the anticipation of nature; that is, by the invention of a hypothesis which, though verifiable, often had little foundation to start with; and not infrequently, in spite of a long career of usefulness, turned out to be wholly erroneous in the long run.'

If this is so, and scientists, logicians, and philosophers of science are in full agreement that these are some of the essential characteristics of scientific endeavour, can we consider psychology and the social sciences as being truly scientific? As a matter of fact, have they reached this stage, or are they still in a pre-scientific stage of gathering isolated facts and other unconsidered trifles? The answer, I think, must be that some parts of psychology have already passed into the scientific stage, others are still in a pre-scientific stage. To those who would doubt the first part of this statement I would like to offer the remainder of this chapter as an example of the possibility of achieving deduction from general laws and empirical verification of such deductions, which we have just seen to constitute the essence of science.

The first thing that strikes us when we look at the field of social attitudes, political behaviour, party strife, and voting is that none of it appears to be innate in any sense, but that all of it is due to some form of learning. However much it may appear at certain moments as if the old jingle were true, and 'Every boy and every girl that's born into this world alive is either a little radical or else a little conservative', yet in our heart of hearts we know that this is not so. Just imagine the reactions of an Eskimo to an election campaign largely waged in terms of the nationalization of the steel industry, or that of a Zulu, whose opinions are sought on the relative importance of Federal as opposed to State rights! We learn our politics as we learn our language, and if we wish to know anything about political attitudes, then we should be able to turn to the laws of learning in our efforts for further clarification.

When we do this, we see that there appear to be two laws rather than one. These two laws have been recognized for a very long time indeed, although it is only in quite recent years that they have been stated in a sufficiently clear form to be amenable to experimentation. We might call these laws the law of hedonism and the law of association. The law of association simply states that we learn that A is followed by B because in the past A and B have always, or often, been associated with each other. The law of hedonism, on the other hand, maintains that we learn things because they have some effect on our well-being. Simple association is not enough; it must be followed by some kind of reward or punishment.

These two views may be summarized in terms of two experiments. To characterize the associationist view we may have recourse to Pavlov's dogs, which we discussed in a previous chapter. The simple association, repeated over a number of times, of bell and meat causes the dog to learn that the bell is followed by the meat, and to respond with salivation to the sound of the bell alone. In the Skinner box, on the other hand, also mentioned in a previous chapter, the rat produces a pellet of food by accidentally striking a bar in its cage which is connected with a food reservoir; the relief from hunger produced by this action causes the rat to learn this particular movement whenever food is desired. These two different types of modification of the animals' nervous system as a result of experience may be called conditioning and learning respectively.

We must now inquire into the consequences in the political field which may be deduced from our knowledge of these two different processes. Let us begin by noting certain facts about the society in which we grew up, facts which every youngster learns in the course of his early life. The first fact we must know is that people differ with respect to their social status. By status we mean such things as the amount of money a man earns, the kind of education he has had, or which he can afford for his children, the kind of house he lives in, and the part of the town in which he lives, his accent, the kind of people he mixes with, and so on and so forth. At the one extreme we have the millionaire, who lives in a huge house, in an exclusive quarter of the town, employs several maids and butlers to look after him, runs several cars, sends his children to Eton and Oxford, sports an old school tie, and speaks with what everybody recognizes as a 'superior' type of accent. At the other end we have a down-and-out, dozing on a bench in the Embankment, with no one to look after him, shabby clothes, little food, and an accent almost unintelligible to anyone not familiar with the particular portion of the country he comes from. Between these extremes there are all sorts of gradations, but, by and large, there is little difficulty in fitting people along a continuum from the one to the other.

For practical purposes it is often useful to group people into a number of status groups. There are many such classifications. Typical of them is that used by the Gallup Poll.

Their top, or Av+ group, is characterized as follows: 'Well-to-do men (or their wives) working in the higher professions, e.g. wealthier chartered accountants, lawyers, clergymen, doctors, professors, or in higher ranks of business, e.g. owners, directors, senior members of large businesses. Almost invariably they will have a telephone, car, and some domestic help.

'Av: Middle and upper middle class: Professional workers not in the top category. Salaried clerical workers such as bank clerks: qualified teachers: owners and managers of large shops: supervisory grades in factories who are not manual workers: farmers, unless their farm is very big when they will be Av+. Many will have a telephone, a car, or employ a "char".

'Av—: Lower middle and working class: by far the biggest group. Manual workers, shop assistants, cinema attendants, clerks, agents.

'Group D: Very poor: people without regular jobs or unskilled labourers or living solely on Old Age Pension. Housing will be poor. They can only afford necessities.'

Many psychological features are correlated with this division of people into different status groups. The average intelligence quotient of the Av+ men (but not necessarily their wives) would be 140–150; that of the Av group would be in the neighbourhood of 120; that of the Av— group would be slightly below 100; and that of Group D would be around 90. I have discussed such relationships in some detail in *Uses and Abuses of Psychology* and will not do so again here. Suffice it to stress that the concept of status is not purely defined in terms of positions, but is also related to psychological concepts.

In addition to status, which is an objective fact which can easily be ascertained with regard to any particular person, we have another concept which is much more subjective in character, but which is also of considerable importance in our analysis. That is the concept of social class. Whatever their objective status may be, people in the democratic countries tend to think of society as being grouped into various classes, and they tend to consider themselves as belonging to one or other of them. This knowledge and this belief can be seen to develop quite early in the lives of our children; by the time they leave school they are as well acquainted with the concepts of class structure as are their parents. While the concept of class is subjectively dependent on each individual's private opinions and beliefs, it does, in fact, have a strong factual relation to social status. The Av+ group tends to think of itself as upper and upper-middle class; the Av group tends to think of itself as middle class; while the Av— group, and more particularly the very poor, tend to think of themselves as working class. The relationship between social status and social class is shown below in Table 3. Figures were obtained on a national sample of about 9,000 people by the British Institute of Public Opinion. It will be seen that social class (as estimated in each case by the person interviewed for himself) and social status (as estimated by the interviewer after talking to the people concerned) do show considerable agreement. In actual fact this Table underestimates the amount of agreement which exists between the two concepts because the interviewer's estimate of a person's status is known to be far from completely reliable. When correction is made for that, agreement becomes considerably higher than is shown in the Table.

TABLE 3

Relationship Between Social Status and Social Class

	Class				
Status	Upper and upper middle	Middle	Lower middle	Working	Don't know
		(per cent)			
Av +	57	36	4	3	—
Av	16	58	13	10	3
Av —	2	20	20	55	3
Very poor	—	7	8	76	11

We thus start our analysis with two widely known and universally accepted facts, namely, that people differ with respect to status and that they are aware of these status differences, and as a consequence of them regard themselves as belonging to certain social classes. We may go on by noting that certain political issues may arise which will further the ends of people belonging to one social class and be opposed to the interests of people belonging to another social class. Indeed, it would be difficult to find many issues which do not in some way fall into this category. This well-known truth is often put in the form of an analogy by referring to a national cake; however it is sliced, some people will receive more than others and the interests of one group will almost infallibly be opposed to the interests of another group. Under these conditions, it seems almost inevitable that political groups should arise to represent these respective interests, and, indeed, as is well known, groups of parties have arisen in all the democratic countries which represent this difference of interests. By long-established custom those parties representing the interests of the high status groups are called conservative parties, or parties of the right, while those parties representing the interests of the low status groups are called radical parties, or parties of the left.

This bifurcation represents an inevitable consequence of the law of learning and can be directly deduced from it. A radical government, acting so as to further the interests of the low-status groups, will thereby benefit members of the low status groups, and thus reward them for having voted for this particular party. Conversely, a conservative government acting so as to further the interests of the high-status groups will thereby benefit members of the high status groups, and thus reward them for having voted for this particular party. A rat in a box which receives food when it presses a red lever and an electric shock when it presses a blue lever will very soon press the one and avoid the other. Similarly, voters who receive benefits from one government and have their status position lowered by another government will soon learn to vote in accordance with their interests. There is nothing very mysterious or difficult about this deduction, and, indeed, the general principle is fairly

universally accepted. Table 4 shows the relationship between
social status and political attitude in Great Britain; again, it
must be remembered that the relationship would be even
closer if estimates of social status were more reliable. Even
as the figures stand, however, there can be little doubt that
in a representative sample of the population there is a close
relationship between voting and social status. There is a
similar close relationship between social class and voting behaviour. Of those who consider themselves to be upper- or
upper middle-class, 79 per cent vote Conservative, whereas
only 20 per cent who consider themselves to be working
class do so. Only 5 per cent of the self-styled upper class
group vote Labour, whereas over 90 per cent of those who
consider themselves working- or lower middle-class do so.

TABLE 4

Relationships Between Social Status and Political Attitude

Status	Conser-vative	Labour	Liberal	Other	Don't Know	Total Number
			(per cent)			
Av +	77	8	11	—	3	447
Av	63	16	12	1	10	1,855
Av −	32	47	9	1	11	4,988
Very Poor	20	52	9	1	18	1,621
Total Number	3,411	3,545	894	60	1,001	8,911

It might be asked why the relationship is not perfect. If
our generalization is true and if the law is as stated, then
surely all working-class people should vote Labour, and all
middle-class people Conservative. This is not so for a number
of reasons. In the first place, in our teaching a rat to press
one bar and avoid another, a large number of repetitions are
required of bar pressing behaviour. Conversely, the number
of elections in which a person takes part is relatively limited;
few people voting this year have voted in more than four or
five previous elections. It follows that the amount of reinforcement received is relatively small, and consequently a
good deal of random behaviour is to be expected.

Furthermore, in the case of the rat experiment, the reward is inevitable and follows immediately. In the case of political actions, the reward is not infallible and may not follow immediately. At a given time the working class may be better off under a Labour government than they would be under a Conservative government at the same time, yet because of world conditions outside the control of any British government, their absolute well-being might be less than that which they enjoyed under a previous Conservative government. Under those conditions, the reinforcement picture is rather confused, and one would not expect a perfect class alignment with voting behaviour.

Another point that arises is that voting behaviour may be used to express feelings and emotions irrelevant to the issues concerned. Thus, the son of a harsh and inconsiderate Conservative father may vote Labour, not because he feels any affinity for the Socialist faith, but simply because he wants to annoy his father. Conversely, the son of an equally harsh Socialist father may vote Conservative for the same reason. Causes of this type are not in any sense systematic and will tend in the long run to cancel out. They do, however, serve to make the correspondence between social class and status, on the one hand, and voting behaviour on the other, to be in less than perfect agreement.

It will now be clear why we would not expect, and, indeed, do not find any kind of correlation between personality and political behaviour as far as the right–left, or conservative–radical continuum is concerned. It may be possible that very stupid people are slower to learn where their real interests lie, thus perhaps voting against the party which would, in fact, benefit them most. It is also possible that some neurotic and emotionally unstable individuals may, for obscure and irrational reasons, be opposed to the party which best embodies their interests. There may be many other individual features which in any given case make a particular person react in ways which are contrary to the generalization which we have established. However, these exceptions are not of a systematic kind; the stupid working-class person who might vote against his interests would be balanced by the stupid middle-class person voting against his interests, and thus there would be no correlation between intelligence and tendency to vote for one party rather than another. Thus, while these individual tendencies make the law less than perfectly applicable, they do not produce any kind of systematic tendencies.

One word should perhaps be said about the position in the United States at the moment. It is often said there that the country is relatively free from conceptions of social class, and that the great political parties are not divided as European parties are on any class basis. Nothing could be further from the truth. Numerous studies have shown that Americans consider themselves members of the working-class or the middle-class to pretty much the same extent as do people in England, France, or Germany. It has also been found that the political tie-up with class and status is quite strong in the United States also. By and large, low-status groups and people who consider themselves working-class tend to vote for the Democrats, while higher-status groups and people who consider themselves middle-class tend to vote for the Republicans. The relationship between class and status, on the one hand, and voting behaviour on the other, is not quite as strong as it is in European countries, but it has been increasing in strength over the years, and there is every reason to believe that in a few years the party structure and party alignment in the United States will in every way duplicate that observed over here.

We have now dealt in some detail with the consequences to be expected from the hedonistic law of learning; we must now consider the consequences to be derived through the associationist law of conditioning. In doing this we must have recourse to the argument already presented in an earlier chapter. There it will be remembered it was shown that the differences in a person's innate capacity to form conditioned reflexes easily and quickly were responsible for marked individual differences in temperament, particularly along the extraversion–introversion continuum. We also saw that the amount of socialization which a given person succeeded in requiring was, to a great extent, determined by his 'conditionability'. Thus, a person in whom conditioned reflexes were formed easily and quickly will tend to become 'over-socialized' in comparison with the average, but a person who forms conditioned reflexes slowly and with difficulty will tend to become 'under-socialized' in comparison with the average.

In the fields of social behaviour and social attitudes the two fields in which socialization should most clearly show itself are the fields of sexual and aggressive behaviour. It is here that we have the most obvious conflict between very strong and powerful individual wishes and desires, and equally strong and powerful social prohibitions and restrictions. Much the greater part of the process of socialization may be said to consist in the erection of barriers to the immediate satisfaction of aggressive and sexual impulses. These barriers are absolutely essential if society is to survive and in some form they exist even in the most primitive type of society. Yet, however essential they may be to society, they are irksome and annoying to the individual, who finds himself thwarted in the expression of what, to him, are perfectly natural wishes and desires. Thus, here is a potential area of great conflict, and it is here, if anywhere, that we would expect the most marked contrast between the extravert and the introvert; the easily conditioned and the poorly conditioned. How would this conflict show itself in the field of social attitudes and political behaviour?

Our expectation follows directly from what has been said so far. We would expect to find a continuum ranging from the introverted type of attitude to the extraverted type of attitude, from the over-socialized to the under-socialized. On the one side we would expect a strong insistence on barriers of one kind or another to the free expression of sexual and aggressive impulses. These barriers might be of a religious nature or an ethical nature, but what would be common to all the beliefs and attitudes on this side would be a desire to restrict the open expression of socially unacceptable behaviour. On the other side of the continuum, we would expect to find the opposite, that is to say, a relatively open demand for a relaxation of prohibitions, an overt desire for the direct expression of sexual and aggressive urges, and the denigration of religious and ethical standards felt to stand in the way of such open manifestations. On the one hand then, we should find a tender-minded regard for conventions and rules protecting society from the more biological drives of human nature; on the other hand, we should find a tough-minded desire to over-ride these conventions and seek direct expression of these animal instincts.

Thus, our hypothesis would lead us to predict the existence, in addition to our conservative–radical continuum, of a tough-minded versus tender-minded continuum, quite unrelated to that of radicalism and conservatism, and therefore cutting clean across the more widely known and popular political schism. Before we turn to the evidence to see whether, in fact, this prediction is borne out, let us first of all look briefly at the structure of political groupings and parties in this country. As Mr Disraeli said: 'Party is organized opinion', and a study of attitude organization as embodied in the major parties will therefore be relevant to our problem.

In considering the mutual relations between the parties, we find that two apparently contradictory theories are quite widely held. The main groups in this country, Conservatives, Socialists, Liberals, Communists, and Fascists, are often thought to be arranged along a continuum from left to right, so that the Communists are supposed to lie at the extreme left, the Socialists a little nearer the centre, the Liberals in the middle, the Conservatives to the right, and Fascists at the extreme right. This theory is represented graphically in Figure 6a.

On the other hand, many people find this arrangement quite unconvincing. They argue that Communists and Fascists have something in common which sets them off against the democratic parties, and that to put them at opposite ends of a continuum is manifestly absurd. Conse-

quently, it is argued, we should really have a different kind
of continuum, at the one end of which we would put Communists and Fascists, at the other end the democratic
parties. Sometimes the argument is taken a little further,

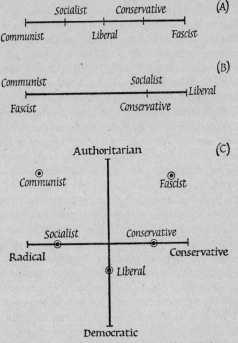

Figure 6: Diagrammatic representation of three
hypotheses regarding the structure of attitudes as
mirrored in the relative positions of different political parties

and it is said that the democratic parties also can be separated out on this continuum, with the Liberals being at the
opposite extreme to the Communists and Fascists, and the
Socialists and Conservatives a little less strongly opposed to
the tenets of these two authoritarian parties. This hypothesis
is shown diagrammatically in Figure 6b.

There is no doubt that most people would find some degree of truth in both these hypotheses, contradictory to each other as they may appear. This contradiction can easily be resolved, however, if we decide that what is needed is not one dimension or continuum but two, placed at right angles to each other. One of these two continua, the radical–conservative one, would sort out the parties in line from the Communist at the left to the Fascist at the right; the other continuum, which we may perhaps call the authoritarian–democratic continuum, would lie at right angles to the first and sort the parties out with the Communists and Fascists at the authoritarian end and the Liberals at the democratic end. This solution is shown in Figure 6c. It is presented at the moment purely as a hypothesis and not as a factual statement; we will see later that the evidence in favour of a hypothesis of this type is rather strong and that Figure 6c does seem to represent reality to a considerable approximation.

We may go one step further and ask ourselves whether we cannot identify this group of political parties with the organization of attitudes which we have deduced from the principles of learning and conditioning. The radical–conservative continuum appears in both hypotheses and we may readily accept the likelihood of our dealing with identical concepts here. Can we go further and identify the authoritarian–democratic continuum with our hypothetical tender-minded versus tough-minded continuum? On *a priori* grounds, and judging from general knowledge and observation, there appears to be some justification for this. The high degree of aggressiveness of the non-democratic parties in this country is well known, as is also the extremely loose sexual morality characterizing so many of the adherents of the two extremist groups. (What is true of Communists in Europe, Great Britain, and the United States does not necessarily apply to the U.S.S.R. or other countries in which the Communists have gained power.) However, common-sense judgements of this kind have no scientific value, and while they may make a particular solution appear reasonable, they cannot serve as proof. Consequently, we must next turn to the task of providing such proof, if, indeed, it can be found.

In looking for proof in favour of our hypothesis we must first of all state a little more precisely what it is that we are asserting. We are asserting that attitudes and opinions on social issues are not independent of each other, but are organized and structured; in other words, they tend to appear in clusters. Furthermore, we are suggesting that there are two main sets of clusters which together account for the major part of the interrelations observed between different attitudes. One of these clusters we have called the radical–conservative one; the other cluster we have called the tough-minded versus tender-minded one. What kind of evidence can we adduce, first to show that attitudes are in fact related to each other, and secondly to show that these relations give rise to the two sets of clusters we have specified?

The answer to the first part of this question is a relatively easy one, and it depends essentially on the statistical method of *implication*. Let us take two logically independent attitude statements. For instance, 'Jews are cowards' and 'The Jews have too much power and influence in this country'. Logically there is no relationship between these two statements. A person may be a coward without having much power and influence in the country, and, conversely, a person may have a good deal of power and influence without being a coward. Therefore, logically, there is no indication that a person endorsing one statement should also endorse the other. We can, however, posit that there is a continuum of anti-Semitism such that some people will tend to endorse all anti-Semitic statements while others will endorse none of them. If that were true, then we would find that, in fact, people would tend either to endorse both statements or to endorse neither; relatively few people would be found to endorse one but not the other. Let us suppose that we have interviewed a thousand people and that, as indicated below, 450 have endorsed both statements, 350 have endorsed neither statement, 100 have endorsed the statement that Jews are cowards, but not that they have too much power and influence in this country, while another 100 have endorsed the statement that Jews have too much power and influence, but not the one that they are cowards (these figures are quite fictitious and put in merely for the purpose of illustration).

		The Jews have too much power and influence	
		YES	NO
The Jews are cowards	YES	450	100
	NO	100	350

It will be seen from this table that there is, indeed, a factual implication from one statement to another. The person who believes that Jews are cowards is four and a half times as likely to believe that Jews have too much power and influence in this country as a person who does not believe that Jews are cowards. We can measure the strength of implication existing in a table of this kind and express it in the form of a single figure. This figure is usually referred to as a coefficient of correlation, and varies from zero, when there is no implication at all, to 1·00, when there is perfect agreement. If the number of people in each of the four cells of our table had been exactly 250 there would have been no implication, and the correlation would have been zero. If the number of cases in the cells agreeing with both statements, had been 500, and 500 disagreeing with both statements, then the implication would have been complete and the correlation would have been 1·00. Knowing the person's opinion on one issue would have determined completely his opinion on the other issue.

In actual fact correlations between different attitudes usually range from about 0·2 at the lower end, to about 0·7 or 0·8 at the higher end. Thus, there is a definite amount of implication in the field of social attitudes, but these implications represent tendencies, not certainties.

When we study, by statistical methods, the actual implications found in large samples of the population we find that they are organized in a kind of hierarchical system. At the bottom of the hierarchy we find a million and one casual expressions of attitude or opinion which we make in the course of our lives. Some of these are characteristic of our long-range views, others are purely ephemeral and may just be the outcome of a temporary annoyance. Thus, the driver who has his new car scratched by an incompetent lady who drives in a rather haphazard manner may be moved to call out some deprecatory remark concerning woman drivers, without, in his more sober moments, necessarily endorsing the anti-feminist position implied. It is only when opinion statements are made on more than one occasion that we

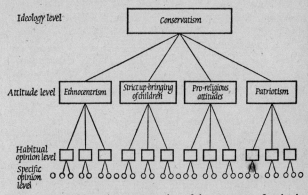

Figure 7: Diagrammatic representation of the structure of attitudes

reach a relative stability of opinion which makes it worth-while to measure and record the expression. Thus, if a person on several occasions gives it as his opinion that children should be seen and not heard, then we may regard this as a genuine expression of opinion.

Such opinions themselves are intercorrelated; we have seen an example in the case of the two views that 'Jews are cowards' and that 'Jews have too much power and influence in this country'. Relationships such as these, which involve a large number of opinions regarding one central issue (attitude towards the Jews in this case) give rise to a somewhat higher-order concept than that of opinion, namely the concept of attitude. Attitudes themselves, however, are not unrelated, and when we analyse their relationships we come to a higher-order construct yet, namely, that of an ideology, such as, for instance, the ideology of conservatism.

A hierarchical system such as this is illustrated in Figure 7. In viewing this figure, it should be remembered that the relationships implied therein are not in any sense arbitrary, or based on *a priori* considerations on the part of the investigator. The Figure simply represents in a diagrammatic form

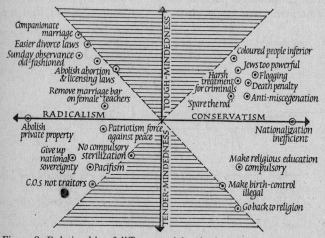

Figure 8: Relationship of different social attitudes to each other and to the two great principles of organization as determined empirically

actual relationships observed between attitudes and opinions held by representative samples of the population. The implication from one opinion or attitude to another is a factual one; its measurement is based on the expressions of points of view made by thousands of people who are selected at random from the general population. This is an important point to remember. What the psychologist contributes is a theory and a method of analysing and organizing the data. The actual content of this scheme, however, is contributed by the people whose opinions and attitudes he is analysing.

His hypothesis may call for a high correlation between two opinions, but whether such a high correlation does or does not obtain is a factual question which only empirical research can answer.

What, then, is the verdict of empirical research of this kind when applied to the hypotheses we are considering at the moment? The result of carrying out detailed analyses of this kind on samples of several thousand men and women, both working class and middle class of all degrees of education, of all ages, and voting for all the different political parties in the country, is shown in Figure 8. We can see there the organization of opinions and attitudes, as objectively determined by the calculus of implication, and it will be seen that the outcome strongly supports our general theory. There are, indeed, two main opposed sets of ideologies corresponding to the radicalism and conservatism and the tough-minded and tender-minded one respectively. Conservative beliefs apparently include the view that nationalization is inefficient; that religious education should be made compulsory; that coloured people are inferior; that birth control should be made illegal; that the death penalty should be retained; and so forth. Radicals, on the other hand, believe that private property should be abolished; that Sunday observance is old-fashioned; that we should give up our national sovereignty in the interests of peace; and so forth. That these items do, in fact, represent conservative and radical opinion can be shown by a very simple calculation. The percentage of endorsements for each item was calculated separately for Conservative and Labour party voters who were equated for social class, education, age, sex, and other important variables. Then the difference in the percentage of endorsements was calculated for each item and it was found that the views mentioned above, as well as the others given in the Figure, did in fact show very marked differences in endorsement between Conservative party voters and Labour party voters. There seems to be no doubt, therefore, that we are here dealing with a genuine radical–conservative continuum.

How about the tough-minded–tender-minded continuum? It will be seen that this bears out very strongly our prediction. On the tough-minded side we have openly aggressive and sexual attitudes. The aggressive ones favour flogging, the death penalty, harsh treatment for criminals; corporal punishment for children; and so forth. The openly sexual attitudes are those in favour of companionate or trial marriage; easier divorce laws; the abolition of abortion laws, thus making abortion easily available to everyone; and so on. On the other hand, attitudes characterizing the tender-minded end of the continuum emphasize ethical and religious restraints and pacifism; the giving-up of national sovereignty; going back to religion; and making religious education compulsory; the making illegal of birth control and the abolition of flogging and the death penalty – these are characteristic of tender-minded views. There appears to be, therefore, considerable evidence in this analysis of attitudes that our deduction is verified.

We have not, however, shown so far that our analysis of the relationships between political parties is as predicted in Figure 6c, and to this task we must now turn. If our hypothesis is correct, then we would expect Communists to be tough-minded radicals; Fascists to be tough-minded conservatives; Liberals to be tender-minded and intermediate with respect to the radicalism–conservatism continuum; Socialists and Conservatives should be intermediate with respect to tender-mindedness between the authoritarian parties and the Liberals, and to the left and right, respectively, on the radicalism–conservative continuum. Proof of this prediction was sought in the following way. Questionnaires were made up of items which best characterized the conservative–radical continuum and the tough-minded–tender-minded continuum; these two questionnaires we shall call the R inventory and the T inventory respectively. These inventories may be considered as reasonably reliable and valid measures of our two continua. They were tried out and refined in a number of studies, and finally applied to large groups of people who were members of, or had voted for, the various party groups with whom we are dealing. Their scores on these two inventories were then determined and plotted. When this was done it was found that our prediction of the relative positions of these various groups were borne out in very considerable detail. The only discrepancy occurred with respect to the Fascist group, which was indeed tough-minded and Conservative, but slightly less conservative than voters for the Conservative party. In all other details, the prediction was precisely fulfilled, and we may therefore conclude that our hypothesis possesses a considerable degree of predictive value.

The reader may be interested in assessing his own and other people's position on these two continua. For this purpose I have given below a 60-item inventory which can be scored for both the R and the T continuum. The reader may like to fill this in first before looking at the key. The instructions preceding the inventory are those normally given with it. The key to this, as well as the method of scoring and the average scores for various representative samples, are given at the end of this chapter.

SOCIAL ATTITUDE INVENTORY

Below are given sixty statements which represent widely-held opinions on various social questions, selected from speeches, books, newspapers, and other sources. They were chosen in such a way that most people are likely to agree with some, and to disagree with others.

After each statement, you are requested to record your personal opinion regarding it. You should use the following system of marking:

+ + if you strongly agree with the statement
+   if you agree on the whole
o   if you can't decide for or against, or if you think the question is worded in such a way that you can't give an answer
—   if you disagree on the whole
— — if you strongly disagree

Please answer frankly. Remember this is not a test; there are no 'right' or 'wrong' answers. The answer required is your own per-

L

sonal opinion. Be sure not to omit any questions. The questionnaire is anonymous, so please do not sign your name.

Do not consult any other person while you are giving your answers.

Opinion Statements	*Your Opinion*

1. The nation exists for the benefit of the individuals composing it, not the individuals for the benefit of the nation.
2. Coloured people are innately inferior to white people.
3. War is inherent in human nature.
4. Ultimately, private property should be abolished and complete Socialism introduced.
5. Persons with serious hereditary defects and diseases should be compulsorily sterilized.
6. In the interests of peace, we must give up part of our national sovereignty.
7. Production and trade should be free from government interference.
8. Divorce laws should be altered to make divorce easier.
9. The so-called underdog deserves little sympathy or help from successful people.
10. Crimes of violence should be punished by flogging.
11. The nationalization of the great industries is likely to lead to inefficiency, bureaucracy, and stagnation.
12. Men and women have the right to find out whether they are sexually suited before marriage (e.g. by trial marriage).
13. 'My country right or wrong' is a saying which expresses a fundamentally desirable attitude.
14. The average man can live a good enough life without religion.
15. It would be a mistake to have coloured people as foremen over whites.
16. People should realize that their greatest obligation is to their family.
17. There is no survival of any kind after death.

18. The death penalty is barbaric, and should be abolished.

19. There may be a few exceptions, but in general, Jews are pretty much alike.

20. The dropping of the first atom bomb on a Japanese city, killing thousands of innocent women and children, was morally wrong and incompatible with our kind of civilization.

21. Birth control, except when recommended by a doctor, should be made illegal.

22. People suffering from incurable diseases should have the choice of being put painlessly to death.

23. Sunday-observance is old-fashioned, and should cease to govern our behaviour.

24. Capitalism is immoral because it exploits the worker by failing to give him full value for his productive labour.

25. We should believe without question all that we are taught by the Church.

26. A person should be free to take his own life, if he wishes to do so, without any interference from society.

27. Free love between men and women should be encouraged as a means towards mental and physical health.

28. Compulsory military training in peace-time is essential for the survival of this country.

29. Sex crimes such as rape and attacks on children, deserve more than mere imprisonment; such criminals ought to be flogged or worse.

30. A white lie is often a good thing.

31. The idea of God is an invention of the human mind.

32. It is wrong that men should be permitted greater sexual freedom than women by society.

33. The Church should attempt to increase its influence on the life of the nation.

34. Conscientious objectors are traitors to their country, and should be treated accordingly.

35. The laws against abortion should be abolished.

36. Most religious people are hypocrites.
37. Sex relations except in marriage are always wrong.
38. European refugees should be left to fend for themselves.
39. Only by going back to religion can civilization hope to survive.
40. It is wrong to punish a man if he helps another country because he prefers it to his own.
41. It is just as well that the struggle of life tends to weed out those who cannot stand the pace.
42. In taking part in any form of world organization, this country should make certain that none of its independence and power is lost.
43. Nowadays, more and more people are prying into matters which do not concern them.
44. All forms of discrimination against the coloured races, the Jews, etc., should be made illegal, and subject to heavy penalties.
45. It is right and proper that religious education in schools should be compulsory.
46. Jews are as valuable citizens as any other group.
47. Our treatment of criminals is too harsh; we should try to cure them, not punish them.
48. The Church is the main bulwark opposing the evil trends in modern society.
49. There is no harm in travelling occasionally without a ticket, if you can get away with it.
50. The Japanese are by nature a cruel people.
51. Life is so short that a man is justified in enjoying himself as much as he can.
52. An occupation by a foreign power is better than war.
53. Christ was divine, wholly or partly in a sense different from other men.
54. It would be best to keep coloured people in their own districts and schools, in order to prevent too much contact with whites.
55. Homosexuals are hardly better than criminals, and ought to be severely punished.

56. The universe was created by God.
57. Blood sports, like fox hunting for instance, are vicious and cruel, and should be forbidden.
58. The maintenance of internal order within the nation is more important than ensuring that there is complete freedom for all.
59. Every person should have complete faith in some supernatural power whose decisions he obeys without question.
60. The practical man is of more use to society than the thinker.

There are one or two more points which should be discussed. The first of these relates to class differences in tough-mindedness. We have seen that from our hedonistic learning field we can predict that working-class groups should be predominantly radical in their sympathies, while middle-class groups should be predominantly conservative. Can we make any prediction about class differences from our association-ist conditioning hypothesis? The answer appears to be in the affirmative. So far we have assumed in our deduction that people who condition easily and people who condition with difficulty are also submitted to a socialization process which is roughly equal in strength or superiority for all of them. This, however, is surely not true to the facts. We know that some children are submitted to a very strict process of socialization, others to a very lax one indeed. The outcome, undoubtedly, will be determined not only by the degree of conditionability of the child, but also of the amount of conditioning to which he is subjected. Given an equal degree of conditionability in a group of children, we would expect those to be most 'over-socialized' who have been subjected to a very strict socialization process and those to be 'under-socialized' who have been submitted to a very lax process of socialization.

Now, there is no reason to assume any differences between social classes with respect to conditionability, but there are

very good reasons for assuming considerable differences between them with respect to the degree of socialization to
which they are subjected. Particular attention has been
drawn, for instance, by Kinsey in the United States to the
different value laid on the repression of overt sexual urges
by middle-class and working-class groups. He has shown
that where, for middle-class groups, parents put very strict
obstacles in the way of overt sexual satisfaction of their growing children, and inculcate a very high degree of 'socialization' in them, working-class parents, on the whole, are much
more lax and unconcerned. In many working-class groups,
for instance, he found pre-marital intercourse viewed as not
only inevitable, but as quite acceptable to the group.

Similarly, with respect to aggression, there is a considerable amount of evidence from a variety of sociological
studies, carried out both in the United States and in Great
Britain, to show a tendency for middle-class groups to im-
pose a stricter standard upon their children than the working-class groups. The open expression of aggressiveness,
which is frowned upon in the middle-class family, is often
not only accepted but even praised in the working-class
group.

There are, of course, many individual exceptions which
will immediately occur to the reader. There are middle-class
families where parents completely fail to impress social
mores and customs upon their children, and where the open
expression of anti-social tendencies is openly condoned, or at
least not strongly discouraged. Conversely, in many working-class families, particularly where there are ambitions
for the children to move in the direction of the higher-status
groups, there is an extremely strong tendency to stress conventional values and inculcate respect for them in the children. However, in spite of numerous exceptions, available
data leave little doubt that, on the average, there are differences between social classes and status groups which, by and
large, allow one to generalize in the direction of stating that
the socialization process is stronger and more complete in
middle-class than in working-class groups.

If that is so, and if we have no reason to expect innate differences in conditionability between the two groups, then we would expect our middle-class groups to be more tender-minded than our working-class groups. This hypothesis has been put to the test by applying the T-inventory to groups of working-class and middle-class individuals, matched on a number of relevant variables. The outcome was exceedingly clear-cut. Middle-class Conservatives were more tender-minded than working-class Conservatives; middle-class Liberals were more tender-minded than working-class Liberals; middle-class Socialists were more tender-minded than working-class Socialists. Indeed, even middle-class Communists were found to be more tender-minded than working-class Communists! Not enough Fascists were available to carry out a comparable study with them, but for all the other groups considerable differences were found in the predicted direction, and we may therefore generalize and say that middle-class people, on the whole, tend to be more tender-minded, working-class people on the whole more tough-minded. There is, of course, considerable overlap, but of the existence of a noticeable average difference there can be no doubt.

Another question that may concern us is that of national differences. Most of the work mentioned has been carried out in Great Britain, and it does not necessarily follow that what is true of Great Britain is true of other countries. Fortunately, a number of studies are available to show that the organization of attitudes in France, Germany, Sweden, and the United States is very similar indeed to that found in this country. Similarly, the relationships of the R and T dimensions to political parties are similar to those observed here.

There are, however, certain differences which in themselves are very enlightening; thus, in Great Britain the major political parties are differentiated almost entirely in terms of the radicalism–conservatism continuum, and comparatively little with respect to tough-mindedness and tender-mindedness. Socialists and Conservatives are approximately equal with respect to their degree of tough-mindedness; the

Liberals are a little more tender-minded, but the difference is not very large. It is only the minority groups, like Communists and Fascists, which show considerable deviation from the norm.

When we turn our attention to France, however, the position is very different. There it has been found that the T-dimension, very far from being negligible, is, on the contrary, even more important than the radicalism–conservatism dimension. Whereas in Great Britain the ratio of importance for these two factors is approximately 10 to 1 in favour of radicalism–conservatism, in so far as the major political parties are concerned, it is 4 to 3 in favour of tough-mindedness–tender-mindedness in France. (This might, indeed, have been expected in view of the well-known strength of the Communist and of various Fascist groups on the French political scene.)

This finding is very important to anyone who wishes to compare the political structure in England and France. In this country parties are divided from each other in terms of radicalism–conservatism; the division between tough-minded and tender-minded usually divides each of the major parties into sub-sections. In France, on the contrary, the major divisions are with respect to tough-mindedness–tender-mindedness, and the radical–conservative dichotomy is frequently found within each of the major parties. The position is not so clear in France as it is in this country because there the two principles, or dimensions, are of approximately equal strength. Nevertheless, a tendency is there, and it will be apparent now why it is so very difficult for British observers, used to our type of political organization, to understand the quite different pattern on the French political scene. If the reader, in studying French politics, will bear in mind these considerations, I think he will find his task considerably eased and his understanding grow correspondingly.

What about countries and nations outside the European circle of circumstance and background? We may expect the tough-minded–tender-minded dimension to remain in some form because it is grounded on relatively universal and permanent characteristics of human beings. We would not, however, expect to find the radical–conservative dimension to emerge in the same form as here unless social conditions have given rise to classes and status groups of a similar nature to those dominating the social scene in the European and North American countries. In a feudal society, for instance, you would not expect to find anything resembling our conservative–radical continuum to emerge.

Only one study has been carried out along these lines in a semi-feudal country. Among mid-Eastern Arabs it has been found that while the tough-minded–tender-minded dimension is still clearly expressed in the relationships observed between different attitudes there is nothing that corresponds to the radical–conservative continuum. It could be of the very greatest interest if studies of this kind could be carried out in countries like China, Russia, and so forth, but the practical difficulties and the financial outlay involved make it unlikely that in the near future our knowledge will grow by an inclusion of these countries in our circle of exploration.

It will have been noticed that nothing has so far been said of an implication in our theory which would link personality with tough-minded and tender-minded attitudes respectively. We have argued, on the one hand, that a person difficult to condition should develop tough-minded attitudes. In a previous chapter we have argued that a person difficult to condition should develop extraverted patterns of behaviour. Similarly, we have argued in this chapter that persons particularly easy to condition should develop tender-minded attitudes, and in a previous chapter we have argued that such a person should develop introverted behaviour patterns. It seems reasonable to expect, therefore, that a tough-minded person would tend to be extraverted, and a tender-minded person would tend to be introverted. This hypothesis has been put to the test several times, and results in each case have strongly supported this hypothesis. There appears to be a definite tendency for extraverted people to develop tough-minded attitudes, whereas introverted people show an equally definite tendency to develop tender-minded attitudes. With this finding our set of hypotheses has indeed come full circle, and we now see in detail the relationships obtaining between personality, social attitudes, and political action. Considering the many sources of error involved in the measurement and determination of personality and of social attitudes, the relationships found are remarkably close. Nevertheless it should be remembered that they are not perfect. We have found that Communists tend to be extraverted, tough-minded radicals, whereas Fascists tend to be extraverted, tough-minded conservatives. It should not be deduced from that that the converse also holds and that all extraverted, tough-minded radicals are Communists and all extraverted, tough-minded conservatives are Fascists. All policemen are over 6 feet tall, but not all men over 6 feet tall are policemen; the argument from the one to the other cannot be reversed. (I understand that regulations about the height of policemen, like most other things, has been subject to change and nowadays one can behold policemen who are only five feet nine inches tall. I have attempted to obtain empirical evidence on this point, but have been awed by the curious headgear worn by policemen which makes any measurement of their height extremely unreliable.)

Indeed, it would not even be true to say that all members of the Communist party, say, are in fact tough-minded radicals. People join a party for all sorts of reasons and it would be unreasonable to expect perfect conformity. To take an extreme case, an agent provocateur, or police spy, might join an extremist party in order to keep an eye on it; you would not expect him necessarily to share its views and attitudes. Again, we have found in several cases that a husband belonging to, say, the Communist party is made to persuade his wife to join also; she may join because she does not want to break up her marriage, but without in fact sharing the beliefs and aims of the party. There will always be a number of people in a party whose membership is based on considerations more or less tangential to the views held by the party and germane to its functioning. These people would not be expected to show identical attitudes with those held by the major set of party members.

Our systematic analysis is relatively complete so far, but we may still feel that a somewhat more detailed analysis of the personality of members of the Communist and Fascist parties might reveal more than is contained in the general statement that they tend to be extraverted. This suspicion is probably well-grounded, but unfortunately it is extremely difficult to obtain the co-operation of members of extremist groups for the purpose of studying their personality structure. Communists, on the whole, are rather more co-operative, but Fascists are extremely suspicious and distrustful, and refuse point-blank any requests for co-operation. In the circumstances, comparatively little has been done, but even the few isolated results which are available are of considerable interest.

One such study carried further the hypothesis, outlined near the beginning of this chapter, that a special characteristic of Fascist and Communist groups would be their aggressiveness, i.e. their failure to become properly conditioned to the social prohibitions regarding the open expression of violence against other people. Forty-three Communists and forty-three Fascists were studied in this particular experiment, and their reactions compared with those of a group of eighty-six people equated with them from the points of view of age, class, and social status, but differing in that they held political views favouring one of the three democratic parties. In addition to being given the radicalism–conservatism questionnaire, these three groups were also tested by means of the Thematic Apperception Test, described in an earlier chapter. Special attention was paid in the analysis of the stories the subjects told to evidence of aggression of both an overt and a covert nature. Scoring along these lines is quite reliable when the scorers adhere to the definition of aggression adopted for this purpose, which was 'To hate, fight, or punish an offence. To criticize, blame, accuse, or ridicule maliciously. To injure or kill, or behave cruelly. To fight against legally constituted authorities; to pursue, catch or imprison a criminal or enemy.' Each person was given a score according to the number of times that clear evidence of aggression was found in his stories. The result of the analysis is shown in Figure 9, where scores on the radicalism–

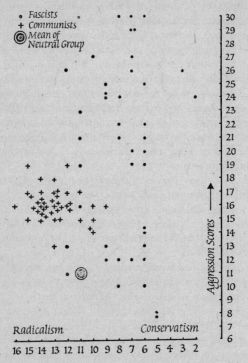

Figure 9: Aggression scores of Fascists and Communists as compared with a neutral group

conservatism scale are shown on the abscissa, and aggression scores on the ordinate. It will be seen that each and every one of the Communists had aggression scores which were in excess of the mean of the neutral group, i.e. the group of people voting for the three democratic parties. The same, with very few exceptions, is true of the Fascists who took part in this experiment; only four of these have aggression scores slightly lower than the neutral group. All the others have aggression scores very much higher than the neutral group.

An inspection of the actual stories told by Fascists and Communists reveals them to be dripping with blood. This is particularly true of many of the stories told by the Fascists; the amount of aggressiveness found in these stories is quite beyond the range of what is found in normal people. It will be seen from the Figure that scores as high as thirty are not unusual among Fascists as compared with the mean for the normal group of about eleven. Communists, by contrast, are somewhat more aggressive than average, but not abnormally so; their mean is in the neighbourhood of sixteen. These data suggest certain differences between Communists and Fascists, but for want of more detailed investigations it is not possible to follow up this lead.

Other investigations of a similar nature have shown Fascists and Communists to be more dominant than members of the democratic parties, to show a certain amount of rigidity, and some intolerance of ambiguity. Suggestive as these findings are, it must be obvious that much more thorough experimental inquiries are needed before we can claim to have gained but a superficial understanding of the personality dynamics which cause a person to become a member of the Communist or Fascist party.

The reader, comfortably seated in his arm-chair in front of the fire, and glancing through the pages describing these results, will almost certainly feel, as does the writer, that they do little more than whet the appetite, and he may wonder why more has not been done in this field. One of the main reasons is the great difficulties which lie in the path of the investigator. Let us take but one example. To have administered the Thematic Apperception Test and a few questionnaires to forty-three Fascists and forty-three Communists may not sound a very considerable task. Yet the student who did this work had to spend approximately a year in simply gaining access to meetings held by these parties, obtaining the confidence of a few members in each, and thus preparing the ground for the heart-breakingly difficult task of individually persuading forty-three members of each group to undergo the testing programme. All this had to be done without revealing the purpose of the experiment, without losing the co-operation of a member once he had been approached (this would have upset the sampling procedure), and without allowing the members of one party to suspect that she was in any way friendly with members of the other party. Almost every Saturday evening, come rain or shine, snowstorm, blizzard, or hail, this intrepid young lady attended open-air political meetings; most of her evenings were spent arguing, debating, and reading party literature so as to be able to talk the accepted jargon. Inevitably, personal complications arose which had to be resolved. All through the time that this work was being carried on there was a risk of personal danger if any suspicions had been allowed to arise with respect to her exact role. Few students are willing, or capable, of carrying out scientific research of a high standard under these conditions, and the majority rest content with the less interesting, but more easily obtainable types of data.

In spite of all these obvious and very great difficulties, it might be possible to induce some of the more adventurous students to take up research of this kind if society showed some interest in the results so laboriously acquired, but unfortunately experimental social science is not welcomed very much in academic quarters, where the quiet somnolence of the reading-room and the dead and forgotten writings of past nonentities are considered much more soothing than the fresh air of empirical investigation, and the intoxicating flood of factual data. Until this general attitude changes, it is idle to expect any great access of knowledge in these complex and difficult fields.

KEY TO SOCIAL ATTITUDE INVENTORY

The scoring key for the two scales is given after each of the items. There are sixteen items for the measurement of R and thirty-two items for the measurement of T; some items are used for measuring both dimensions. Some items in the scale are 'filler' items and are not scored at all. As regards scoring, the R scale is always scored in the radical direction. For items marked R+ in the key, agreement (+ or ++) is scored 1, and any other response 0. For items marked R−, disagreement (− or −−) is scored 1, and any other responses 0.

The T scale is always scored in the tender-minded direction. For items marked T+, agreement (+ or ++) is scored 1, and

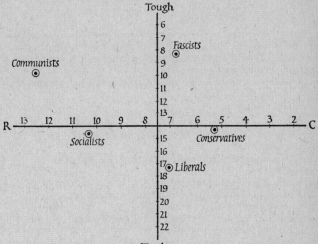

Figure 10: Empirically determined positions of Communists, Socialists, Liberals, Conservatives, and Fascists on two main dimensions

any other response 0. For items marked T−, disagreement (− or −−) is scored 1 and any other response 0. The range of scores in the T scale is from 0 to 32; the range of scores in the R scale is from 0 to 16.

In comparing these scores with those of members of various political groups, the reader will find Figure 10 useful. In this are shown the actual mean scores of Communists, Fascists, Socialists, Liberals, and Conservatives on the R and T scales. By entering his own score in this table, the reader will be able to see how he stands with respect to the major political organizations in this country.

Below are given sixty statements which represent widely-held opinions on various social questions, selected from speeches, books, newspapers, and other sources. They were chosen in such a way that most people are likely to agree with some, and to disagree with others.

After each statement, you are requested to record your personal opinion regarding it. You should use the following system of marking:

+ + if you strongly agree with the statement
+ if you agree on the whole
o if you can't decide for or against, or if you think the question is worded in such a way that you can't give an answer
— if you disagree on the whole
— — if you strongly disagree

Please answer frankly. Remember this is not a test; there are no 'right' or 'wrong' answers. The answer required is your own personal opinion. Be sure not to omit any questions. The questionnaire is anonymous, so please do not sign your name.

Do not consult any other person while you are giving your answers.

Opinion Statements   *Your Opinion*

1. The nation exists for the benefit of the individuals composing it, not the individuals for the benefit of the nation.
2. Coloured people are innately inferior to white people.
3. War is inherent in human nature.
4. Ultimately, private property should be abolished and complete Socialism introduced.   R+
5. Persons with serious hereditary defects and diseases should be compulsorily sterilized.
6. In the interests of peace, we must give up part of our national sovereignty.
7. Production and trade should be free from government interference.   R—
8. Divorce laws should be altered to make divorce easier.   T—
9. The so-called underdog deserves little sympathy or help from successful people.   T—
10. Crimes of violence should be punished by flogging.   R—   T—
11. The nationalization of the great industries is likely to lead to inefficiency, bureaucracy, and stagnation.   R—
12. Men and women have the right to find out whether they are sexually suited before marriage (e.g. by trial marriage).   R+   T—
13. 'My country right or wrong' is a saying which expresses a fundamentally desirable attitude.   R—

Opinion Statements – contd   *Your Opinion*

14. The average man can live a good enough life without religion.   T—

15. It would be a mistake to have coloured people as foremen over whites.

16. People should realize that their greatest obligation is to their family.

17. There is no survival of any kind after death.   T—

18. The death penalty is barbaric, and should be abolished.   R+   T+

19. There may be a few exceptions, but in general, Jews are pretty much alike.   T—

20. The dropping of the first atom bomb on a Japanese city, killing thousands of innocent women and children, was morally wrong and incompatible with our kind of civilization.   T+

21. Birth control, except when recommended by a doctor, should be made illegal.   T+

22. People suffering from incurable diseases should have the choice of being put painlessly to death.   T—

23. Sunday-observance is old-fashioned, and should cease to govern our behaviour.

24. Capitalism is immoral because it exploits the worker by failing to give him full value for his productive labour.   R+

25. We should believe without question all that we are taught by the Church.   R—

26. A person should be free to take his own life, if he wishes to do so, without any interference from society.   T—

27. Free love between men and women should be encouraged as a means towards mental and physical health.   R+   T—

28. Compulsory military training in peace-time is essential for the survival of this country.   T—

29. Sex crimes such as rape and attacks on children, deserve more than mere imprisonment; such criminals ought to be flogged or worse.   R—

30. A white lie is often a good thing.   T—

31. The idea of God is an invention of the human mind.   T—

32. It is wrong that men should be permitted greater sexual freedom than women by society.

33. The Church should attempt to increase its influence on the life of the nation.   T+

34. Conscientious objectors are traitors to their country, and should be treated accordingly.

Opinion Statements – contd   *Your Opinion*

35. The laws against abortion should be abolished.
36. Most religious people are hypocrites.   T—
37. Sex relations except in marriage are always wrong.   R—   T+
38. European refugees should be left to fend for themselves.   T—
39. Only by going back to religion can civilization hope to survive.
40. It is wrong to punish a man if he helps another country because he prefers it to his own.   R+
41. It is just as well that the struggle of life tends to weed out those who cannot stand the pace.   T—
42. In taking part in any form of world organization, this country should make certain that none of its independence and power is lost.   R—
43. Nowadays, more and more people are prying into matters which do not concern them.   T—
44. All forms of discrimination against the coloured races, the Jews, etc., should be made illegal, and subject to heavy penalties.
45. It is right and proper that religious education in schools should be compulsory.
46. Jews are as valuable citizens as any other group.   T+
47. Our treatment of criminals is too harsh; we should try to cure them, not punish them.   R+   T+
48. The Church is the main bulwark opposing the evil trends in modern society.   T+
49. There is no harm in travelling occasionally without a ticket, if you can get away with it.   T—
50. The Japanese are by nature a cruel people.
51. Life is so short that a man is justified in enjoying himself as much as he can.   T—
52. An occupation by a foreign power is better than war.   R+   T+
53. Christ was divine, wholly or partly in a sense different from other men.   T+
54. It would be best to keep coloured people in their own districts and schools, in order to prevent too much contact with whites.
55. Homosexuals are hardly better than criminals, and ought to be severely punished.
56. The universe was created by God.   T+
57. Blood sports – like fox-hunting, for instance – are vicious and cruel, and should be forbidden.   T+
58. The maintenance of internal order within the nation is more important than ensuring that there is complete freedom for all.   T—

59. Every person should have complete faith in some
    supernatural power whose decisions he obeys with-
    out question.
60. The practical man is of more use to society than
    the thinker.

8

THE PSYCHOLOGY OF AESTHETICS

THERE can be few topics more certain to lead to furious discussion than those related to aesthetics; there can be few topics within the realm of aesthetics more certain to arouse normally peaceful artists, philosophers, and aestheticians to a pitch of uncontrolled indignation than that which has given this chapter its title. The idea that objects of beauty, as well as their creation and appreciation, are subject to scientific scrutiny appears abhorrent to most people, even as the idea that the physicist might study and analyse the colours of the rainbow with his objective methods was abhorrent to their grandparents. There appears to exist a fear that clumsy handling might crush the butterfly's wings; an idea that analysis may destroy what it is intending to study.

Associated with this fear is perhaps another. Most people hold views regarding aesthetics which they are extremely unwilling to give up, although these views are not based on any objective facts. Indeed, the very idea that one's views ought to be related to factual evidence is usually dismissed, and it is asserted that subjectivity reigns supreme in this field. This, of course, is a tenable view; it is contradicted, however, by the well-known tendency of most people to argue about their aesthetic views, often with great acerbity, always with great tenacity, never with that humility which the hypothesis of complete subjectivity should engender in them. If aesthetic judgements are completely subjective, there would appear as little point in argument as in scientific experiment; if the one is permissible, so surely is the other. Perhaps the objection to scientific investigation is in part due to a fear that facts may be more potent than arguments in forcing one to give up a cherished position, and to acknowledge certain objective factors which one would prefer to overlook.

However that may be, there can be little doubt about the

hostile reaction which psychology has experienced on all sides when it attempted to introduce scientific methods into the study of aesthetics. A good deal of this hostility is probably based on misunderstanding, and it will be the purpose of this chapter to explain in some detail just what the psychologist is trying to do, and how he sets about his task. I shall try to avoid arguments and comparisons with philosophical procedures and problems as far as possible; these often seem to resemble those attacked by psychologists, but the similarity is only superficial. The reader familiar with modern aesthetic doctrines, and with the long history of discussions in this field, will easily be able to apply the facts of psychological research to the solution of such philosophical problems as interest him.

How, then, does the psychologist start? He notices that certain types of judgement are made frequently of certain objects; these judgements are phrased in terms of 'beautiful' and 'ugly', or some synonymous terms, and apply to various combinations of colours and shapes, as in the visual arts; words, as in poetry; or sounds, as in music. The essential datum with which he deals, therefore, is a relation – a relation between a stimulus (picture, poem, piece of music) and a person who reacts to this stimulus in certain conventional ways. Usually the response is a verbal one, but it is possible, and has been found useful in certain situations, to record physiological reactions indicative of emotion, such as heartbeat, pulse-rate, skin temperature, or changes in the electric conductivity of the skin.

In analysing this relation, the psychologist encounters a twofold problem. In the first place, he must ask himself: Just what is the physical property of the stimulus which causes a favourable reaction as opposed to an unfavourable reaction in the majority of the subjects with whom he is working? In the second place, he must ask himself: Just what is the reason why one person reacts favourably to a given stimulus, while another person reacts unfavourably? Possible answers to the first question might be in terms of certain 'laws of composition', as for instance that the centre of interest of a picture ought to lie at the intersection of the 'thirds', i.e. of lines drawn parallel to the side and bottom of the pictures, and dividing it into three equal parts either way. Answers to the second question might be in terms of temperamental traits or types; thus it might be argued that introverts prefer classical, extraverts romantic music. I am not here arguing that these examples in any way correspond to fact; they are merely quoted to show possible methods of answering psychological questions.

Inevitably, the psychologist will start his work by experimenting with the simplest possible stimuli – simple colours and colour combinations, simple proportions of lines, and so forth. In doing this he is following the usual path of scientific progress from the simple to the complex. It is here that he frequently encounters the first serious objection on the part of the philosopher and aesthetician, who claims that judgements regarding the relative beauty of simple colours or lines are not in any way related to judgements of more complex stimuli, such as a landscape by Cézanne or a portrait by Rembrandt, and that consequently rules and laws derived from simple stimuli can have no relevance to what are considered 'real' works of art. No proof is offered for this rejection of evidence, other than the subjective feeling of the critic that these judgements are 'qualitatively' different. I shall not attempt to argue this point here, but shall defer discussion until later on, where evidence will be cited to prove quite definitely that there are essential similarities linking aesthetic judgements of 'simple' with aesthetic judgements of 'complex' stimuli.

How does the psychologist design his experiment? Usually he will provide a series of stimuli whose physical properties are known, and ask his subjects to rank these in order of aesthetic merit, i.e. from best liked to least liked. Alternatively he may offer his subjects two stimuli at a time, with the request to say which of the two is more pleasing aesthetically; all possible combinations of stimuli are shown in this manner. Either procedure will result in an average order of preference, and experience has shown that this order will be pretty much the same regardless of the exact method used for deriving it. From this average order of 'aesthetic' merit, certain deductions may be made regarding the physical properties associated with high-ranking and low-ranking objects respectively.

It is here that a second objection will often be made. Psychologists, it will be said, are treating the perception of 'beauty' as if it were essentially similar to some 'objective' property like greenness, or size, or shape. But this can hardly be permissible; surely 'beauty' is not a property belonging to an object in the same way that one might say the colour green, or the triangular shape, belonged to the object. Beauty, in other words, is essentially subjective; colour, shape, and other properties of a stimulus are objective. How can one reasonably use methods appropriate to the study of one type of stimuli in the study of other, different types?

This objection is based on an essential fallacy, a fallacy whose hoary age does not prevent it from coming up again and again in modern discussion. An object does not 'contain' the colour green in any meaningful sense of the term; it reflects light of a certain wavelength which some people experience as 'green', others, who happen to be colour-blind, as 'grey'. Similarly, an object does not 'contain' beauty in any meaningful sense of the term; it reflects light in certain combinations of wavelengths which some people experience as 'beautiful', others as 'ugly' or 'indifferent'.

Some people, harking back to Locke's distinction between primary and secondary qualities, are willing to concede the force of this argument with respect to colour, but balk at its extension to shape. Here, they would say, there is complete correspondence between stimulus and experience; everyone sees a circle as round, a triangle as different from a square. Alas, the facts contradict even this confident assertion. Experiments with people whose congenital blindness was removed surgically in later life, and who thus experienced sight for the first time, have shown them to be quite incapable of distinguishing between a circle and a square, or of recognizing triangles and other simple figures. Weary months of learning were needed for them to make even such very simple discriminations, and the disheartening slowness with which such learning proceeded bore ample testimony to the absurdity of the notion that 'roundness' or 'squareness' were inherent qualities in the object, just waiting to be perceived. Rules for the perception of these qualities had to be acquired, just as we have to acquire rules for the perception of beauty; without these rules there is literally no perception at all.

This fact was brought out with particular clarity in experiments on animals, mainly chimpanzees and rats, where the animal was reared in darkness. Although there was no interference whatever with the physiological apparatus of vision, the animals, when brought into the light, behaved to all intents and purposes as if they were blind; they could not learn to avoid a large, distinctive object from which they obtained strong electric shocks, and they failed to learn to recognize the white-clad attendant to whom they were attached, in spite of the fact that he stood out conspicuously from the uniform grey background. Perception of colours, shapes, and other physical properties is a learned activity, and what is perceived depends very strongly on the type of learning and the amount of learning which the animal – or the human – has gone through. In this respect the perception of 'beauty', therefore, is no different from the perception of other qualities.

These facts make it necessary to inquire into the precise meaning of those terms, 'objective' and 'subjective', which are so often used to mark the distinction between properties which are supposed to be capable of being investigated by scientific techniques – such as colour and shape – and others which are not – such as beauty. 'Objective' is usually taken as synonymous with 'real', 'subjective' with 'unreal'. But we have shown that to call a stimulus 'green' is far from being an 'objective' description; all that we can say objectively is that the stimulus object reflects light-waves of a certain periodicity. The experience 'green' is subjective, i.e. inherent in the observer rather than a characteristic of the stimulus. If it is nevertheless permissible to try to link up the subjective experience and the objective stimulus in the case of colour or form perception, it is difficult to see why it should not be permissible to do the same in the case of our perception of 'beauty'.

Here the argument often changes its content, and the term 'objective' assumes a different meaning. It is said that everyone is agreed on the experience of 'green' when his eyes are stimulated by a light of the wavelength of 515 millimicrons, while he will report an experience of 'red' when the wavelength changes to 650 millimicrons. But there is no such agreement with respect to experiences of 'beautiful' and 'ugly'; one man's meat is another man's poison, and *de gustibus non est disputandum*. In other words, 'objectivity' is now defined in terms of agreement among observers; where such agreement obtains, as it does in the case of colour judgements among individuals with perfect colour vision, the judgement is said to be objectively based. Where there is no agreement, judgement is said to be subjective. We may accept this type of definition, but we should be aware that in so doing we abandon the absolute distinction between 'objective' and 'subjective', and recognize instead degrees of 'objectivity' depending on the amount of agreement observed among our subjects. In other words, our decision as to the 'objectivity' of a judgement ceases to be determined by philosophical argument, and becomes instead an empirical and experimental question, to be settled by observations regarding the degree of agreement found. This is the sense in which the term will be used here.

As an example of experimental work in this field, let us take the numerous studies on colour preferences. In order to appreciate their outcome, we must first of all be able to specify exactly the colour stimulus; unless we can do this, we cannot describe our experiment completely, thus enabling others to repeat it, and we cannot state any laws relating preference judgements to the physical properties of the stimulus. Now essentially there are three dimensions along which colours can differ from each other (black, white, and grey are called 'colours' here in addition to red, green, yellow, blue, and the other chromatic colours). These three dimensions are known as hue, saturation, and brightness, and their relationship is shown in the accompanying diagram. *Hue* refers to the chromatic quality which distinguishes red from yellow, or blue from green; it is measured

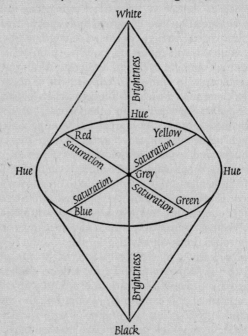

Figure 11: Showing the three-dimensional
nature of colours

in terms of wavelength. *Brightness* refers to the amount of light reflected by the colour, while *saturation* refers to the amount of chromatic colour shown (its vividness). Hues are arranged in a circle (the so-called 'colour-circle') in such a way that colours at opposite poles of the circle (complementary colours) give grey when mixed together.

If we take coloured chips representing the various parts of

the colour circle, being careful to have them all of the same brightness and saturation, and ask a number of people to rank them in order of preference by means of either of the two methods described earlier, we find that there is considerable agreement between different people. This agreement is still manifest when we are less careful to keep brightness and saturation equal for all our colours, but it is much less strongly marked, because judgements are now based not on one characteristic (hue) only, but on a combination of several. Nevertheless, considerable agreement is still found, even when we compare European subjects with savage tribes, American whites with Red Indians, and subjects from Oriental with subjects from Occidental cultures. There thus appears some strong biological foundation for judgements of colour preference, a foundation which may occasionally be overborne by cultural influences but which asserts itself in all the many diverse groups studied.

There seems to be a definite physical property in the stimulus which is responsible for this universal order of preference. Short wavelengths are generally preferred to long wavelengths; the correlation between wavelength and preference is almost perfect. For young children this relationship does not appear to hold, but for adolescents and adults it appears to constitute a natural law.

If people differ in their preference judgements – and agreement is far from perfect – then it would follow that some people's judgements are more in accord with the average order of colours than are the judgements of other people. If, in accordance with our definition of the term 'objective', we call this average order of colour preferences the 'objective' or 'true' order, then we can perhaps call those who agree with it most the 'best' judges, and those who agree with it least the 'poorest' judges. Alternatively, we may say that our 'best' judges have good taste, while our 'poorest' judges have had bad taste; we would, in that case, be defining the terms 'good' and 'bad' taste in a somewhat unusual way, and the reader is of course free to reject that definition of the term. Evidence will be brought forward later on to show that this suggested usage agrees quite well with common usage in many ways; for the moment let us just note this new way of defining the concept.

We have dealt with preference judgements of hues of a given saturation and brightness; what happens if we give the same subjects a test involving hues at different levels of saturation and brightness? What would happen if we gave them tests in which preference judgements were to be made between colours of different degrees of saturation, keeping hue and brightness constant, or between colours of different degrees of brightness, keeping hue and saturation constant? The outcome of these experiments is in line with the 'hue' experiment already described; there is substantial agreement between different judges, and those people who are 'good judges' (have good taste) in one test are on the whole those who are 'good judges' (have good taste) in the other tests. The quality we have denoted as 'good taste' thus is not dependent on any one particular test; it applies generally to all the tests which can be constructed in the field of colour preference.

What happens if we extend our work to colour combinations – say combinations of two colours of equal brightness and saturation, to keep the problem at a manageable level? The answer to this question is important, for two reasons. In the first place, aestheticians often maintain that judgements regarding single colours are not aesthetic judgements at all; it is at the level of complexity represented by colour combinations that the simplest form of aesthetic judgement begins. Thus a demonstration that what is true of simple colour judgements is also true of judgements regarding colour combinations is important in showing that the aesthetician's argument is possibly wrong, and that we may generalize from simple colour experiments to more complex stimuli.

Even more important is another argument. There is an important school in psychology, the holistic or 'Gestalt' school, which maintains that complex units or 'gestalten' are not built up atomistically from simpler units or 'atoms';

rather, the more complex unit shows 'emergent' qualities which cannot be predicted from knowledge of the simpler constituents and the relations obtaining between them. If this argument were true, then our whole attempt to derive laws governing appreciation of complex works of art from experiments dealing with relatively simple objects would be doomed to failure. Here we have an ideal testing ground for the 'atomistic' hypothesis. If we can predict preferences for colour combinations on the basis of knowledge of preferences for single colours, and knowledge of the relation on the colour circle between the colours in each combination, then we would have disproved the 'Gestalt' argument, and might with reasonable assurance go on with our general plan. If such prediction should prove impossible, then we would have to abandon our 'atomistic' approach, and look around for a different methodology.

First of all, let us note that with respect to colour combinations we again find a certain marked degree of agreement or 'objectivity'. Secondly, let us note that again those who prove to be 'good' judges on one test involving colour combinations also turn out to be 'good' judges on other tests involving colour combinations. Thirdly, let us note that these 'good' judges of colour combinations are precisely those who earlier on were found to be good judges of single colours and their aesthetic values. Whatever constitutes 'good taste' in the one experiment obviously constitutes 'good taste' in the other; we can justifiably generalize from simple to more complex stimuli.

But even more important than this is another demonstration. It is possible to show that preference judgements of colour combinations depend on two factors. The first is the simple sum of the preferences for the individual colours; if both the individual colours making up the combination are liked, then the combination will on the whole be liked. If both colours are disliked, the combination will tend to be disliked. If one colour is liked, the other disliked, or if both are neutral, then the affective value of the combination will tend to be neutral.

The second factor relates to the position of the two component colours on the colour circle. The closer together the two colours are on that circle, the lower will be the aesthetic ranking of the combination; the further apart they are, the higher will be the ranking of the combination. Best liked of all are pairs of complementary colours, i.e. colours exactly opposite each other on the colour circle.

If we combine these two factors – liking of the individual colours, and knowledge of their separation on the colour circle – then we can predict with very great accuracy indeed the aesthetic ranking of the colour combination. Thus the evidence decisively favours the atomistic hypothesis, and does not agree at all with the holistic view that in the appreciation of complex objects 'emergent' qualities come into play which cannot be dealt with in terms of simple qualities and their relations. This conclusion may of course have to be modified when dealing with objects of very high complexity, like landscape paintings or portraits, but even so this finding is certainly encouraging.

So far we have been dealing exclusively with colours, and the question must be faced: can we extend our findings to other properties of works of art? One such set of properties is dealt with in the 'laws of composition' referred to already, and it seems worth while to inquire into the possible relation between 'good taste' as defined in our experiments so far, and 'good taste' as it might be defined by these laws.

Fortunately there exist tests constructed for the express purpose of obtaining a measure of this ability to judge the factors entering into good composition. This is usually done by contrasting two line drawings, or two designs, one of which purposely violates one of these rules, while the other is unimpeachable on this account. Great care is taken in the construction of these tests to obtain the best advice available from artists, art teachers, and art critics, and only if these experts are practically unanimous as to the respective aesthetic value of the two designs making up each test item are they included in the test. Here, then, we have rather a different criterion of 'good taste', one much nearer to the way in which the term is used in ordinary speech. It would of course still be possible to argue that the unanimous verdict of all the experts who had devoted their lives to the practice and study of painting was mistaken, and that their standards were quite arbitrary; such a nihilistic view would find it very difficult indeed to account for some of the findings to be reported presently.

In the first place, tests of this type predict with considerable accuracy which students in the arts school make a success of their studies, and which fail ignominiously. The tests, be it noted, do not predict whether the person with a high score is likely to paint in the classical manner, or whether he will become a revolutionary; they merely predict that he is likely to paint well regardless of the particular manner he chooses, or the style which he finally adopts. The controversy over 'modern' painting has blinded many people to the fact that paintings differ in quality as well as in style, and that one can paint well or badly in any style; it is this *quality* which tests attempt to predict, and the evidence shows that they are successful in doing so at least to some extent.

In the second place, and this point cannot be stressed too strongly, it has been found that people who show good taste in their judgements of simple colours and of colour combinations also do well on these completely achromatic tests of composition. This finding must certainly be somewhat unexpected to the subjectivist; it is accountable in terms of the hypothesis that there exists some property of the central nervous system which determines aesthetic judgements, a property which is biologically derived, and which covers the whole field of visual art. People would on this hypothesis be expected to differ with respect to 'good taste' in the same way in which they are known to differ with respect to acuity of vision, ranging from an extreme of Philistine lack of all aesthetic appreciation – a true 'blindness' to all that is beautiful – to the other extreme of almost instinctive appreciation of the good and beautiful, and abhorrence of the bad and ugly. Admittedly, this is only a hypothesis at this stage, but it appears to be the only hypothesis to account for all the facts, and it is scientifically valuable in that verification or disproof can be very easily arranged. One deduction, for instance, might be that this ability should be very strongly determined by heredity; there is already some evidence in favour of this view, but it would require experiments with identical and fraternal twins to make the proof conclusive.

Another deduction might be that a person who showed good taste (as defined) with respect to one type of visual art should also show good taste with respect to any other type of visual art. This deduction has been verified by constructing tests involving a great variety of different types of visual stimuli – portraits, landscape paintings, book-bindings, silverware, statues, landscape photographs, carpets, and many more. In each case it was found that the person showing good taste on one test tended also to show good taste on the others, just as predicted by our hypothesis. This finding also is very difficult to account for in terms of any alternative hypothesis, although several such may have suggested themselves to the reader.

In the first place, it might be argued, this agreement may be due entirely to intelligence; the more intelligent may also be the more 'artistic', and perhaps the more knowledgeable regarding aesthetic values. This hypothesis falls to the ground because intelligence correlates only to a very slight extent with 'good taste'; certainly the correlation is much too low to account for the findings.

A more reasonable hypothesis might be one which referred the observed correlations to cultural factors entirely; the argument might run something like this. A person who is knowledgeable with respect to current views about the aesthetic value of certain paintings would also be knowledgeable with respect to current views about the aesthetic value of different types of carpets, or statues, or book-bindings. Thus the tests might merely measure 'cultural knowledge', rather than something more fundamental.

This argument also cannot be defended. The specimens used as test objects were all unknown to the subjects taking part in the experiment; they had been selected with particular care in order to obviate any criticism of the experiment along the lines of the 'cultural' hypothesis. When pictures were taken from the works of an artist relatively well known, then the whole test was made up of pictures taken just from that one artist, so that there was no 'cultural influence' or 'general attitude' determining the relative value of the different items. Even more conclusive is the last consideration; how could cultural influences create a correlation between aesthetic tests of the type described, and simple colour judgements? There is no cultural ruling which some subjects might know, and with which they might conform, in the field of colour rankings. Indeed, most of the subjects doubted if there was any agreement at all among people in this field, holding strongly to a 'subjectivist' position. But an influence which is absent in the case of one type of test cannot possibly cause a correlation between that test and others; consequently we must dismiss the 'cultural' argument, in spite of its superficial appeal.

This point should not be stretched too far; it certainly is not denied that cultural influences have very great importance indeed. When we look at the factors which determine the judgements of many people in the field of art, we find that some of these factors are not of an aesthetic nature at all. The monetary value of the picture, its fame, the fact that it is exhibited by the Royal Academy, knowledge of the position of the painter in the hierarchy of his colleagues – all these and many other extraneous considerations determine what people will say when asked: 'Do you like this picture?' But the psychologist – no more than the aesthetician and the philosopher – is not particularly interested in these irrelevant factors; he wishes to isolate the determinants of genuinely aesthetic responses. In order to do that he has to select his material carefully, so that considerations of the type described cannot influence his subjects. Such control of irrelevant factors is absolutely essential; without it we would be lost in a welter of contradictory and non-aesthetic determinants.

Similar arguments apply to another troublesome question.

M

If we make up a test consisting not only of pictures of widely different quality, but also contrasting strongly in style – including, say, Old Masters and works of the Picasso–Matisse school – then style preferences would to some extent obscure the differences in quality which are the main object of our interest. Consequently, such a test would not be a good test for our purpose; we would have to split it into two, making up one test exclusively of Old Masters, the other exclusively of works of the Picasso–Matisse school. In this way we would prevent style differences from interfering with our measurement of differences in our subjects' ability to judge the quality of the pictures.

Can we justifiably neglect such important factors as those associated with the Ancient *vs.* Modern controversy? The answer is surely that we cannot neglect them in any orderly description of the whole of aesthetic appreciation, but that we must pass them by in our attempt to isolate and measure one particular aspect of aesthetics, namely the qualitative one, which appears to be largely independent of the controversy. We cannot give an adequate description of a person's body by measuring his height alone, but when we are measuring his height we disregard for that purpose such factors as his weight, his flat feet, and the wart on his nose. For certain purposes measures of height are valuable, for others they are almost useless; what we want to measure depends upon our purpose. If quality and style of painting are independent variables – and the evidence in favour of this view is very strong – then we must measure them independently and in isolation. If there are still other factors, then they also must be investigated and measured, each in its turn.

In actual fact, measurement of style preferences is very much easier than measurement of quality judgements. The usual method has been to select sets of two pictures, both of which depict a similar scene, a windmill, say, or a waterfall; one of these is taken from the paintings of a well-known modern painter, the other from the paintings of an equally well-known classical painter. In this way we may hope to keep under control interest in the subject-matter, the quality of the painting, and the acceptability of the artist's name; preference judgements as between the two paintings should then be strictly a measure of 'style' preferences. Studies along these lines have shown fairly convincingly that these preferences are related to temperament; introverts tend to prefer the older, extraverts the more modern works. Interesting as this finding is, we cannot stop to discuss it here, as it is somewhat outside the main argument.

To return, then, to our muttons, we may be said, in a way, to have taken the average order of preference of the population as our standard of 'good taste'. This motion is so alien to the most cherished tenets of aestheticians and philosophers that it is liable to be ridiculed on irrelevant grounds. Thus it might be said that surely Mozart is a greater composer than Irving Berlin, in spite of the fact that the great majority seem to prefer the latter's productions. A Hollywood musical is aesthetically inferior to the *Midsummer Night's Dream*, however many more customers may be attracted to the former. How, then, can we use the average judgement of the masses as the arbiter of aesthetic excellence?

This criticism misses the whole point of the argument. The average rank order of works of art is a good criterion of excellence *only under carefully specified conditions*; all irrelevant and extraneous factors must first be ruled out before we can accept the average judgement as having any value at all. Preference for a 'leg show' or the more 'bosomy' Hollywood productions over Shakespeare may be a good measure of strength of sexual interest; it is irrelevant to the respective aesthetic values of these two productions because the judgement is not based on aesthetic grounds. The usefulness and value of an average in science depend entirely on the question asked, the conditions of the experiment, and the precise nature of the figures averaged; under appropriate conditions, such an average may be of the greatest value, under other conditions it may be useless and misleading. Criticisms of the notion that the average ranking of aesthetic objects can furnish us with an acceptable criterion of aesthetic value are usually based on examples in which all the rules for obtaining a meaningful average are broken; this may make for a good knock-about argument, but it does not help much in the search for scientific criteria of 'beauty'.

One last point should be considered. In addition to general 'good taste' and style preferences, aesthetic judgements are often determined by highly individualistic and idiosyncratic factors. A man may like yellow because his girl always wears yellow; or he may show an inordinate preference for Pechstein's 'Lupowmündung' because this picture reminds him of sunny summer holidays on the sandy beaches of the Baltic. These are extraneous factors which may be of interest in themselves, but which do not affect the determination of our average order; being specific to one individual, they tend to cancel out over large numbers. Essentially, this type of preference determinant is non-aesthetic in nature, being mainly based on associations with particular events which have brought happiness or pain to the individual concerned.

I have no space here to deal with the considerable body of experimental work that has been done in the fields of music and poetry; by and large, findings there are similar to those in the visual arts. Nor is it possible to discuss aesthetic creation; too little is known in that field, apart from some ingenious but unlikely Freudian speculations, to make any reasonable conclusions possible. On the whole, we may say that experimental work in aesthetics has unearthed a number of facts which cannot be disregarded by anyone interested in the problem of the formation of aesthetic judgements, and that these facts all point with remarkable unanimity to a theory of aesthetics which is firmly anchored in biology and derives judgements of 'beauty' from inherited properties of the central nervous system. Over-simplified and inadequate to deal with the tremendous complexities of great works of art? Certainly. But nevertheless a beginning which promises to lead us to a more adequate account in due course.

It will be noted that our concern has been almost entirely

with what are called formal elements of art. Would it be possible to go a step further than we have done so far and actually try to describe a formula, of a completely objective nature, for the measurement of beauty? The attempt to do this is not essentially modern in origin; it will be remembered that Pythagoras attempted to base the beauty of music on mathematical relations obtaining between the lengths of the strings used in striking a chord, and other writers of antiquity have at times made similar attempts. Thus, Plato has this to say in the *Timaeus*: 'That triangle which we consider to be the most beautiful of all ... is that of which the double forms a third equilateral triangle.' His reason, as will be seen from Figure 12, was that out of this triangle could be built the equilateral triangle, the rectangle, the parallelogram, the diamond, and regular hexagon

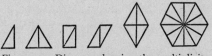

Figure 12: Diagram showing the multiplicity of relationships which caused Plato to call the triangle on the extreme left 'the most beautiful of all'

among polygonal figures, as well as three of the five regular solids. This power in combination was peculiarly significant to Plato, who valued it for purposes of cosmological speculation.

We would hardly be content to agree with this or regard his reasons as being of an aesthetic nature. This capacity for missing the point has, of course, always been characteristic of philosophers. (One of the extreme examples of this is Schopenhauer's well-known essay on humour. He spends some sixty pages in an attempt to analyse the particular excellence of what he regards as the best joke he has ever come across. This joke, apparently – and it is here that there is an interesting parallel with Plato – consists of a tangent to a circle. The exquisite humour of the line approaching the circle and then receding from it again provokes rhapsodies

326 · Part Two · Personality and Social Life

of appreciation from Schopenhauer, which, however, have not been echoed by most readers!)

It would be boring to review the whole history of attempts of this kind, but we must mention one psychologist who may be said to have elevated the study of aesthetics into a scientific discipline. Fechner was particularly interested in the experimental determination of preferences for proportions, and tried to relate these to a well-known aesthetic doctrine; namely, that of the golden section. This section of a linear segment is that which divides it into two segments in such a way that the longer segment is the mean proportional between the shorter segment and the whole segment. Fechner's particular interest concentrated in the so-called 'golden rectangle', i.e. a rectangle whose sides are in the ratio of the golden section. These rectangles, with the ratio of the longer to the shorter side of 1·618, or very nearly 8 to 5, were supposed to have some occult beauty by philosophers and aestheticians, which made them quite outstandingly superior to other types of rectangles.

Experimental work by Fechner, and many of his successors, has shown that rectangles having proportions somewhat similar to the 'golden rectangle' are indeed well liked. It has also been found, however, that the exact proportion of the sides required by the alleged law is not conspicuously superior to neighbouring ratios, and, in fact, it is often found to be inferior to them. Thus, there appears nothing very occult or mystic about this ratio, and the general theory endowing it with special beauty must remain very suspect.

In recent years, an American mathematician, George D. Birkhoff, has taken up this problem of an aesthetic formula again in his book on 'Aesthetic Measure'. In this he has made a thoroughgoing attempt to provide a general formula for the measurement of works of art (visual art, poetry, music). Three elements enter into this formula and are related to the three phases in the aesthetic experiences which he distinguishes: (1) a preliminary effort of attention, which is necessary for the act of perception, and which increases in proportion to what he calls the *complexity* (C) of the object; (2) the feeling of value or *aesthetic measure* (M) which rewards this effort; and finally (3) a realization that the object is characterized by a certain harmony, symmetry, or *order* (O), more or less concealed, which seems necessary to the aesthetic effect. Taking his cue from the well-known aesthetic demand for 'unity in variety', he maintains that this analysis of the aesthetic experience suggests that the aesthetic feelings arise primarily because of an unusual degree of harmonious interrelation within the object. He goes on to say, 'More definitely, if we regard *M*, *O*, and *C* as measurable variables, we are led to write

$$M = \frac{O}{C}$$

and thus to embody in a basic formula the conjecture that the aesthetic measure is determined by the density of order relations in the aesthetic object. ... If we admit the validity of such a formula, the following mathematical formulation of the fundamental aesthetic problem may be made: *Within each class of aesthetic objects, to define the order O and the complexity C so that their ratio M = O/C yields the aesthetic measure of any object of the class.*'

Much of Birkhoff's work is concerned with defining precisely how this order in complexity elements may be measured. In the case of polygonal figures, for instance, complexity is defined as 'the number of indefinitely extended straight lines which contain all the sides of the polygon'. Order elements are analysed into the following: *V*, or vertical symmetry, *E*, or equilibrium, *R*, or rotational symmetry; *HV*, or relation to a horizontal-vertical network; and *F*, or unsatisfactory form, which is a kind of rag bag involving factors such as the following: too small distances from vertices to vertices or to sides, or between parallel sides; angles too near 0° or 180°; other ambiguities; unsupported re-entrant sides; diversity of niches; diversity of directions; lack of symmetry. All the terms used in this formula are precisely defined, and it is possible for any given polygonal figure to arrive at a measure M which, in terms of Birkhoff's theory, should give its degree of aesthetic measure.

The crucial question, of course, is a factual one. Does the formula actually work? We may agree or disagree with the theoretical development, and we may like or dislike the whole orientation of Birkhoff's work. If he should happen to succeed in predicting aesthetic preference judgements on the basis of a formula, however, we could hardly neglect such an important contribution. The answer seems to be that the formula does work up to a point, but that it does not work very well. Agreement with actual expressed preference judgements by large numbers of people is relatively slight.

There appear to be three main reasons for this. In the first place, Birkhoff bases part of his theory on an assumption which is not, in fact, borne out. In his discussion of the complexity elements in aesthetic appreciation he links it with the effort made by the observer in the act of perception, and he seems to equate this effort with the actual amount of muscular exertion. This is what he says: 'Suppose that we fix attention upon a complex polygonal tile. The act of perception involved is so quickly performed as to seem nearly instantaneous. The feeling of effort is almost negligible while the eye follows the successive sides of the polygon and the corresponding motor adjustments are effected automatically. Nevertheless, according to the point of view advanced above, there is a slight feeling of tension attendant upon each adjustment, and the complexity C will be measured by the number of sides of the polygon.' Now even a very elementary knowledge of psychology would have taught Birkhoff that in actual fact the eye, in perceiving any kind of figure, polygonal or otherwise, does not, in fact, 'follow the successive sides'. By photographing actual eye-movements during reading, during the perception of pictures, of polygonal figures, and of other objects, it has been established that the eye does not smoothly follow along the lines constituting the percept, but that rather it rests for a brief moment and then, by means of a so-called *saccadic movement*, jumps to another point, resting there again for a fraction of a second before jumping off again. In viewing Birkhoff's hypothetical polygonal tile, the direction of these jumps would be quite irregular and would certainly not follow the lines of the figure being observed. There is, consequently, no possibility of deriving the complexity element from such pseudo-physiological considerations as those employed by Birkhoff. (It is interesting to note that several other mathematicians and philosophers, in attempting to build up some coherent account of visual perception and appreciation of beauty, have fallen into the same trap. The notion that one is free to make any kind of postulation in psychology seems to die hard. Much time and effort, which at present is wasted, could be put to better effect if, before making assumptions of this kind, the writers bothered to find out what the known facts of the situation are!)

Where Birkhoff's first error was a factual one, his second appears to have been a theoretical one. He makes the aesthetic measure of an object equal to the number of order elements, and inversely equal to the number of complexity elements. This is a purely *a priori* notion; Birkhoff does not appear to have carried out any experimental work whatsoever to check the truth of his hypothesis, or the accuracy of his aesthetic measure. In a long series of experiments, the conclusion was forced upon the present writer that the general formula was wrong, and that the aesthetic measure was not the ratio of the order and complexity elements, but their product. In other words, $M = O \times C$, not O/C. This conclusion is best illustrated, perhaps, by looking at the polygon having the highest M value in Birkhoff's table, namely, the square. This figure is not particularly liked by the majority of subjects, for the precise reasons which caused Birkhoff to give it such a high rating. The square has a low order of complexity and a relatively high degree of order. The majority verdict seems to be that such an object is 'boring', 'uninteresting', 'too regular', and 'uninspired'. In other words, it possesses too little diversity and too much order to appeal. The most preferred objects seem to be those having a high degree of complexity *and* a high degree of order. When formulae were constructed on this basis, agreement with observed preference judgements rose to a respectable height, and in terms of this new and changed formula it is possible to say that we can predict aesthetic reactions in terms of a simple objective mathematical formula, thus apparently confirming the notion expressed in the ancient rhyme:

> For he that reades but Mathematicke rules
> Shall finde conclusions that availe to worke
> Wonders that passe the common sense of men.

The third reason why Birkhoff went wrong lies in his failure to take into account some additional complexities. In addition to the general preference judgements characteristic of human beings in the group, we must take into account also considerable individual differences. These differences seem to relate particularly to preferences for order or complexity elements respectively. In other words, some people appear to prefer aesthetic objects having a relatively high degree of complexity, whereas others prefer aesthetic objects having a relatively high degree of order. I may perhaps illustrate this from some experiments done with the appreciation of poetry. Those with a strong liking for a preponderance of order elements tended to prefer poems with a simple regular beat; a simple straightforward rhyming scheme having a regular and heavily accentuated rhythm. The following stanza may serve as an example of this:

> Into the Silence of the empty night
> I went, and took my scorned heart with me,
> And all the thousand eyes of Heaven were bright;
> But Sorrow came and led me back to thee.

By contrast, here is a stanza from a poem preferred by those generally liking more complex types of phrase forms, i.e. an unorthodox irregular rhyming scheme, and a much less obvious rhythm:

> Thou art not lovelier than lilacs – no,
> Nor honeysuckle; thou art not more fair
> Than small white single poppies, – I can bear
> Thy beauty.

On the average, the two poems from which these stanzas were taken would be liked equally well, but there would be considerable disagreement between subject, those liking the one disliking the other, and vice versa. There is some evidence to suggest that in part, at least, these differences are due to temperamental factors. Extraverts tend to prefer the simple type of poem with a regular rhyming scheme, and the heavily accentuated rhythm; introverts prefer the more complex type of poem with the irregular rhyming scheme and the less obvious rhythm.

In addition, there is some evidence to suggest that practice and familiarity also play a part in determining a person's appreciation. It has been found, for instance, that when subjects were asked to make preference judgements for simple and complex chords struck on the piano, their preferences tended to go towards the simple and more familiar types of chords. However, when the experiment was repeated a large number of times the simple familiar chords began to lose their appeal and the more complex, unfamiliar ones began to become more popular. Much the same has been found with respect to other types of art objects, as indeed one might have suspected on common-sense grounds. Apparently, familiarity itself must be counted as an additional order element in the formula, so that simple repetition, of viewing, or hearing, may change the aesthetic measure of a given object. These additional complications can all be taken into account in the final formula, of course, but it can be seen that the method is by no means as simple as suggested by Birkhoff. Unfortunately, there is at present little interest among psychologists in the experimental study of aesthetics, and the very promising beginning made in the fields of colour preferences and the aesthetic measure are not likely to be followed up on a sufficient scale to make rapid progress in this very difficult field likely.

Throughout this chapter we have been concerning ourselves with formal aspects of art. These have always been of major interest to psychologists because they alone lend themselves easily to measurement and, hence, to the formulation of laws and the accumulation of experimental evidence so desirable when exact statements of relationship are required. However, rightly or wrongly, the man in the street, the literary critic, and the artist have usually shown much more interest in a rather different kind of analysis. This type of analysis deals with content rather than with form. It is subjective rather than objective. It does not make exact statements in a numerical form, but rather tries to convey impressions by means of words. These features, which render it somewhat suspect to the scientist, make it much more readily acceptable to a wide variety of people who are more interested in the humanities than in science, and who do not look kindly upon any attempt to make aesthetic experiences amenable to scientific laws.

Much of the kind of analysis I have in mind here has been done in the fields of the novel and drama, perhaps largely because, in these fields, content is very much more important than form, just as scientific analysis has been most prominent in the fields of visual arts and music, where form is more important than content. Best known among the different types of analysis of content is probably that carried out by psychoanalysts, who have concentrated a considerable amount of energy on this field. An example may show just precisely what these writers are attempting to do, and we can then go on to discuss how far what they are trying to do is feasible and successful.

As we cannot discuss in detail all the many attempts that have been made by psychoanalysts, we shall have to restrict ourselves to one or two examples, and in order to be fair I have chosen as my first exhibit what has been universally considered to be the most successful of all these attempts. I refer to Ernest Jones's attempt to explain what he calls 'Hamlet's mystery' in terms of the Oedipus complex. In this he has but followed in the footsteps of Freud himself, who made a similar suggestion in a footnote to one of his books.

What, then, is 'Hamlet's mystery'? This, according to Jones, is the peculiar hesitancy shown by Hamlet in seeking to obtain revenge for the murder of his father. Three types of hypothesis have been put forward to explain this 'Sphinx of modern Literature'. The first of these hypotheses sees the difficulty in the performance of the task in Hamlet's temperament, which is not supposed to be suited to effective action of any kind. This view, seeking to account for Hamlet's inhibition by some difficulty in his constitution, was originally advanced by Goethe, Schlegel, and Coleridge. This view roughly maintained that because of his highly developed intellectual powers, and his broad and many-sided sympathies, Hamlet never took a simple view of any problem, but always saw a number of different aspects and possible explanations. Hence, no particular course of action ever seemed unequivocal and obvious, and therefore his scepticism and reflective powers tended to paralyse his conduct in practical life. In terms of the concepts discussed in detail in an earlier chapter, we might say that Hamlet was a highly introverted person, probably with strong neurotic tendencies – a person liable to lose himself in abstract trains of thought at the expense of contact with reality.

The second hypothesis seeks for a cause, not in the personality of Hamlet, but rather in the difficulty of the task itself. There are many sub-varieties of this kind of hypothesis, but they all agree in suggesting that, to depose a reigning sovereign without, at the same time, losing one's own life, was an extremely difficult matter, particularly if, at the same time, an attempt is to be made not only to slay the murderer but also to convict him of his murder.

Jones rejects both these hypotheses as accounting for Hamlet's vacillation, and goes on to say:

If this lies neither in his incapacity for action in general, nor in the inordinate difficulty of the task in question, then it must of necessity lie in the *third* possibility, namely in some special feature of the task that renders it repugnant to him. This conclusion, that Hamlet at heart does not want to carry out the task, seems so obvious that it is hard to see how any critical reader of the play could avoid making it.

What Jones has, in fact, suggested is that Hamlet had some repugnance to carrying out the task of revenge, but he is handicapped in maintaining this view because nowhere in the play is there any evidence in Hamlet's soliloquies of such repugnance. This, however, presents no difficulty to Jones; if there is no evidence in Hamlet's words of any repugnance, of any cause for his inhibition, then the simple conclusion is that he himself was unaware of the nature of his repugnance – in other words, that he was unconscious of it. Having thus thrust the explanation of the mystery which he is seeking into the unconscious, Jones goes on to try to find out what it is that has been repressed. He makes a start by stating a law which runs like this: 'That which is inacceptable to the herd becomes inacceptable to the individual unit.' He goes on to say,

> It is for this reason that moral, social, ethical, or religious influences are hardly ever 'repressed', for as the individual originally received them from his herd, they can never come into conflict with the dicta of the latter. ... The contrary is equally true, namely that mental trends 'repressed' by the individual are those least acceptable to his herd.

It would follow from these considerations that what has been repressed, and what caused Hamlet to hesitate, is something which is not acceptable to him or to his herd.

This 'something' Jones looks for by examining Hamlet's attitude towards the object of his vengeance, Claudius, and to the crimes which have to be avenged. These are first Claudius's incest with the Queen, and second his murder of Hamlet's father, Claudius's brother. In trying to explain Hamlet's attitude towards Claudius, Jones claims that this is not simply one of mere execration, but that there is a complexity arising in the following way:

> The uncle has not merely committed *each* crime, he has committed *both* crimes, a distinction of considerable importance, for the *combination* of crimes allows the admittance of a new factor, produced by the possible inter-relation of the two, which prevents the results from being simply one of summation. In addition it has to be borne in mind that the perpetrator of the crimes is a relative, and an exceedingly near relative.

Having taken us this far, Jones now explains the mechanism of the so-called Oedipus complex, which he believes will, at the same time, explain Hamlet's hesitancy. Briefly, this complex is supposed to arise because of a strong sexual link between the boy child and his mother. (Girls are somehow left out of this intriguing constellation, and although Freud has, at times, made perfunctory efforts to fit them in, these cannot be said to be anything like as striking as those leading to the concept of the Oedipus complex.) In this liaison, the father is experienced as a successful rival who comes between the child and his mother. Consequently, the boy wants to kill the father and marry the mother, a feat actually accomplished by Oedipus in the Greek legend and tragedy of Sophocles. It is because of this similarity between the story of Oedipus and the alleged desires of young boys that this complex has received its name.

It is in terms of the Oedipus complex then that Jones would explain Hamlet's mystery. Having in his youth repressed his aggressive feelings towards his father, and his sexual feelings towards the mother, he now receives news of the father's death and the mother's second marriage. As a consequence, Jones points out,

The long-'repressed' desire to take his father's place in his mother's affection is stimulated to unconscious activity by the sight of some one usurping this place exactly as he himself had once longed to do. More, this someone was a member of the same family, so that the actual usurpation further resembled the imaginary one in being incestuous. Without his being at all aware of it these ancient desires are ringing in his mind, are once more struggling to find expression, and need such an expenditure of energy again to 'repress' them that he is reduced to the deplorable mental state he himself so vividly depicts.

Add to all this the ghost's revelation that the uncle is also the murderer of his father, and Hamlet's unconscious is clearly in a considerable turmoil. According to Jones, his attitude towards Claudius becomes a very complex one. He detests his uncle, but it is the jealous detestation of one evil-doer towards his successful fellow. This makes it difficult for him to denounce his uncle, because the more vigorously he does so, the more powerful does he stimulate the activity of his own unconscious and 'repressed' complexes. This, then, is Jones's explanation for Hamlet's failure. He cannot obey the call of duty to slay his uncle because this is linked with the call of his nature to slay his mother's husband, whether this is the first or the second; the latter call is strongly 're-pressed', and therefore necessarily the former also. In other words, Hamlet, having as a young boy repressed his (hypo-thetical) desire to slay his father, now, for no obvious reason, transfers this repression to his mother's second husband and therefore is prevented from carrying out his vengeance.

This explanation may or may not appeal to the reader, but before discussing it, let us first of all try to get clear pre-cisely what it is that is being said. Jones appears to suggest that Hamlet is suffering from an Oedipus complex, which in some way which is not very clear and seems to rest on a quite arbitrary assumption, causes him to hesitate to kill Claudius. But as a statement, of course, this has no meaning. Hamlet, after all, is a non-existent person, a figment of the imagina-tion, and to assert that a non-existent person is activated by an Oedipus complex is not a very enlightening statement. It clearly is impossible to refute or to support in any meaning-ful way, but Jones, of course, only uses this statement as a stepping-stone. He wants to inquire into the relation of Hamlet's complex to the inner workings of Shakespeare's mind. Thus, he goes on to say, 'It is here maintained that this conflict is an echo of a similar one in Shakespeare him-self, as to a greater or less extent it is in all men.' In other words, Jones is asserting that Hamlet is a kind of Thematic Apperception Test which can be used to diagnose Shake-speare's neurosis. As nothing whatever is known of Shake-speare's personality such an assertion, of course, can be made quite confidently. It also can neither be proved or dis-proved. In particular, any kind of disproof is ruled out be-cause the conflict connected with the Oedipus complex is, inevitably, an unconscious one, and therefore must for ever remain hidden.

But this is not the end of the story. If Shakespeare, unconsciously and unwittingly, endowed Hamlet with unconscious desires which make it impossible for him to carry out his duty, he also produced a drama which appeals to us because the same conflict (unconsciously, of course) is present in our own minds. Thus, Shakespeare's unconscious, through the unconscious of Hamlet, is calling to the unconscious of the various members of the theatre audiences who hear the play and who unconsciously recognize and appreciate all these unconscious determinants.

But the matter does not rest there either. Freud and Jones both explicitly assert that the Oedipus complex is characteristic of all human beings. In view of that, it is a little difficult to see how the Oedipus complex can be adduced to explain the actions of any particular person. This point has often been mentioned in criticism of Freudian theories; by making their conceptions universal, i.e. by applying them to all human beings, they also make it quite impossible to use these conceptions in an explanatory manner. Only that which affects different people differently can be made into an explanatory principle to account for differences between them. If everyone has an Oedipus complex, then the possession of one does not differentiate Hamlet from Claudius or Laertes. Nor does it differentiate him from Shakespeare, or any member of the audience during the play.

Perhaps the diagnosis has to be more detailed still, but how is that possible? Freud himself makes it clear that only by detailed analytic sessions, extended over many years, and assisted by procedures of dream interpretation and free association, can reliable diagnoses be made. To make such a diagnosis of a person, 300 years dead, of whose life practically nothing is known, on the strength of a very esoteric interpretation of a few lines probably, but not certainly, written by that person, on the basis of a story already existing at that time in several different forms, seems to be a somewhat extravagant claim. Whether the reader feels that the explanation given by Jones is a likely one or not, he will agree that the whole process of arriving at this explanation is a literary rather than a scientific device, and, while it undoubtedly is more colourful than the more sober scientific types of research, it can hardly aspire to the same degree of confidence in its conclusion.

Much the same may be said about a slightly less widely known psychoanalysis conducted by Schilder on *Alice in Wonderland*, and through her on Lewis Carroll. Schilder bases himself on a saying by Freud, according to which non-sense in dreams and so-called unconscious thinking signifies contempt and sneering. He therefore says, 'We may expect that nonsense literature is the expression of particularly strong destructive tendencies of a very primitive character.' Whence do these destructive tendencies come? Schilder maintains that they arose because Carroll, being one of a large family, never got the full love of his parents and therefore hated and wanted to destroy his various brothers and sisters. Carroll, as Schilder points out, liked to play with toads and snails and earth-worms, while Alice is in continuous fear of being attacked or blamed by the animals. 'Do the insects', asks Schilder, 'represent the many brothers and sisters who must have provoked jealousy in Carroll?'

Somewhat inconsequentially, Schilder then goes on to ask, with respect to Lewis Carroll, 'What was his relation to his sex organ, anyhow?' The answer he gives relates to a theory adumbrated by another well-known psychoanalyst, Fenichel, who suggested the possibility that little girls might become symbols for the phallus. In support of this view, Schilder points out that Alice changes her form continually. She is continually threatened and continually in danger. Thus, apparently, Lewis Carroll is suffering from a castration complex, which thus appears as a strong motivating factor in his writings.

What about the reader? Schilder declares that to him Carroll appears to be a particularly destructive writer. He asks whether such literature might not increase destructive attitudes in children beyond the measure which is desirable. Thus, *Alice in Wonderland* and *Through the Looking Glass* join the ranks of the horror comics, a somewhat curious juxtaposition!

This is by no means the only psychoanalytic interpretation of *Alice*; others are available which make use of quite different hypotheses and emerge with quite different conclusions. The reader who has a fertile imagination and some knowledge of the psychoanalytic system will find many hours of unalloyed amusement by going through the adventures of Alice, trying to link them up with the more obvious psychoanalytic concepts which they may call to his mind. Such a procedure may do little to throw light on the psychology of aesthetics, but it will convince the reader of the unparalleled fertility of analogies to be found in the Freudian system, and of the utter impossibility of subjecting these analogies to any rational test of truth or falsehood.

RECOMMENDED FOR FURTHER
READING

1. WEITZENHOFFER, A. M, *Hypnotism. An Objective Study in Suggestibility*. New York: John Wiley & Sons, Inc., 1953. (for Chapter 1)
2. INBAU, F. E., and REID, J. E. *Lie Detection and Criminal Interrogation. Third Edition.* Baltimore: The Williams & Wilkins Company, 1953. (for Chapter 2)
3. WEST, D. J. *Psychical Research Today.* London: Duckworth, 1954. (for Chapter 3)
4. HALL, C. S. *The Meaning of Dreams.* New York: Harper & Bros., 1954. (for Chapter 4)
5. EYSENCK, H. J. *The Structure of Human Personality.* London: Methuen & Co. Ltd., 1953. (for Chapter 5)
6. PAVLOV, I. P. *Conditioned Reflexes.* London: Oxford University Press, 1927. (for Chapter 6)
7. EYSENCK, H. J. *The Psychology of Politics.* London: Methuen & Co., 1954. (for Chapter 7)
8. BIRKHOFF, G. D. *Aesthetic Measure.* Cambridge, Mass.: Harvard University Press, 1933. (for Chapter 8)

INDEX

SOME PELICANS ON PSYCHOLOGY
AND RELATED SUBJECTS

—

SOME MORE PELICANS ON PSYCHOLOGY
AND RELATED SUBJECTS

—